DYNAMICS OF SANCTIONS IN WORLD AFFAIRS

S.J.R. BILGRAMI

ATLANTIC
PUBLISHERS & DISTRIBUTORS

Published by
ATLANTIC PUBLISHERS AND DISTRIBUTORS
B-2, Vishal Enclave, Opp. Rajouri Garden, New Delhi-27
Phones : 25413460, 25429987, 25466842

Sales Office
7/22, Ansari Road, Darya Ganj, New Delhi-110 002
Phones : 23273880, 23285873, 23280451
Fax : 91-11-23285873
web : www.atlanticbooks.com
e-mail : info@atlanticbooks.com

ISBN 81-269-0313-9

Typeset at
APD Computer Graphics, Delhi

Printed in India at
Mehra Offset Press, Delhi

TO MY DAUGHTERS

SAMEETA AND SAMEERA

Who may face such dynamics and dilemmas in their lives.

PREFACE

A few words of apology and explanation are called for if this book is to escape even more severe censure than it doubtless deserves.

Apology is due to the specialists and individual contributors. Every point of view, discussed, is better known to some others than to me. If, however, different case studies and varied perspectives are to be covered in a single book, it is inevitable since those who write such books should spend less time on any one aspect or part than can be spent by a man who concentrates on a single perspective or a brief period. Some, whose scholarly austerity is unbending, will conclude that books covering a wide field should not be written at all, or, if written, should consist of monographs by a multitudes of authors. There is, however, something lost when many authors cooperate. If there is any unity in the theme, if there is any intimate relation between what goes before and what comes later, it is necessary that earlier and later periods should be synthesized in a single mind. Galtung's suggestions and Nixon's implementations are little known today. The current 'Smart Sanctions,' which the globalization and the technological development facilitate, could not be conceived of a decade earlier. Or, Drezner's Conflict Expectation Model, which illustrates the degree of the effectiveness of sanctions, is a definite improvement over the earlier literature which overlooks such nuances in simplistic dichotomy of success and failure, based mainly on the criterion of return to *status quo*. The comparative assessment is necessary to comprehend the relative progress. To bring out such relations is one of the purposes of this book, and it is the purpose, which only a wide survey can fulfill.

The theorists and specialists on sanctions are both 'effects' and 'causes:' effects of the politics and institutions of their time (Galtung, Green, Drezner); causes of beliefs which mould the politics and the institutions in accordance with changing situations or for better consequences (Interlaken, Bonn-Berlin and Stockholm Processes), the efforts of which are going on. Each one of them is the outcome of the milieu in which are crystallized and concentrated thoughts and feelings, which in a vague and defused form are common in the community of which they are the part. It is but natural that a theme such as the subject of this book is inevitably weighted by texts, case studies and theoretical formulation, which act as the 'rational ambassador' of community's feeling. As such this book owes its existence to all such contributors. But since the sanctions affect the very life of the community and such effects have been seen, discussed and analysed from different perspectives, an attempt, however trifling, has been made to present the "collectivity" of such impact. If there is any merit of this book, it is from this point of view that it is derived.

S.J.R. BILGRAMI

Contents

1

Humanitarian Intervention: Sanction Fixation

I. CONCEPT

Humanitarian intervention is an act, which seeks to intervene to stop a government murdering its own people. Traditionally intervention has been defined in terms of 'coercive breach of the walls of the castle of sovereignty.' Such a breach violates the cardinal norm of sovereignty and its logical corollary the principle of non-intervention, which is enshrined in customary international law and codified in Article 2 (7) of the UN Charter. This prohibits the UN from intervening in matters, which are essentially within the jurisdiction of state. The majority of international lawyers argue that the prohibition on the use of force in Article 2 (4) of the UN Charter renders forcible humanitarian intervention illegal. The only legitimate exception is the right of self-defence in Article 51 of the UN Charter on the basis of which it is argued that there is a legal right of unilateral and collective humanitarian intervention in the society of states. But this position is controversial.

Conventionally, humanitarian intervention is defined in terms of intervention motivated by humanitarian consideration, but this raises the question as to what counts as humanitarian? The International Court of Red Cross defines humanitarian acts those that 'prevent and alleviate human suffering.' This definition of humanitarianism is claimed to be non-political and impartial in the sense that all human beings are included as worthy of concern irrespective of sex, race and nationality. The problem with this definition is that it assumes that humanitarian acts are the same across time and space; that a capacity of humanitarianism naturally inheres in all humans by virtue of a common human nature. Critics of this position argue that what counts as human suffering changes from one historical epoch to another. There is nothing natural of inevitable about who gets defined as human/inhuman. Thus slavery was regarded as perfectly natural in one century and identified as scourge against humanity in the next. What this example illustrates is that our conception of humanitarian intervention is culturally specific and has its own biases.[1]

The emerging norm of humanitarian intervention against such 'specificity and biases' challenges the principles of sovereignty, non-intervention and non-use of force, which are the established bases of international society. The pressure of circumstance has moved the society of states towards "human rights culture" which outlaws genocide, torture and massive human rights abuses. But these principles of humanitarianism conflicts with principles of sovereignty and non-intervention. It is argued that sovereign states are expected to act as guardian of their citizen's security, but what happens if states behave as 'gangsters' towards their own people, treat sovereignty as a license to kill? Should murderous state be afforded protection of the norms of sovereignty and non-intervention? What responsibilities do other states have to act as guardians of human rights in the society of states?

These questions, which are the self-answered justifications for the international intervention, prompted few pro-active states to rescue the Kurds in Northern Iraq. But such early euphoria subsided as a result of UN failure in Bosnia and Somalia and West's inaction and indifference to the on-going genocide in Rwanda. Failures in Bosnia and Somalia raised doubts in the efficiency of military force in promoting humanitarian ends. Some suggested greater willingness to employ military force in defence of humanitarian ends, while others emphasize non-violent means for rescuing of suffering humanity since the use of force is always counter-productive. On one hand, the debate is: whether the use of force can promote humanitarian values and long term reconstruction in murderous and/or failed states. On the other hand, the debate is : whether the states can be trusted with responsibility to act as agents of common humanity. The abdication of moral responsibility by Western States in the face of the genocide in

Rwanda suggests that too much faith cannot be reposed in state leaders as guardians of human rights in world politics. For both these reasons, analysts argue reconceptualisation of humanitarian intervention and suggest non-forcible, non-violent and collective humanitarian intervention. But any such attempt is contingent upon two inter-related factors: Since the expression of humanitarian intervention in world politics is product of 'changing historical and social process,' 'the legality of the forceful humanitarian intervention' is a matter of dispute between supporters and opponents.

II. SUPPORTERS

The defenders of humanitarian intervention argue that the maintenance of international peace and security is not the exclusive purpose of the United Nations; the declaration of the UN Charter—"promoting and encouraging respect for human rights and for fundamental freedoms for all," "social progress and better standards of life in larger freedoms," "the UN to be the centre for harmonizing the actions of the nations in the attainment of...common ends"—provide a legal right and a moral duty of humanitarian intervention. The defenders are little impressed by legalistic arguments about the "domestic jurisdiction" of any state and impatient with protracted negotiations and lack of agreement between representatives of national governments. Such impatience led some of them to go even further, assessing that if the UN fails to take remedial action—as is so often the case—the individual states, on the basis of the Articles 1 (3), 55 and 56 of the UN Charter, have the legal right to intervene with force to reduce human suffering. If it is not the case, they stress, the very explicit purposes, for which the United Nations was established, shall be defeated. They point out that as the right to self-defence, under Article 51, humanitarian intervention is the legitimate exception to the non-use of force principle found in Article 2 (4) of the UN Charter.

An additional ground to a legal right of unilateral humanitarian intervention is found in the assertion that a customary legal right exists independently of the UN Charter. Customary International Law is the law of the state practice. If over a period of time, states act in a certain way and come to regard that behaviour as required by the law, then a norm of customary international law has developed. Not only must states actually engage in the practice that is claimed to have the status of customary law but must believe that this practice is required by law. This is described in the language of international law as "Opinion Juris." Thus, states are permitted under pre-Charter customary international law to engage in humanitarian intervention.[2]

The legal and customary instruments for intervention can, by itself, not determine the quantum of abuses. How should the society of state decide when the level of human rights abuses has reached the point where the use of such instruments for forcible intervention is justified? The defenders could never provide the satisfactory answer to this crucial question. J.R. Vincent has, however, dropped some him:[3] "If the threat of life becomes a systematic killing and reaches feminine proportion in which local governments were implicated by failing to meet their responsibilities, then there might fall to international community a duty of a humanitarian intervention." As regards morality of state, Vincent points out: "States ought to satisfy certain basic requirements of decency before they qualify for the protection which the principle of non-intervention provide." Despite ambiguity on this score, defenders draw much inspiration to justify the ground of humanitarian intervention.

III. OPPONENTS

Opponent's objections to legitimizing humanitarian intervention may be summarized as follows:[4] First the reciprocal recognition of sovereignty and non-intervention are usually the norm of interactive behaviour of states. But humanitarian intervention prefers individual justice to the norm of sovereignty and non-intervention. In the face of disagreement about what constitutes extreme human rights violation and in the absence of legitimized consensus on what principle should govern a right of individual or collective humanitarian intervention, if such a right were permitted it would undermine the international order. In the absence of consensus on what consideration are to count as humanitarian, the viability of international order and hence the general well-being of all individuals is better served by upholding the principle of non-intervention. Otherwise the humanitarian intervention shall always remain the cultural preferences of the powerful. Moreover, in the absence of an impartial mechanism for deciding when humanitarian intervention is permissible, the state cannot act even if convinced of theoretical and speculative justification of J.R. Vincent. In such situation state might spouse humanitarian motives as a pretext to cover the pursuit of national interests. Thus the humanitarian intervention will always be a weapon that strong will use against the weak.

Second, states are usually motivated to intervene, not by the sentiments of humanity, compassion or fellow feeling, but by what they judge to be their national interests. As states are governed by what they judge to be their national interest, they will always intervene only when they deem this to be at stake. It means that they will always apply the principle of humanitarian intervention selectively, resulting in an inconsistency in policy. The problem of selectivity arises when an agreed moral principle is at stake in more than one situation, but national interest dictates a divergence of responses. A good example of selectivity of response is the claim of Muslim states that the West is guilty of double standards in failing to respond as effectively to the plight of Bosnian Muslims as it had in the case of Iraqi Kurds. The differentiated treatment of Israeli and Palestinian interactive behaviour is also cited in this respect. Selectivity of response is the problem of failing to treat like cases alike.

Third, the responsibilities, obligations and duties of state are limited to its own citizens. If civil society has broken down or is behaving in an appalling way towards its citizens, this is the responsibility of that state's citizens and its political leaders. Outsiders have no moral duty to intervene independently even if they would be able to improve the situation and stop the killing. The condition of prior consent from the host country in peacekeeping operation is the recognition of this consideration.

Fourth, some specific and extraordinary situation apart, states do not normally risk their soldier's lives on humanitarian crusades. The military itself is not always to participate in humanitarian efforts. Soldiers are in fact keen to react quickly and aggressively. They are not neutral. But in humanitarian intervention, they are often called upon to work with the people whom they would otherwise want to arrest. Their hierarchical culture and prescribed standard operating procedures are quite distinct from those of their civilian counterparts who clearly do not operate like this.

Fifth, the United Nations is a treaty organization, not a government. While its Charter begins with "We the People," its structure is built on sovereign nations that have ceded little real authority. The United Nations has no independent source of financing—it must rely on voluntary compliance with assessments. Consequently it can decide and act only when there is sufficient support not only for a favourable veto or consensus, but also, and more significantly, for necessary financial, military and diplomatic support of action. Finding justifications on the basis of the declared objectives, expressed in the lofty language of the Charter, shatters on such factual grounds.

Sixth, the prohibition on the use of force in Article 2 (4) of the UN Charter is already vulnerable to states abusing it in the name of self-defence under Article 51. The UN members, under Article 56, pledge to "take joint or separate action in cooperation with the organization." The defenders assert that "joint or separate action" justify arbitrary action and presume that the condition of "cooperation" is implied if such arbitrary action fulfils the purposes set forth in Article 55. Thus, the concept of cooperation is attached with the 'consequence,' not with the 'procedure.' The artful detachment of cooperation from the procedure and attachment with the consequence provide space to "separate action" to be interpreted as "arbitrary action." It amounts to taking liberty with Article 56 of the UN Charter in order to justify unilaterally the humanitarian intervention.

As for as the existence of the pre-UN Charter customary international laws are concerned, they virtually belong to the colonial phase, which has already passed away. The UN silence over such customary laws should not be presumed as 'silent approval;' it is the 'oversight of irrelevance.' Any attempt to regard these customary laws of the discarded phase will amount to re-colonisation of de-colonisation process by other means. The non-Western world is sensitive to this danger, which involves in invoking the customary laws to justify "humanitarian" intervention.

Thus the opponents are convinced that the ground of humanitarian intervention lacks the consensus, the provisions of the UN Charter are stretched too far and the invoking of the customary laws are out of context in the present situation. The Charter provisions are based on check and balance, for instance Article 51 and Article 2 (4). Any effort to highlight the one and downplay the other would render the interpretation doubtful. The attempt of gaining the universal legitimacy of the customary laws of the colonial powers is controversial. In short the over all case of the defenders is not only weak but 'tailor-made' and full of conscious effort.

IV. INTERACTION

The interaction between supporters and opponents culminated when in his September 20, 1999 address to the UN General Assembly, the Secretary General, Kofi Annan identified four aspects of armed intervention in resolving future conflicts. Since such identity represents, in nutshell, the main pleas of the defenders of the principle of humanitarian intervention it evoked much "reaction" in the General Assembly. The summary of Kofi Annan's arguments is as follows:[5]

(a) A strategic irony of many of the crises, that continues to go unnoticed and unchallenged today, is that they could be dealt with by far less perilous acts of intervention than one we witnessed recently in Yugoslavia.

(b) The sovereignty alone is not the only obstacle to effective action in human rights or humanitarian crisis. No less significant are the ways in which the members of the UN define their national interests in any given crisis. Thus, the national sovereignty and a state's interpretation of its national interests can be challenged in the interests of humanitarian intervention.

(c) If forceful intervention becomes necessary, we must ensure that the Security Council, the body charged with authorizing under international law, is able to rise to the challenge. He argued that the case should neither be that of Rwanda when the Council never achieved a consensus and therefore the genocide of the Tutsis went on unchecked, nor that of Kosovo, when group of states took military action outside the established mechanism for enforcing international law.

(d) If states, bent on criminal behaviour, know that frontiers are not the absolute defence, if they know that the Council will take actions to halt crimes against humanity, then they will not embark on such a course of action in expectation of sovereign impunity. So long this sovereign impunity shall continue to be regarded as exclusive preserve, the sanctions shall continue to harm the civilian population more than the Iraqi leaders for whom the sanctions were originally intended.

Predictably enough, India and China, along with several other countries, which had earlier opposed NATO aerial bombing of Yugoslavia, rejected promptly the "humanitarian intervention theory." Directly challenging the Secretary General's thesis, the External Affairs Minister, Jaswant Singh told the UN General Assembly on September 22:[6] "It would be an error to assume that the days of state are over. The state continues to have a crucial role and relevance; also therefore national sovereignties. The UN was not conceived of as super state; it will not even become so, principally because there is no viable substitute to sovereign state. Significantly, the call to strengthen the Security Council for an effective armed intervention in an humanitarian crisis suits those permanent members who led the NATO action in Yugoslavia, the US and UK."

The Indian representative to UN pointed out:[7] "Secretary General's forceful plea for intervention, citing the catastrophes in Kosovo and Rwanda to press home his case, comes at a time when aggressive elements are espousing ideologies supporting enforced homogenization or separation of ethnic groups as against support for ideals of multi-cultural and pluralistic societies which respect human variety."

The reaction to Secretary General's proposal may be summarized as follows:[8] The underlying premise of the proposal is based on a dubious presumption that external forces can resolve all problems in every part of the world when the UN and the international community have neither the resources nor capability to undertake it; under the pretext of defending human rights, the rising international impulse runs the danger of exacerbating conflict between and within states; what some regard as humanitarian actions others would consider as war crimes; the emergence of the principle of armed intervention to redress humanitarian issues would set the world as a perilous slope. In principle, at least, there would be no limit to it; deep concern at humanitarian crisis should not obscure the reality that such action is prone to being viewed through a political prism; theories of interventions seeking to justify interference and use of force to fight alleged repression might end up strengthening the hands of covert interventionists.

It seems, no doubt, convincing that genocide or other egregious civilian suffering turn conditions so bad that it almost becomes upright to ignore the fundamental tenet of non-intervention in the domestic affairs of a sovereign state. These are the compelling reasons to justify military humanitarian intervention. But the fact is that the intensity of the situation cannot be determined and the consequences remain blurred. As a result there is still reluctance to intervene in most armed conflicts; areas such as Tibet and Chechnya are considered off-limits. Use of air power in Kosovo and on an ongoing basis in Iraq have simply increased civilian suffering in the name of humanitarianism.

As such, extreme caution is necessary and all options, other than military, should be explored. For instance, arms embargoes may be one policy option. Or instead of virtually impossible task of intervening between and among warring factions, perhaps it would be better to seal borders, prevent the delivery of weapons and create truly safe heaven—thereby quarantining violence and minimizing civilian casualties. It is generally believed that fighting simply cannot be allowed to continue when genocide is taking place, that more imaginative solutions can and should be found.

V. ASSESSMENT

The pleas of supporters and opponents as well as their inter-active behaviour create the impression that the term "humanitarian" has been stretched so far that the adjective's currency is de-based. It is virtually a "military intervention for humanitarian purposes" rather than "humanitarian intervention."[9] It is also revealed that the legitimacy of humanitarian intervention remained mainly confined to Western states; the wider legitimacy of humanitarian intervention has been challenged by non-Western states. These states are sensitive to the danger of being seen to legitimize exceptions to the non-intervention principle. However, the ramification of the international system and the invocation and application of the UN provisions are essential pre-requisites for a viable assessment of humanitarian intervention.

As the international system is what major nations conceive of it, they arrogate to themselves the right of intervention in the name of concern for international community. The process of legitimacy of intervention under international law has already started through advocacy as well as the precedence of interventions around.

An inherent contradiction exists between interdependence and lone superpower after the end of cold war. The growing inter-dependence seeks accommodation of racial interests for managing the equitable distribution of resources whether of security or development. The increasing domination and control of the lone superpower develops the temptation to take arbitrary action in the name of international community, which, in turn, amounts virtually to profiting, incidentally or intentionally, of other people's hostilities. Reciprocity, so beneficial in the interdepending phase is, thus, destroyed by such arbitrary intervention.

United States fixes missile at Bin Laden but not at his main sponsor who heads the Taliban; it eases its 46 years old sanctions on North Korea under the deal which debars North Korean missile tests but not missile export to Pakistan; the US nuclear cooperation deal with China adjures missile transfer to Iran but not to Pakistan; despite acknowledgment by China and confirmation by US intelligence, Washington failed to invoke sanctions, mandated by its domestic laws, on China for transfer of M-11 to Islamabad.[10] With such ambivalent behaviour pattern a strange mismatch emerges:[11] "Those promoting internationalism and seeking to enforce international norm in the name of international community are riding a wave of nationalism at home. The biggest exponents of economic liberalization protect their own markets with non-tariff barriers. Political and economic unilateralism goes hand-in-hand with multilateralism". On one hand, the 'covert fragmenting trends' within the 'overt globalisation' are generating religious orthodoxy, ethnic applications and even xenophobia, which are spreading terrorism. On the other hand, the coincidence between globalisation and humanitarian intervention is being portrayed as a return to 18th century colonialism when the imperial powers set out to civilize other societies and append them to their capitalist economy. Thus the overt intervention is little different from Taliban type of covert intervention. After all, both overt and covert interventionists justify interference and use of force on the ground of combating repression. They can only exacerbate inter-state and intra-state conflicts besides setting the stage for a war between themselves.

In an interdependent world, the increasing incidence of internal war carries implications beyond national boundaries. As such non-interference cannot remain inviolable in all circumstances. This challenge to the principle of non-intervention is significant because the European colonial powers, which had created some modern states through fusion of ethnic and tribal states, have started foreseeing the bloody ethnic conflict and collapsing states in 21st century. The increasing number of armed conflicts in 1990s with external intervention taking place in several cases justifies such danger.

As the international system is based, not on collective security but on national security, the advocacy of right to intervention against the 19th century concept of absolute sovereignty raises some troubling questions:[12] Who will judge when and how to intervene? How do we ensure that such an intervention does not make matter worse or create new tragedies as has happened in the Balkans or elsewhere? Without sanctity to the principle of non-interference, how can the international community seek to discipline states sponsoring terrorism or proxy war against a rival state? If signatories of peace agreement do not respect their commitments, should they not be left alone? Whether an intervention in the American civil war would have been a good idea? Belligerents should not be stopped because unless they are ready and willing to settle, they are not going to settle. This view is not callous but sensible for instigating more imaginative solutions.

In the context of international system these issues are very significant for the critical assessment and reconceptualisation of the humanitarian intervention principle. The other base of evaluation is the UN provision.

The United Nations has tried to curb the possible arbitrariness, which the international system promotes. The UN General Assembly resolution of 1966 enumerated the following grounds to justify intervention: (a) Enforcement of treaty rights; (b) Self-defence or right to exist; (c) Right over protectorate; (d) In pursuance of UN Charter; (e) In violation of international law; (f) In protection of person or property abroad; (g) On humanitarian ground; (h) In civil war situation.

All such exceptional rights of intervention are permitted on the basis of 'collective decision.' Under no circumstances the 'arbitrary intervention' is allowed. No matter how moral or plausible sum of the foregoing justifications of intervention may have appeared in specific instances, the fact remains that intervention, in essence, is a hostile act which is rendered possible only because of superior force of intervening state which shall provide licence to arbitrary act if not checked collectively.

The permanent members of the Security Council are assigned the task of maintaining the international peace and security; decision cannot be taken without their concurrence and once decision taken, shall be binding on all the members of the United Nations. This arrangement of the collective security system provided enough space for unilateral intervention and was legitimized when the arrangement was found operationally imperfect. It is but natural that the territorial, commercial and other ambitions of permanent members continue to clash with their sense of responsibility for maintaining international order. But the system stopped working when a single member was sufficiently powerful to dominate the rest. If five permanent members of the Security Council are mandated to act as "Trustees" of the entire membership of the United Nations, the logical conclusion is that the first among them, emerged to be so under the pressure of circumstances, would automatically behave unilaterally on behalf of the entire international community. It so seems as if the British Cabinet model has emerged at the international level: "The First Among Equals" is acting as Prime Minister. The danger invokes in this situation is not merely that the prior condition of getting approval of the UN does not require but the unilateral and arbitrary action are such in which the legitimacy of the collectivity is falsely supposed to be taken for granted.

The enforcement action, under Chapter VII of the UN Charter, is concerned with the "inter-state" aggression and in case the aggression is proved the military operation can take place without any subsequent consent. But the "intra-state" conflict is a new situation, which is not covered under Chapter VII. In order to deal with such situation, the United Nations has been innovative to develop peace-keeping operation which lies somewhere between the pacific settlement of Chapter VI and enforcement action of Chapter VII of the UN Charter. This arrangement requires the consent of parties concerned.

The outside forces, which are intervening in intra-state conflict in the name of humanitarian intervention, can neither legitimize their action under Chapter VII which is automatically binding nor can be regarded as peace-keeping which necessitates prior permission from a host country. Such arbitrary operation on the part of multi-national forces does not only clash with the established norm of sovereignty and non-intervention but does not confirm to either enforcement action against the aggressor or peace-keeping operation in an intra-state repression. Moreover, such arbitrary behaviour does not only threaten the effectiveness of the United Nations but actually violates the International Committee of the Red Cross's (ICRC's) principles of classic humanitarian action—consent, neutrality and impartiality.

Iraq's invasion of Kuwait, 1990, is the kind of situation requiring intervention anticipated by the Chapter VII of UN Charter. But the Council's monitoring of post war development within Iraq's border is a clear violation of Charter's prohibition on interference in domestic affairs. The US missile attack on Afghanistan and Sudan and ongoing US-British military assault on Iraq and Serbia are the examples of unilateral intervention without even the technical regard of either the principle of collectivity or the existence of any regime. The stationing of UN human rights monitors in Haiti was without any reference to whether or not there was any threat to international peace and security under Chapter VII. Similarly it was an innovation when the Council decided that a humanitarian emergency caused by a natural disaster or by the collapse of state such as in Somalia, bringing about chaos, social unrest and human suffering, is adequate to intervene. The greatest departure from the traditional ground for intervention came in Libya when the Council decided allegedly that state-sponsored terrorism justified intervention. The culmination is the independent and unqualified declaration of war against all such countries, which allegedly sponsor, indulge or harbour terrorism.

These examples and such developments are supposed to be the evolutionary enlargement of the concept of "threat to international peace and security." But these arbitrary and selective characters serve more the strategic interests of some great powers rather than contribute to the expanding jurisdiction of the concept of threat to peace and security. Moreover, while violation of human rights, humanitarian emergencies and even terrorism should engender UN response, it should not be done under the rubric of a threat to peace and security. The United Nations should change the Charter to authorize intervention on other clearly defined grounds.

Against background of the international system, which generates the arbitrary behaviour and the UN system, which provides the space for unilateral action, the arguments of "humanitarian" intervention may better be examined. Such arguments runs as follows: Under no circumstances can government claim it is lawful to massacre its own population under the protective umbrella of 'internal matter;' all states have agreed in a sovereign manner the principle of right to life and illegality of genocide, so they must respect these principles in a sovereign manner too; where massive violence of the people's most basic rights occur, the retaliatory measures and reprisals can be taken in political, diplomatic, economic and financial ways. The actions, motivated by such arguments, have been undertaken to justify intervention in Argentina, Afghanistan, Haiti, Burundi, Iraq, Somalia, Rwanda, Bosnia, Herzegovina, Liberia, Sierra Leone, Albania, Kosovo, Cuba, Iran, Korea, Lebanon, Mexico, Nicaragua, Grenada, Panama,

Jordan, Dominican Republic, and Serbia. These operations have been carried on by the international community through either United Nations or by certain states, which are prepared to defend this principle on humanitarian ground.

But the contradictions between justifications and actions are too glaring: While the justifications are regime-based and of collective nature, the actions are arbitrary and unilateral; while the justifications are exceptional, the actions are frequent; while the amount of interference is increasing, the number of interventionists are decreasing from multilateral to bilateral to unilateral; while the large canvas of intervention is justified as the 'expanding jurisdiction' of humanitarianism, the character of the volume of intervention has practically reached to internecine proportion. No doubt, it is justified to say that under exceptional circumstances the 'sovereignty' of state cannot be used as licence to kill. But it is equally true to say that the superior force of state, without which the intervention is not possible, cannot be used as licence to arbitrary and unilateral action.

Another justification is based on historical precedents. It is argued that the Western military action against the Ottoman empire as well as in Africa and Far East have been justified in the past on the humanitarian ground and the United Nations has not put an end to such practices. Thus, on the basis of historical continuity it is emphasized that the traditional international law is not inadequate for intervention.

But this adequacy of international law collapses on the factual ground that the right to exercise veto in the Security Council means that nobody is going to claim that international law is perfectly adequate for arbitrary intervention on behalf of international community. Moreover this historical precedents ignored the entire phase of anti-imperialist and anti-colonial movement which resulted in the liberation of colonies which, in turn, for the first time in human history, democratized and universalized the international system. To ignore such transformation phase of historical precedent means to insist on a return to a situation where there was a right to intervene, the legacy of which manifests in side-stepping the UN decision and its involvement today. It means that the world's most powerful states, on the basis of 'pick and choose' phases of historical precedents, aspire to arrogate to themselves the authority to act as the judge of what humanity supposedly needs. The net result is that once again the 'might is right.'

The worst part of it is that such unilateral intervention is not uniform: The use of terms such as "Unique," "Extraordinary" and "Exceptional" do not characterize the intervention principle but manifest the attempt to differentiate the humanitarian crisis, say in Somalia, from other cases of failed states, hence, reducing the chance of setting precedent for future humanitarian intervention. They seem to have been inserted specifically to appease the fear of states such as China, which may have otherwise blocked a Chapter VII enforcement action.[13]

Such added adjectives cannot cover up the selective and therefore discriminatory aspect. The term itself is permanently over-loaded with the adjective 'humanitarian,' which cannot automatically become the echo of international community to the extent of justifying unilateral intervention on its behalf as if carrying the spirit of Rousseau's "General Will."

A compound situation, which often remains out of sight, is the direct result of such arbitrary action. A state which seeks to induce another to observe the law of its own volition protests an impending or actual violation and takes a retaliatory actions of various kinds—in the mode of a traditional balancer—, thus blurring the distinction between intervention and non-intervention. There is a considerable justification in Talleyrand's remark that:[14] "non-intervention is a political term meaning virtually the same as intervention." As such an amalgamating process serves the interests of few alone. In this process, the non-intervention and collective intervention may coincide, but non-intervention and unilateral intervention may contradict despite the ambiguous or 'maneuvered' approval of the international community.

The principle of 'invitational'[15] intervention has also provided pretext to major powers to use smaller states as a pawn on the chess board of power politics. After the collapse and disintegration of Soviet Union, this principle of 'invitational' intervention has become an added excuse to the only superpower to dictate terms even to the Security Council of the United

Nations, to compel other major powers like Britain and France, to work as allies of the United States in specific situations. Such postures threaten the sovereignty and independence of smaller states. The fact is that in the case of strife, which is primarily internal, and particularly, where the outcome is uncertain, the mere invitation by either faction to an outside state to intervene does not legalize an otherwise improper intervention.

Thus, the doctrine of humanitarian intervention, which might seem attractive in theory, has led to and is still leading to many abuses in practice. The reason is that the humanitarian intervention is usually sanctioned under legal provisions, customary laws and historical precedents. But the policy has become controversial as a result of arbitrary, unilateral and coercive use, the frequent application and the consistent failure. Under such distressing circumstances, the "sanctions" which had so far been used as "verb," acquired the status of "noun." It gradually emerged as "policy" itself for the imposing state and "issue" itself for the targeting state. Soon the policy aspect developed into an "Art of Diplomacy" for the former and the issue aspect developed into the "Science of State-Craft" for the latter. In such transformation the "GENE" of humanism remains intact. It is in this sense that humanitarian intervention is "Sanction Fixation."

REFERENCES

1. Nicholas J. Wheeler, "Humanitarian Intervention and World Politics" in John Baylis and Steve Smith (eds.), *The Globalisation of World Politics*, Oxford University Press, 1997, p. 393.
2. *Ibid.* p. 396.
3. *Ibid.*, See Box 20.2, p. 396, Vincent defined intervention as set out in Box 1. *Ibid.*, p. 393. He was not writing specifically of humanitarian intervention but his definition sums up the traditional view. For the overview of the case of supporters see Policy Bulletin: Using "Any Means Necessary" for Humanitarian Crisis Response, 36th United Nations of the Next Decade Conference, The Stanley Foundation, 2001. The full report is available online at http://reports.stanleyfoundation.orge.
4. For detail on intervention see Nicholas J. Wheeler, *Ibid.*, pp. 391-407. For key concept on the theory of humanitarian intervention see *Ibid.*, Box (Box 20.3), p. 397; Paul Taylor, "The United Nations and International Organisation—particularly subheading: The United

Nations and Intervention within States, in John Baylis and Steve Smith (eds.), *Ibid.*, pp. 273-84; "The UN Role In Intervention: Where do we go from here?, 28th UN of the Next Decade Conference, The Stanley Foundation, June 13-18, 1993, pp. 6-31; Vernon Van Dyke, *International Politics*, Vakils, Feffer & Simons Pvt., Bombay, 1969, pp. 265, 280, 382; Olivier Corton, "Humanitarian Intervention: A Controversial Right, vide hllp://www.UNESCO,org/courier/1999 o8/ UK/ethique/txt1.htm. pp. 1-3; Fernando Teson, "Humanitarian Intervention: An Inquiry into Law and Morality," New York, Transitional Publishers, 1988.

5. *Hindustan Times*, 27-9-1999.
6. *Ibid.*, 8-10-1999.
7. *Ibid.*
8. *Ibid.*
9. Report of the Fortieth Strategy for Peace, US Foreign Policy Conference, The Stanley Foundation, 1999, p. 39.
10. Brahma Chellaney, "Foreign Policy Challenges," *Hindustan Times*, 22-9-1999.
11. *Ibid.*
12. *Ibid.* For some of the questions already mentioned and other queries see The UN Role In Intervention, *op. cit.*, p. 12; and the Report of the Fortieth Strategy, *op. cit.*, p. 43.
13. Nicholas J. Wheelar, *op. cit.*, p. 402.
14. Palmer Perkin, *International Politics*, CBS Publishers, Delhi, 1985, p. 226.
15. See S.J.R. Bilgrami, "Resistance to Arbitrary Intervention" in Pramila Srivastava (ed.) NAM: Extending Frontiers. NOIDA Publishing House, NOIDA (U.P.), 2000, p. 156 (Full article: pp. 151-57).

2

Sanctions Paradox

I. ILLUSTRATION

Economic Sanctions, as Miroslav and Wallensteen, illustrate[1] are economic pains inflicted by one government on another in order to attain some political gains. If the aim of intervention is purely economic ends, just as to trigger prices in order to protect steel producers, it will not come under sanctions unless associated with political goals. Similarly, bombing of an economy's industrial installations is an economic warfare, not an economic sanctions. But sometimes the distinction is blurred when purely an economic action is directed to a military objective and the time between political and military goals are intermingled; even when an adequate distinction is made, both objectives—military and political—is pursued by the same means. For example the purpose of US control of its export and those of its allies to Soviet Union had been to undermine Russian military capacity by depriving it of relevant technology; control, however, had also been designed to demonstrate distaste for Soviet communism, to punish specific policies, to display toughness in cold war dispute etc. So this is the admixture of economic warfare and economic sanctions.

Still distinction can be made on the basis of 'coerciveness.' At the least coercive end, there is a diplomatic bargaining based on the reciprocity and often coupled with persuasion. At the opposite end, adjustment in other nations policies can be pursued by military force, by the direct destruction of life and property. Economic sanctions occupy the middle ground between the two extremes. They are coercive but not directly destructive. This middle ground is infested with infiltration, propaganda and the clandestine support of population groups. While such covert interventions remain within the purview of many nations, the effective economic sanctions is the practical prerogative of few members of the international community.

It is generally presumed that by inflicting the economic pains the target state would abandon the course that provoked economic retribution. A loss of external markets of needful goods and capital would lead the target state to reason. Thus, the costs of controversial policy outweigh its benefit. For instance, the sanctions imposed by 17 Arab nations against Egypt because of support to Camp David, were mainly intended to force the Egyptian leadership to renege on its accommodating policy. The apparent intent of Washington's sanctions against Nicaragua was to pressure the Sandinistas to withdraw their military support of El-Salvador's leftist rebels and loosen Managua's ties to Castro.

This main function is usually attributed to economic sanctions. But often the target states adhere so steadfastly to its chosen policy that it creates doubts in initiator's own ability to force the government, via sanction, to abandon policies to which they are firmly committed. Under such compulsions, official declaration notwithstanding, the ousting of the recalcitrant government and replacing it with a more compliant set of leaders may become the real intent. The idea is that the other politically potent actors as well as the nation's public will blame the incumbents for bringing the economic difficulties upon them, resist their clinging to such costly policies, and ultimately remove them from power by any measures necessary.

When Stalin recalled technical advisers from Yugoslavia, cut-off trade with it, cancelled promised loans and forced Soviet allies to follow his example, that expectation was not that Yugoslavian leaders would repent but that they would be overthrown. Similarly the motivation behind US action against Cuba seems to be more of causing Castro's downfall rather than forcing him to reform. Although neither of the regimes has fallen as a result of sanctions, the externally created economic dislocation may have indeed increased some governmental instability. Also, whereas economic pressures may hasten political decay in a highly polarized society, it may produce the opposite effect in a nation where cleavages run less deep. Numerous examples may satisfy to this possibility.

The sanctions directed against Sadat by the hard line nations may, for instance, have strengthened the domestic support for the Egyptian government which is reflected in the statement: 'Other Arab states grew rich while Egypt bore the brunt of the conflict with Israel'. Tito's internal popularity was also enhanced by Russian belligerence and a similar conclusion might apply to Castro's position in the face of US pressure. In fact a hostile superpower, wielding its economic might against a weak and beleaguered nation will usually rouse the patriotic indignation of its population and generate a 'rally-round-the-flag' effect to the government's benefit. On the whole, the success of economic sanctions remains doubtful if the purpose is to face a significant policy change or to cause the removal of an unpalatable government. Their overall usefulness has not, however, been refuted.

Sometimes the purpose is to deter objectionable future policies by demonstrating an ability to retaliate rather than modify extant behaviour. If undesirable is punished with sufficient severity it may not be repeated by the target state. In addition, the example of punishment may discourage other countries from engaging in the unacceptable activities. The interest of the sanctioning state can thus be promoted although the initial offence has not been undone. For example, another purpose of the measures against Cuba was to discourage other Latin American nations from emulating Castro's policies. Despite the thin prospects of forcing Russian withdrawal from Afghanistan through pressure, if the policy continued the more plausible intention of Carter administration might have been to deter further instances of Soviet aggression. Stalin probably hoped to cause the disintegration of Tito's regime. But the wish to discourage similar displays of independence on the part of other communist countries—some of which were of greater strategic importance to the Soviet Union—may have been the more potent motive for the economic retaliation.

The success of the sanctions with the aim of deterring others cannot be confidently assessed. How can it be proved that the memory of sanctions in the wake of invasion of Afghanistan may be helpful in explaining why Poland was spared the fate that befell Czechoslovakia in 1968; or the failure of Soviet economic pressure against Yugoslavia in 1948 may have led Moscow to opt for military action against Hungary in 1956; or the economic coercion to which Yugoslavia was once subjected may have played some part in discouraging emulation of Tito's independent path elsewhere in the Soviet bloc? Such speculative analysis may at best be 'plausible' but cannot be taken as a 'definitive proof' of the sanction effectiveness.

Sometimes the purpose of the initiator's government may not be either to change the behaviour of the target state or to prevent it to repeat the objectionable policy in future or to deter other nations but to address the desire of the domestic political group or incumbent's own political interests. For instance the forceful US action against the Soviet Union aimed at to demonstrate to American public that the aggression in Afghanistan would not be met with passive acquiescence; at the same time it produced a surge of domestic support for the US President. Thus, sanctions, in this respect, may be more valuable for the symbolic content they convey domestically and added support that this may mean for the political elite. As the *New York Times* observed following the US ban on imports of Iranian oil in 1980: "The decision...appeared to many to be more effective in bolstering the President than in bringing the release of the hostages."[2]

Miroslav's and Wallensteen's illustration of 'what is and what is not' sanction and its varied purposes, the summarized version of which is presented above, leaves doubt about the efficacy of sanction. However the co-authors are realistic enough when they admit:[3] "Of all the ends that sanctions can plausibly be intended to promote, the objective to advance the interest of the government applying it seems to be more effective. Not all the effects of sanctions can be anticipated, however, and many of those that should be expected may actually be counter productive to initiator's interests."

Galtung has tried to compress all the illustrative ramifications when he defines that[4] "a sanction is an action initiated by one or more international actors (the senders) against one or more others (the receivers) with either or both of two purposes: to punish the receivers by depriving them of some value and/or to make the receiver comply with certain norms the senders deem important." He miniaturized the ramified dilemmas when he raised the querry:[5] "If one cannot have both, which outcome is preferable: punishment without compliance or compliance without punishment?" In an effort to overcome this dilemma, he propounded the following classification of sanctions:[6]

(1) Sanctions—negative (punishment) or positive (compliance);
(2) Sanctions aimed at 'individual' or 'collective' involving nation as a whole;
(3) Sanctions—'internal' (as a result of inside changes) or 'external' (as a result of interaction pattern with other nations);
(4) Sanctions—'unilateral' or 'multilateral' or 'universal';
(5) Sanctions—'general' or 'selective';
(6) Sanctions—'total' or 'partial' and
(7) Types of Sanctions—diplomatic, communicative and economic.

If the goal is to damage the economic system of receiving nations without similarly damaging the sending nations, Galtung has enumerated the following conditions, required to be fulfilled:[7]

(a) Imports have a very high loading on the important sectors of the economy of the receiving nations;
(b) There is no internal substitute for the imports;
(c) The high loading of the important imports from the sending nations;
(d) There is no external substitute for these imports so that the receiving nations cannot threaten to change trade partners;
(e) The import make up a very small part of the exports of the sending nations and/or the products cannot be exported to other nations;
(f) The exports from the receiving nations are sent mainly to the sending nations and there are no easy substitutes from them so that receiving nations cannot obtain income easily;
(g) These exports from the receiving nations can easily be obtained elsewhere by the nations so that the sending nations are not hurt economically and can threaten to change trade partners or the export cannot be obtained

elsewhere by sending nations so that the sending nations can demonstrate that they would rather suffer deprivation than touch products from the receiving nations and

(h) Trade relations can easily be supervised and even controlled (as when the receiving nation is an island or is surrendered either by impenetrable terrain, such as swaps or desert or by nations that participate in boycott).

A small economic satellite of a major economic power can alone fulfil these conditions. In most of these cases, barring few, this situation has actually emerged. Even ninety per cent of both import or export of the smaller country may be with the big country, yet this trade volume may still be less than one per cent of the big country's total trade. This trade structure occurs in the present world, and it gives a major potential for control by the big nations of those small nations in their 'sphere of interests', particularly, since the power of any weapon lies in its potentiality than in its actual use.

The crucial concept here is 'vulnerability', which has external and internal components. The key to the understanding of vulnerability, as Galtung has pointed out, seems to be 'concentration:'[8] "The more a country's economy depends on one product, and the more its exports consists of one product, and the more its imports and exports are concentrated on one trade partner, the more vulnerable is the country. Since vulnerability is more a property of small power than a property of a poor nation, economic sanctions as a source of power, tend to preserve the existing power structure."

The least vulnerable are big countries such as USA, Europe, Japan, China, Brazil, Mexico, India, Argentina, Columbia etc. Bigger countries, of course, have in general more diversity in raw material and bigger domestic markets; hence they have more potential for diversified domestic industries, which can be converted to export industries. The three factors of concentration—in economy, in commodities and in trade partners—are of equal weight in determining external vulnerability. But in the context of classification such concentration is qualified. As Galtung has pointed out:[9] "If sanctions are universal (and not unilateral) geographic concentration will not count; if sanctions are general (and not highly selective) commodity concentration will not count; and if sanctions are both universal and general (and total) then only the trade percentage of the G.N.P. will count."

The 'illustration' leaves a contradictory situation: While the existing power structure encourages the imposition of sanctions, the ramifications keep their goals elusive. Naturally the question arises: What should be the proper sanctioning level—above which the sanctions remain a threat to small states, below which, they remain a temptation to major powers? The subsequent sections, which further de-codify the 'Sanctions Paradox,' may perhaps provide some clue to such query.

II. OBJECTIVES

Sanctions, as mentioned, are measures directed to political objectives. In this respect, James Barber has explained certain ambiguities:[10] The primary-ambiguity is the relationship between sanctions and use of force. While some see the sanctions as alternative to force, others view that sanctions can be effective when force is available and ready to be used if required. This ambiguity creates confusion. For example, when League of Nations was preparing in 1935 to impose sanctions against Italy, some members were opposed to blocking the Suez Canal or cutting communications with Italy because the League was 'a great instrument of peace.' In contrast others believed that 'collective security' could only be ensured if force were available. Some of those who opposed the use of force believed in the organized moral force against the aggression. Other supporters are more pragmatic. They recognize that sanctions are limited in terms of means as well as ends. In many situations force may be unacceptable methods. Such diversity of views has rendered the objectives of sanctions somewhat haphazard.

The initiative in imposing international sanctions normally rests on one or two particular governments; but to make the sanctions effective they usually attempt to recruit other states and to involve international agencies. Thus, sanctions may be employed by a single government—the United States against China; or by a group of national community as a whole through an instrumentality of an international organization—the League of Nations against Italy or United Nations against Iraq. The range of sanctions and the intensity with which these are imposed varies considerably which, in turn, manifests differentiated objectives.

Apart from the question of number of states imposing sanctions there is also the question whether the sanctions are employed selectively, concentrating a particular aspect of the economy such as oil supplies or whether they are applied on a much wider basis. Another issue is that of authority which may lack the sanctions. This may be only a recommendation by an international agency to its member states—and inside state by a government to business organization—or alternatively there may be an attempt to make the sanctions mandatory even to the extent of imposing them by law. Rhodesia is an example in which an effort has been made to maximize sanctions on each of these three scales—universal, comprehensive and mandatory. It took thirty months to reach that position and even then the applications of sanctions did not gain universal support. As such the objective remain ambiguous.

Changes in the behaviour of government, against whom sanctions are directed, are much less clear. There has always been diversity of consideration which remain concealed behind the declared goals but which, in fact, play an important role in imposing, retaining and even intensifying sanctions. As such the objectives for which sanctions are imposed are far from simple or straightforward.

Against such amalgamating objectives, discussed, James Barber stated:[11] There are 'primary objectives' which are concerned with the action and behaviour of the state or regime against whom the sanctions are directed—the target state. There are 'secondary objectives' relating to the status, behaviour and expectations of the governments imposing sanctions—the 'imposing state.' And there are 'tertiary objectives' concerned with international considerations relating either to the structure and operation of the international system as a whole or to those part of it which are regarded as important by the imposing state.

He clarifies:[12] It was the primary objectives of sanctions to stop Italy attacking Ethiopia; it was the secondary objective for the labour government to counter attacks by the conservatives over Rhodesia; it was the tertiary objective for the USA to seek in Cuba to stop the spread of communism to the Western hemisphere. When the sanctions are applied over a lengthy period, the relative weight of these different categories of objectives may shift. Such shift may be noticed in Rhodesia and Iraq when secondary objectives emerge prominent as hopes of achieving the primary objectives dwindled. Each category contains diverse dimensions, which require some detailed discussion:

(i) ***Primary Objectives:***[13] The primary objectives are themselves diverse. They include to induce internal political change within the target state, as the USA sought successfully to do in the Dominican Republic; to force an erring member of a regional alliance back into the fold, as the Russian tried to achieve with Yugoslavia; to deter target state from action beyond its border, which is what the United States sought to do against Japan in 1930; to weaken or punish the target state as in the case of Arab boycott of Israel; to force a target state to accept broadly agreed international norms as in the argument over sanctions against South Africa.

Even if the purposes of sanctions are precisely identified, their application cannot be isolated from other factors. Circumstances change over time and diversity of objectives always remain against which success or failure may be measured. Moreover, there are important and damaging side effects of sanctions such as denial of international legitimacy and encouragement of the revolutionary group effect, which may not always have been intended when the sanctions were imposed but which have had an adverse impact upon the target state. American sanctions against Cuba had a reverse effect of that intended for they helped to bolster Castro's position and opened up opportunities for Russian involvement. In the case of Dominican Republic, though sanctions succeeded to topple the regime but replacement was not to the liking and acceptance of the United States. So economic sanctions are not only ineffective but, in some cases, counter productive.

When sanctions are imposed, the issue for the imposing state is how to achieve the political result by economic pressure and the issue for the target state is how to resist the proposed political changes even if it suffers economically. The single most economic reason for the difficulty to achieve the primary objectives of sanctions appear to be the failure of the imposing state to anticipate fully the response to the sanctions within the target state. In Rhodesia and Iraq cases, a roughly proportional relationship was assumed between economic deprivation and political disintegration. But such assumption of political collapse following economic disaster proved to be unfounded. Indeed economic sanctions have generally had the opposite effect of creating a sense of community and solidarity in the target state. Reluctance to accept change may become stronger and population may be ready to accept a high degree of economic punishment. The alternatives which are offered to target states—whether it is abandoning Italian imperial aspirations or dissolving the Castro government in Cuba, or accepting black rule in Rhodesia or replacing Jewish state of Israel with a secular Palestine or changing the Saddam regime in Iraq—may appear so unattractive that privation of sanctions are well worth bearing.

Naturally the target states also try to neutralize the impact of sanctions by stock-piling, by finding alternative markets and suppliers, by diversifying the domestic economy, by buying illegally even if it is more expensive, and by diverting the economic impact away from the politically dominated social groups. In some cases the application of sanctions has been stimulated sectors of economy. The statistics of various case studies prove so. Defeating sanctions become a major national activity with businessmen who protest against the risk of sanctions being imposed and try to undermine and circumvent them.

By contrast in the imposing state, the situation is ambiguous because the objectives for which sanctions are imposed are diverse and the price to be paid is not always evenly distributed. As a result some imposing states will suffer more than others and within any particular country, some sectors of economy will be affected while others may escape unscathed. While sanctions are decided by government, compliance is required at all levels—individuals, groups, firms, financial organizations—and the greatest compliance is demanded of those who have to pay the highest price, providing a strong motive for avoiding or modifying the sanctions. But these same people resent and have doubts about the effectiveness of the political justification of sanction. Thus, in contrast to the situation in the target state, there may be great difficulty in the imposing state in creating and even sustaining the psychological climate for a national effort in involving sacrifices.

The problem of maintaining a commitment to sanctions increases when the governments and commercial enterprises breach them; even superpowers ignore aspects of sanctions when it suit their interest to do so. It initiates skepticism and generates tension between governments such as differences of perspectives between USA and Europe over Iran and between USA and China on India and Pakistan. Such a skepticism and resentment generates another problem of checking and policing sanctions. Some states have to introduce the legislation, which takes time and produces areas of uncertainty. Machinery has to be set up to administer sanctions. When sanctions are prolonged such as in Cuba or Rhodesia, the implementation of blockade becomes a detailed, almost a routine governmental task.

When international organizations become involved, they also set up their own machinery, although they normally have to rely on information fed to them by their member states. Both national governments and international organizations have to face the headaches of the administrative, bureaucratic and legal supervision of sanctions such as seen in respect to Iraq. Even when there is strong commitment, member states often actually create a legal mess either because of lack of skilled men-power or a desire to have the best of both the worlds. As such they are largely ineffective.

The fact is that the implementation of sanctions cannot be isolated from other international and domestic issues. They may clash with other goals of imposing states. The best example is the sanctions against Italy. The French and British wanted two incompatible things—to protect Ethiopia and the Covenant but still more to protect themselves against Hitler. Thus falling between the two stools becomes the inevitable fate, not only of the imposing states, but also of their imposed sanctions.

(ii) ***The Secondary Objectives*:**[14] The secondary objectives of sanctions are those which concerned with the status, reputation and position of governments imposing them. In broad terms these objectives have positive and negative aspects. Positively, they are intended to demonstrate the effectiveness of the imposing government. Negatively, the purpose may simply be to anticipate or deflect criticism or to ward-off threats of action by other states as to avoid domestic criticism on the score of ineptitude or indifference.

(iii) ***Tertiary Objective***:[15] Sanctions, in the context of tertiary objectives, becomes the means of upholding the international norm by deterring, and if necessary, punishing those who might be tempted to break them. Black states regard white regimes as deviators because they break the norm of racial equality; Arab states legitimize their action against Israel by branding it as 'racialist.' The way the international relations are perceived—to defend a balance of power or to ensure the coherence of a regional grouping or to counter the extension of ideological or religious doctrine—will determine the form of particular international structure, the support of which is included among the tertiary objectives. The actions of Americans in Central or South Africa or the Russians in Eastern Europe can be interpreted in each or all of the three stated ways. The Structural considerations also affect either the diplomatic relations between states or establishment and support of international organizations. In the support for the League against Italy and the UN against Rhodesia, the broader issue of how international relations are handled is super-imposed on the particular problem.

When international structure and norms are changing, the sanctions may also be used to ensure that the new dimension is accepted. For instance the emerging norm of 'humanitarian intervention' in respect to genocide or extreme human rights abuses is a new dimension in the protection of which sanctions are supposed to be justified, particularly when 'intervention' and 'sanctions' are mutual substitutes. Sometimes the abrupt development in international system is to be resisted which justify sanctions. For instance, sanctions imposed on India can be interpreted as to prevent her from gate crashing into the sanctum sanctorum of the five permanent members of the Security Council of the United Nations who happen to be the nuclear powers as well and who, by virtue of such membership and power, have the exclusive jurisdiction over the international system.

Comparing to primary and secondary objectives, the evaluation of tertiary objectives is most difficult. In view of range of factors to be taken into account in examining changes and development, it is impossible to isolate the particular part played by sanctions from the momentum, dimension, degree and direction of changes; such opening to wide interpretation cannot precisely determine the role of sanctions. Tertiary objectives serve, in fact, as deterrent to others than the target state, carrying the message that action will be taken against similar behaviour. But what can be the effect of this on others can be the matter of speculation.

Evaluation. Generally sanctions are not successful in achieving their primary objectives. The reasons are: the problem of agreement and implementation among the imposing states; a failure to appreciate the reactions inside the target state; and to much reliance on a naive theory of economic pressure leading to political disintegration. The importance of secondary and tertiary objectives has often been under-valued. Yet even when their importance is recognized, the evaluation of their success is very difficult because some of the aims are so elusive such as reputation of an imposing state while others are so complex such as the structure of an international system. Despite such difficulties, sanctions are regarded the preferred policy options in trying to achieve a range of objectives than pursuing them through direct recourse to force.[16]

The obsession of the professed objectives of the sanctions—to weaken the position of the target state pursuing the objectionable policy—occupies the mind so much that the reverse impact, it produces, often remains obscure. The domestic support that otherwise might have been denied, is readily granted by the government when it suffers an external assault. In the short run at least, the major beneficiaries of economic measures could be the target state.

Sanctions often drive a nation into the arms of the initiator's adversaries—weakening the international position of an imposing state. Soviet attempt to jeopardize Yugoslavia's economy drive that country into much closer commercial ties with the capitalist world and toward a non-aligned foreign policy. Similarly the UN sponsored economic boycott of Rhodesia re-enforced the commercial bonds between Salisbury and Pretoria.

More frequently the effect of sanction is to provide one's rival with a new partner or ally, injuring the commercial interest of the initiator's own friends and thus weakening the solidarity of his own camp. The attempt of the US administration to increase Soviet Union's economic difficulties by pressurizing a number of West European countries to down grade their economic relations with the Soviet met with substantial resistance and did not advance the cause of Western unity.

Quite contrary the sanctions consolidate the solidarity among the allies of target state if the aim is to weaken the rival group's overall economic capacity. Heightened intra-bloc solidarity could stem from a bolstered sense of common purpose and destiny. External pressure may also make it easier for the group's leader to assert his authority and control. For example other Latin American nations may have suffered the indirect consequences of the US-European attempts to apply economic punishment to Argentina for its invasion of Falkland Islands. But most of these countries viewed the Argentina's action an instance of the struggle against the vestiges of colonialism and granted it their political support.

It is also conceivable that the hostility of the member states could be directed to the country whose behaviour caused the sanctions rather than the nation imposing them. But it depends up to what extent other members of the group identify with the policies that provoked the external relations. Generally the intra-hostility of the member nations remain submerged in the face of hostile external pressure, which diminishes the initiator's benefit despite possible increased maneuverability. In the face of Israel-Palestine conflict, the hostile relations among Arab nations remain submerged.

It should also be recognized that the total punishment in the expectation of instant good behaviour, may be undermined partly because the target is forced to find other economic partners or to enhance its self-sufficiency, but also because the initiator's means of economic coercion may be exhausted and there is little left with which the initiator can inflict additional economic pain to get desired responses of the target state.

Even if under total denial, some change of policy or abstention of future misconduct of a target state is perceived, the imposing state cannot relax the pressure which may be considered unacceptable by an aroused public. This should be true even if the initiator also suffered from the sanctions since it could be feared that a retrenchment would signal an inability to absorb costs and hence weaken the credibility of future threats. Thus there may be incompatibility between short-term and long-term interests.

A contradiction of another sort is noteworthy: A favourable domestic impact, imposing government's image and incumbency, require that sanctions should be overtly applied and well advertised. But more conspicuous it is, the more difficult it may be for the target government to capitulate in terms of its own internal politics. Although it may be more important for the initiator to bolster its internal position than to force compliance on other nation, the two goals may be mutually inconsistent.[17]

Unless such reverse impacts are taken into consideration, the sanction policies may backfire and objectives, whether primary, secondary or tertiary, may remain elusive.

III. THE INSTRUMENT OF FOREIGN POLICY

The recent emergence of sanctions as the instrument of foreign policy can be traced back to two major circumstances[18]—the first involving, principally, the superpower, the second concerning the nature of international economy. In the wake of cold war and rival military blocs, a comprehensive strategic embargo was initiated against the Soviet Union and its Western Pact allies. Curtailment of grain deliveries, oil and pipeline equipments, air traffic and movements of people were associated with this embargo. Apart from the direct economic pressure against the Soviet bloc, each superpower extended the use of economic pressure to the third world nations wherever this has been deemed suitable tool for East-West confrontation. The end of cold war provided much space to pursue foreign policy ends through economic coercion. The United States has sought to influence specific policies by economic sanctions as when economic aid has been made contingent upon attainments in human rights or on measures of nuclear proliferation by the recipients. Between 1992 and 1996, the United States imposed or threatened economic sanctions sixty times against thirty-five different countries, affecting 42 per cent of the world's population.[19] These sanctions are estimated to expect an annual cost of close to $ 20 billion in lost exports.[20] What is noteworthy is not just frequency with which sanctions are used but their centrality; economic sanctions are increasingly at the core of US foreign policy.[21] As public resistance to military interventions increase and foreign aid budget are slashed, policy makers are turning more and more to economic coercion as an attractive substitute to advance the national interests.

The USA has not been alone in its readiness to pursue foreign policy ends through economic coercion. Arab nations, opposed to the Cemp David, have sought to punish Cairo's adherence to accord by curtailing economic cooperation with Egypt. The European Economic Community responded to Argentina's invasion of Falkland Islands with economic sanctions. When relations between Moscow and Peking deteriorated, the Soviet Union withdrew the substantial assistance it had promised to its ideological rival. The Russian also mustered all their capacity for economic relations against Yugoslavia when that nation embarked on an independent path as well as against Albania when Tirana sided with China in Sino-Soviet rivalry. China curtailed its own economic relations with Albania when latter refused to support its invasion of Vietnam. Such prolificacy of sanctions as the tool of foreign policy is the result of the changed circumstances: Since military power is not only costly but sometimes counter-productive, it is the economic power, which is less violent.

Growing international economic inter-dependence has been a second circumstance encouraging the resort to external coercion. Foreign trade and flow of capital among nations have generated vulnerabilities. This has led, in fact, to increased leverage among like-minded nations with similar economies, but it has been more relevant to relations between less compatible states. Still inter-dependence is the knife that cuts the two ways for it means that any disruption of an economic relationship may ramify further than intended, and in particular, that it will create costs for the initiator as well as the target. The networks of international economic relationships, associated with significant inequality and asymmetrical levels of dependence, has actually increased vulnerability and damage for the target state and as such initiated the surge in economic pressure. It is in this respect that Joseph Nye appropriately remarks:[22] "Inter-dependence does not mean harmony. It means unevenly balanced mutual dependence. The less vulnerable of the two states may use subtle threats to their relationship as a source of power." This has been as true of East-West relations as of those between developed and developing nations.

From the view-point of the political use of economic sanctions, two questions are crucial: (1) Can economic pressure more likely to operate through restriction of imports from the target or export to that nation? (2) Are certain types of goods more apt to be the object of sanctions than others? Miroslav's and Wallensteen's answer to these questions, along with illustrations, are summarized as follows.[23] Exports are the most frequently chosen tools as US blocked grain shipment and restricted transfer of advanced technology to the Soviet Union following the invasion of Afghanistan. Imports too are sometimes used as Britain's sanctions against Rhodesia by depriving its Tobacco industry of Britain and other foreign markets.

Similarly US sugar imports from Cuba were barred in 1960. Yet it is unlikely that sanctions could selectively involve only imports or exports. Counter sanctions by the target states will typically lead to a reduction in both, independently of the initiator's own emphasis. Even without explicit counter sanctions, it will be difficult for the target to keep importing from a country where its exports earnings have been significantly reduced.

A goods or service may not be valuable from the perspective of economic coercion if it is easily available from a source other than the initiator. Supply may be concentrated and accounted for primarily by the initiator or by nations over whose policies the initiator exercises sufficient control. The greater the number of suppliers of a commodity, the more difficult it is to politicize its availability. On the other hand, a credible sanction should hurt the target more than the initiator and this may not be the case if the power represents the latter's principal market. From initiator's point of view the ideal situation is thus of near monopoly coupled with a marginal dependence on the target as an outlet for the good. From the reverse perspective, a high level of supply dispersion, associate with a very concentrated demand, puts the potential target in the least vulnerable position. This is the idea behind the consumer cooperatives within many nations or for example, of the International Energy Agency, which strives to coordinate the oil needs of rich industrial nations in order to avoid consumer competition and unnecessary concession to oil producing countries.

Not only should supply be concentrated, but the good in question should have no obvious substitute. Even a monopoly over some commodity will yield little political leverage if the need that it satisfies, can be adequately met by another good. Tea and Coffee are clearly mutual substitutes and to a certain extent iron or tin or copper and aluminum. On the other hand, there are few obvious substitutes for the petroleum or advanced microchips.

Finally the need associated with the goods in question should be experienced as vital may depend on social cultural considerations as well as on a nation's level of economic development—neither of the previous conditions will have any practical meaning if the goods addresses a need that is irrelevant or redundant. In the US-Cuban case, the target's position was further weakened by the ready availability of sugar from non-Cuban sources. The United States could, at the minimum cost to itself, inflict considerable economic damage on Cuba by shifting its imports to other Caribbean and Central American countries. In another view, American use of grain as a political weapon has suffered from the ability of other nations such as Argentina to replace it as a supplier to the Soviet Union and from the fact that the Soviet market is clearly major outlet for the American grain. It has benefited for the vital need that grain satisfied, especially given the nature of Soviet diet.

Food, oil, raw materials and agricultural products are frequently used for economic coercion. Here the source of goods is easily identifiable and usually involves rather asymmetrical trade relations. However the more advanced the goods exchanged, the more symmetrically integrated are the relations involved. Indeed the more advanced the product, the more difficult it is to determine its origin: it may be designed in one country, require the material of another, the labour of the third, and the finance of the fourth. Although this part of international division of labour associated with multinational cooperation, it makes it more difficult to define a discrete target and decreases the political feasibility of the sanctions. Thus, in US-Japan commerce, we encounter embargoes on soyabeans but not on cars. American efforts to get West European countries to withhold technologically advanced pipeline equipment from the Soviet Union threaten an entire international economic network.

Military transfers represent a particular case of highly sophisticated goods that are, nevertheless, often the object of economic sanctions. Unlike many other modern industrial goods, weapon production follows national boundaries rather closely. At the same time supply is relatively concentrated while demand is dispersed. The fact that the security needs that military goods supposedly meet are deemed vital (and that there is often much surgery involved) makes the manipulation of supply an attracted tool of political influence.

But there are other sides of this kind of goods as well. Given in the intense demand for arms, a target will try very hard to circumvent sanctions. Although supply of the most sophisticated military equipment is quite concentrated, this is less at slightly lesser levels of technological complexity. Thus, other suppliers may seek to supplant the initiator either in search of economic gain or of political influence.

Denial of excess to capital is a new form of sanction. Capital is the fuel of the economies and it tends to follow political boundaries very imperfectly. Measures to control private credits to the Soviet Union are an example of the foreign policy of economic capital. The decision to freeze Iranian financial assets in the United States, in response to the taking of American hostages, is an example of other sorts.

The international mobility of the people, rather than capital, can also be manipulated for the purpose of diplomatic coercion. Indeed for many years US citizens were prohibited from travelling to certain communist countries, presumably as a part of comprehensive embargo efforts. The same has applied to the travel of citizens of a number of Arab nations to Israel.

Finally, the curtailment of communication can also be used as part of campaigns of economic coercion. For example trade can be affected by withdrawing transit privileges, or by revoking the docking and landing rights. The visibility of this form of economic retribution has made it popular component of sanctions designed for demonstrative purposes.

Each form of sanction is likely to be part of future pattern of international influence and coercion. The circumstances that have made sanctions increasingly used tool of foreign policy in the post war-period, are likely to exist during coming decades. There is indeed little indication that economic inter-dependence will be reduced in the foreseeable future; or the contrary, the multilateralisation of industrial production, the reliance on the external sources of new materials and trans-national integration of financial markets are likely to grow. Also there is little indication that this inter-dependence will assume a more symmetric nature, maintaining at least the possibility of unilateral pressures. Moreover, the reticence of the major powers, and the superpower in particular, to use military force will probably not diminish; the seemingly inexorable nuclear proliferation, as well as the spread of highly sophisticated conventional arms, will make the consequences of even limited conflict increasingly impalpable. Some of these trends may make certain types of goods, such as industrial products, created through multi-national efforts, less appropriate an instrument of economic pressure. Others such as control of capital-flows may be experimented more frequently.

Sanctions will continue to be associated with many such dilemmas. Normal learning patterns suggest that they may be used in a more carefully calculated manner, but many of their problems and counter-productive efforts are simply inherent in the nature of economic tools of external pressure. Whether one regards sanctions with equanimity or misgivings will depend upon how one assess options. A new form of coercion is only as attractive or unattractive as are its alternatives.

IV. STRATEGY

Strategy is the operational part of the foreign policy. There are always two different ways of influencing another nation's actions: the one is economic engagement, the other is economic sanction. Franklin L. Lavin[24] identifies these two strategies as "Oxygen" and "Asphyxiation" respectively. Under 'Oxygen' strategy, the economic policy can reduce trade barriers like tariff and quotas and adopt more active measures such as loans, credit, trade and investment and foreign aid. Under 'Asphyxiation' strategy, the exports to and from the target country are impeded, financial flows are restricted, trade is degraded, privileges of Most Favoured Nation (M.F.N.) are withdrawn, the projects of International Monetary Fund (I.M.F.) or World Bank are blocked and trade blockage or embargoes are imposed.

The choice between these two strategies is not simple because of the surrounding politico-economic factors and advocate's own political perception. For instance in 1980 the conservatives of the USA tended to favour 'Asphyxiation' for Cuba and 'Oxygen' for South Africa while liberals advocated, some of them very tougher, 'Asphyxiation' for South Africa than the Soviet Union. Both approaches have their own arguments.

The 'Oxygen' school argues that the great economic activity leads to positive political consequences such as growth, development and prosperity; de-stabilizes the traditional order by creating increased diversity of occupation and status, rendering highly centralized rule or self-sufficient localism inadequate and necessitating the division and share of authority in complex way; creates a group that seeks greater political freedom; ends isolation; gains, beyond prosperity, the familiarity and mutual benefits which can induce authoritarian governments to behave better. And finally the oxygen approach is, after all, more humane since it is likely to improve the day-to-day lives of people in the subject country.

The 'Asphyxiation' school has its own points: It argues that the economic costs of sanctions limit the government's capacity to engage in the offending practices and can even topple the government through mass discontent or unhappiness within a leadership faction, thereby ending the bad behaviour. Even if the sanction is an empty gesture it results in side benefits: Fifty years old Arab economic boycott of Israel has had minimum economic impact, but it has promoted Arab solidarity. In general Asphyxiation is more effective than Oxygen because government policy can more readily disrupt market forces of trade and investment than encourage them.

Successful examples of either approach can be found. The asphyxiation camp claims: After year's of economic stagnation the South African business establishment realized that apartheid was increasingly untenable and their prospects for preserving their position lay in changing the *status quo* rather than preserving it. They shifted to majority rule not so much from a democratic impulse but so that boycott would be ended.

The oxygen camp claims: The moves towards democracy and Western style human rights standard relaxed political controls, continued stability, increased economic growth and promoted the establishment of educated middle class in South Korea and Taiwan. All these developments are actually facilitated by oxygen strategy, which resulted in an overall prosperity, achieved by these two countries in 1980s.

Similarly failed examples of each approach can also be found. On the asphyxiation side the examples of failure are as follows: Despite inflation of 2000 per cent a month, economic sanctions could not prevent Serbia to meddle in Bosnia. In 1979, President Carter banned the sale of grain to Soviet Union but had to backtrack when its farmers, who faced bankruptcy, turned hostile against their own government and next, the Reagan administration had to persuade Brezhnev to come to rescue of American farmers.[25] The US trade sanctions against Vietnam failed when its European partners made a beeline to Vietnamese market.[26] Cuba survived; Iran neutralized the effect of US sanctions by establishing relations with European countries; Iraq managed to overcome the US led sanctions.[27] The sanction initiators failed to overthrow Saddam Husein; realised the futility of prolonged sanctions; had to resort to military action and occupied Iraq against the basic tenet that sanctions are not prelude but an alternative to war. Such actions on their part is virtually an acceptance of the defeat of the very purpose of sanction, *i.e.*, to avoid war.

On the oxygen side the example of failure is as follows: Despite West Germany's Ostpolitik which employed deliberate policy of economic engagement, due to contiguity and special relationship, the East Germany remained most Stalinist in structure and most enduringly loyal to Soviet Union. The East German leadership was aware that the interaction with the West might infect the body-politic, they erected a massive security apparatus. It is often argued that West's effort of subsidizing the East had actually prolonged the Soviet system in decline. Thus economic interaction by itself does not seem to guarantee a political opening.

The success and failure in each school depends, in fact, upon the particular circumstances at play. Franklin L. Levin[28] has identified four criterion—sufficiency, economics, confluence and cohesion/proportionality—discussed below in brief, which, according to him, must be met for the policy of sanctions to succeed.

The sanctions must reach a level of sufficiency, which is determined by the degree to which the flow of goods is restricted. In cases such as North Vietnam, a partial success in closing the border is no success in restricting the flow of goods. Two core determinants of sufficiency are geography and alliance solidarity. A country is land-locked or has few neighbours will be more vulnerable than one that is littoral or extensive. Geography is a given fact; solidarity depends on allies showing the same perception of a problem and the same prescription. Otherwise countries will agree to subscribe only when the costs are so low as to make their participation symbolic, such as Japan's support for the US blockade of Haiti. Thus the most important requirements for successful sanctions are largely outside the control of policy makers.

The next is the economic dimension of the policy of sanction, which contains several vital components. First, a country's susceptibility to sanction is contingent upon fuel (which military people call POL for Petroleum, Oil and Lubricants), hard currency and high technology weaponry. In this respect, the target country's self-governance, its petrol storage and consumption rates, the percentage of its gross domestic product that is derived from export must be taken into account in order to assess the extent to which a country's susceptibility to sanctions can be manipulated.

The UN Security Council imposed broad economic sanctions against Iraq, which succeeded on one level in that geography and alliance solidarity were sufficient for a near total economic blockade of Iraq, involving fuel, hard currency and high-tech weaponry. But sanctions did not induce Iraq to withdraw from Kuwait, nor did they have a particular impact on war itself. The denial of weaponry to Iraq was of little military significance because Iraq had stockpiled all the weapons it needed.

Second, prohibition of food, water and medicine inflict hardship on the general population. These morally questionable tactics, whether direct or as an indirect consequence bring disgrace to the initiator country from the international community and harms its standing. The desperate civilian population of Iraq, facing shortage of food and medicine, as a result of continued sanctions, is virtually causing the opprobrium to the implementers within the United Nations and outside.

Third, the impact of sanction goes beyond these criteria for disrupting the target country's economy. In fact one has to consider relative disruption: Will the target country be hurt more than the implementer or the implementing alliance? There is a Newtonian dynamics to sanctions: Every action has an equal and opposite reaction that can make it less cost effective than a military attack. A one million cruise missile can paralyze target country's communication network, causing, may be, $ 100 million worth damage. But in order to deprive the target country of $ one million worth of petroleum, it can cost the implementer $ one million in foregone profits.

The economics involve the co-relation between the size of the economies of the initiator and target state. Economically sanctions hurt the target country less than the implementing country. When the United States imposed a grain embargo on the Soviet Union in 1980, the Soviet easily found other suppliers but the United States found no alternative buyers as well. It is easy for the United States to support an economic blockade against Serbia, but it is much more difficult for the neighbouring states of Bulgaria, Greece, Hungary or Romania to do so. Yet without their support the blockade is meaningless. Therefore, one key to analyzing the relative disruption of sanctions is to compare the size of the target country's economy with that of the implementer. A small country will have difficulty in enduring economic disruption.

Beyond the question of sufficiency and economics comes the issue of confluence. Sanctions can raise the cost of action and exacerbate problems but is rarely successful by itself. South Africa and Nicaragua both eventually changed policies while being subjected to trade sanctions. The implementers simply brought to the surface more serious pre-existing problems, such as government lacking popular support and engaging in a costly insurgency campaign. The proponent of continued embargo of Cuba argue that the policy would be effective now that the Soviet Union is gone and Russia can no longer subsidize the Cuban economy. Such prediction too proves wrong; Castro exists very much. Since sanctions exert only a marginal impact on a country, one of the keys to the success is to target countries already burdened with other problems.

A fourth determinant of success relates to the issue of national cohesion, internal political structure, presentation of the sanction and the proportionality of the action. Trade sanctions like neutron bomb, destroy the economy and wrecks misery on general population but leaves the political establishment intact. It even bolsters support to the government of target state, which cashes on the impingement upon sovereign prerogatives. UN and the British sanctions against the white minority-run government of Rhodesia from 1965 to 1979 stand out as an example where a government's domestic position was actually strengthened by sanctions.

Economic sanctions have been attempted in efforts to fulfil a range of foreign policy goals, already explained, such as winning a war, toppling a government, punishing a country for support of terrorism or encouraging it to change some policy. If other fundamentals of sanctions noted above are not in order, sanctions will be successful in pursuit of only modest goals. Because sanctions are the marginal tools, they are most effective when applied to marginal issues such as technical trade matters.

The goals outsiders sought in Rhodesia and Indonesia were vastly disproportionate to the economic tools applied. The goal in Rhodesia was to overthrow the government. The goal in Indonesia was nothing less than a radical change in Indonesia's policy towards East Timor,[29] a former Portuguese colony seized by Indonesia. What country would choose national humiliation over economic hardship? Since even seemingly minor issues—a fishing dispute for example—can be perceived as a test of sovereignty and integrity of government, sanctions must be implemented in such a way as to not back the country into a corner. It illustrates the principle of proportionality and links it, as well, with presentation. Presentation becomes important so as to ensure that the threat of sanction is not perceived as a challenge to a country's sovereign integrity. Peculiarly, political sensibilities make sanctions more effective tool in dealing with friendly countries than with unfriendly ones, for with the former there is no issue of sovereignty at stake. The prospects of sanctions can be held out with regret, and not as a threat.

Against his illustration of these four cardinal principles, Franklin L. Levin has evaluated the Asphyxiation and oxygen approaches as follows:[30]

Asphyxiation represents a philosophy of making thing worse before they get better and of inflicting hardship on a broad population. This raises the question of moral dimension of sanctions. In Nicaragua and South Africa economic manipulation worked out but economies crippled which could not recover easily. Although US backed sanctions were imposed in Haiti for only three years, the economic disruption remained long after the political dispute had ended.

Oxygen requires that a country in question must have some openness that will allow the economic benefits to flow broadly to the general population. It will do little good for the international side of country's economy to be open if the domestic side is closed. South Korea and Taiwan are the examples of openness where the policy of oxygen succeeded while East Germany is the example of closed economy where it failed.

While so characterizing, Franklin selects two cases of North

Korea and China in order to illustrate the debate between Asphyxiation and oxygen policy choices:[31]

North Korea worries US policy makers because of its nuclear programme and China because of its military assertiveness, human rights policy, weapon proliferation and trade practices. What would be the impact of Asphyxiation strategy in each country?

If the United States degraded its trade relations with China, it would stand-alone. Other important trading partners—Japan, Taiwan (China's political rival), Hong Kong and the European Union—have stated that they do not agree with US approach. Since China's economy grew about 10 per cent in 1995, the loss of M.F.N. could reduce its rate of growth in 1996 to 9.5 per cent. With or without M.F.N., China will have one of the fastest growing economies in the world.

The denial of M.F.N. would cause economic dislocation in the export-oriented sectors, hurting the international business community, the more modern littoral provinces, and specially Hong Kong. But it would not hurt China in a broad way, and there is no reason to believe that it would make China more responsive to US demands. Because of the way the United States presents its human rights goals—in a highly publicized and accusatory fashion—Chinese leaders interprets US goals as a challenge to their sovereignty.

China's loss of M.F.N. would hurt broad sectors of US economy: Wholesalers; shippers; retailers; and consumers of apparel, footwear and textile. Because of the structure of these exports, more Americans than Chinese would be affected. More Americans buy shoes than the number of Chinese making them. If China were an island whose hard currency earnings came from the sale of a single commodity, then such sanctions might have the desired effect.

A strategy of asphyxiation towards China violates all four cardinal rules. The action must have a degree of sufficiency, which in China's case would necessitate the active cooperation of many other countries. It must exacerbate existing problems, but China enjoys a booming economy and a stable polity. It must respect the laws of economics by exacting more disruption from the target than from the implementer, which in China's case is an open question. Finally, goals must be proportionate to the costs. But since Chinese government interprets US human rights concerns as a challenge to its leadership, it cannot afford to back-down. The principle of not backing down vastly outweighs the importance of the human rights issues themselves.

The fundamental issues of size and geography are much favourable to adopt asphyxiation policy towards North Korea. Countries unwilling to antagonize China are more willing to take a tough line towards North Korea since it plays such a marginal role in world affairs. Its geography and trade patterns are such that economic sanctions would depend on the cooperation of the United States, China and Japan, although it is unclear to what extent the latter two countries would participate. What about North Korea's susceptibility to sanctions? It is difficult to estimate the probable economic impact on North Korea of a substantial reduction in fuel or hard currency. Fuel is currently transported by ship and across a relatively porous border with China, and the largest source of hard currency is the expatriate Korean community in Japan. Suffice it to say that even in a state-directed 1950 style economy, these deprivations would have an impact. North Korea faces another problem. Its economy is shrinking as it grapples with the withdrawal of financial and political support from China and Russia. The fundamentals, therefore, are in order; asphyxiation is feasible.

It is but natural to assume that the North Korea, as one of the most militarized countries in the world, would react violently to tough sanctions. In this respect, on one hand it is stated that sanctions are a bad choice because either they would not have much impact or they would precipitate a violent reaction. On the other hand, it is stated that since the issue is North Korea's attempt to develop a nuclear capability, it is better to confront a non-nuclear or a quasi-nuclear North Korea today than a fully nuclear North Korea tomorrow. At this initial phase, it is considered to implement economic sanctions incrementally; instead of full economic sanctions, it is appropriate to gradually restrict currency remittances to North Korea from Japan.

As to the principle of proportionality, the United States stated repeatedly that it does not challenge North Korean sovereignty but simply seeks its compliance with IAEA requirements. While abiding an inspection but always falling short of requirements, North Korea continually places new demands on the United States. It is suggested that the United States, instead of conceding to the next demand, should attach costs to North Korea's behaviour and should be ready to abandon the economic sanctions as soon as North Korea abandons its nuclear weapon programme. And it would be wise to offer some modest symbolic benefits to North Korea, should it comply on the nuclear issue. Economic sanctions have to be offered not as a prelude to conflict but as a stepping-stone to peace.

In contrast what would be the impact of oxygen strategy of economic engagement with each country? China meets the fundamental conditions of having a successful open economic system; North Korea does not. China is one of the fastest growing economies in the world, one that has transformed its society in little more than a decade. Indeed the protests at Tiananmen Square and elsewhere were not peasant revolt; students, professionals and businessmen—the newly educated and newly affluent, led them. Even China's most bitter ideological enemy, Taiwan, encourages its private sector to conduct business in China, presumably not just for reasons of profit. Deng also recognized the connection between economic growth and political evolution when he remarked: "When you open the window, flies and mosquitoes come in."[32]

In North Korea, however, the economy is not open, but entirely state directed. The interaction with foreigners is tightly controlled because the leadership requires and fears the potential impact. In sum, asphyxiation will not work in China but it might in North Korea. Oxygen is already succeeding—and will continue to succeed—in China but it will not succeed in North Korea until it moves from Stalinist economic model to a Gorbachev or Deng style one. The fact that China and North Korea are both labelled 'communist' states show how meaningless that term has become at the end of the twentieth century.

Comparing the two strategies the fact is that asphyxiation disrupts another country's economy, the oxygen stimulates it. But though difficult it is for any government to disrupt the economy of other country, it is still easier than stimulating it.

The reason is that oxygen strategy takes more time than asphyxiation. The full emergence of the middle class can takes decades and only then does pressure begin to build on the authorities to relax an authoritarian political structure.

It is often argued that sanctions or engagements both do not work because economic mechanism, whether positive or negative, are slow and indirect. Economic strategy provides incentives or disincentives. The concerned country may not react quickly; or these incentives or disincentives may not react the way they are desired to act. Then it would be very difficult calculus of self-interest than that for which the implementation of sanctions had hoped. But over the long run, countries—one odious one—tend to act rationally. Thus, these strategies may not be effective in the short run, they influence the behaviour in the long run.

Franklin concludes:[33] History has shown that sanctions are not always economic, not necessarily peaceful, not silent, and deadly only at the margin (in conjunction with other factors) and over the long run. But some times they do the trick. Similarly the engagement offers no automatic prospect of success, but sometimes it, too, is the right formula. Sanctions tend to be effective in response to trade issues, and engagement in response to human rights problem. Neither is terribly effective response to aggression. Either strategy can work, given the circumstances. The challenge for the policy makers, as always, is to avoid a dogmatic approach and choose the right tool for the job.

V. COUNTER-STRATEGY

The reward or punishment through the use of economic engagement or economic sanctions, identified as oxygen and asphyxiation, are, in fact, the initiator's choices for economic influence of other countries, in the context of which, the responsive action of the target state has, no-doubt, been discussed as well. But there are ways to fight back, independent of initiator's strategy. Galtung has developed the 'counter-strategy' as an independent variable by undertaking public interviews during Rhodesian case study. These down-to-earth public responses, in nut-shell, are as follows:[34]

First, a family having two cars and receives petrol for both, puts one car in garage. Families living in countryside and having offices in Salisbury, form a car pool and go together. Even if this should not work, the city develops adequate collective transportation and even that does not work, walking is a better way. Some may not have refrigerators, others may not have the latest model but most will have refrigerators and technicians can ensure spare parts to keep them operational. The population has never been familiar with the luxury goods since the colonial days. So if such goods are not available under sanction, it makes no difference. Beside one family has some and another will borrow. So this has been the regular pattern of sacrifice since war days.

Second, economic boycott in general applies a rapid decrease of import-export business and a change towards home-made production. The question is whether the trade sector, which stands to loose some of its significance, is more or less amenable to compliance than are the emerging new economic elites of home-made industry or agriculture.

Changes in the economy put power more and more into the hands of the farmers; they increasingly become the symbol of national survival. Moreover, when an import-export firm has to close down, there is little alternative use to which it can be put, whereas it makes a great deal of sense for the government to subsidize the conversion of Tobacco land to grain field or pastures. If such efforts fail, the sanctioning state is to be blamed; if they succeed, the local ingenuity ensures independent potentiality. The self re-enforcing power, like the possibility of making automobile fuel out of sugarcane or even out of coal, are such inventiveness which will probably lead to chain reaction both in inventiveness and in feeling of autonomy.

Third, the blessed sanctions enhance our talent once again to figure out how products can be brought in by middle men, how firm will loose their markets forever, if they do not help, how goods can eventually be smuggled into the country if that is necessary and how to get petrol more cheaply than from the Portuguese merchants who set up filling stations across the border from Umtali and charge exorbitant prices for the gallon.

If the sending nations are able to ensure that, regardless of how much talent is invested in smuggling, very few goods will, in fact, materialize, the reward from this mechanism will dwindle away. But in countries like Rhodesia, with its extensive adjoining friendly territories, even moderate talent should be able to adopt counter-strategies in order to mitigate the impact of sanctions.

The cost of economic sanctions may be prohibitive and boycott under it may extend from unilateral through regional to a universal action, Galtung, qualifying upon such interviews, has pointed out that the receiving nation is left with three counter stratgies:[35]

(1) To retain itself in 'sacrifice' by doing without certain commodities and preferably even liking it;

(2) To 'restructure the national economy' so as to absorb the shock of the boycott by producing locally the imported commodities, denied it or by making some substitute for them and

(3) To organize changes of trade with third parties or via third parties or if the boycott is truly universal, to engage in 'smuggling.'

Galtung, on the basis of these counter strategies—sacrifice, restructuring and smuggling—has drawn some conclusion contrary to common belief:[36]

It is generally presumed that the more value deprivation, the more political disintegration; the political disintegration is more or less proportionate to economic disintegration; and the economic disintegration cannot be counteracted.

Against such common presumptions, Galtung observes that it is quite possible that value deprivation may initially lead to political integration and only later—perhaps much later, or even never—to political disintegration. The basic point here is that value deprivation creates the social conditions under which much more sacrifice is possible so that the limit for political disintegration will be reached much later.

He remarks that it would be naive to think that economic sanctions—once they are economically effective—will, automatically, cause either partial or complex surrender. Drawn on the case studies, cited above, he has reached very balanced conclusion:[37] "The thesis that the economic sanctions, at least to start with, will have a tendency to create social, political integration rather than disintegration seems relatively strong one though it is not free from conditions and circumstances."

It is interesting to note that in 1973 and 1974, seven years after Galtung's article was published, as Bruce Russett and Harvey Starr mention,[38] the Nixon administration's energy policy, that attempted to counteract the Arab oil weapon, matched Galtung's recommendations point for point. The major defensive strategy set out is one of self-sufficiency; just as Nixon announced that the American aim had to be self-sufficiency by 1980. Until self-sufficiency is reached, it is suggested that a people learn to sacrifice, and preferably even learn to like it. One of the first suggestions by the Nixon administration was to turn down thermostats in homes, with the added information that cooler temperatures were healthier. The speed limit on American highways was cut to 55 mph and it was argued that in addition to saving fuel, this speed was also safer. Galtung also suggests changes in trade with other parties and perhaps even some form of smuggling. At this time the United States organized the consumer states into the International Energy Agency, referred earlier, as a means to coordinate energy policies, stockpiling and means by which to aid each other if another embargo occurs. The United States also begin or continued oil-oriented negotiations with non-Arab-oil producing states. Finally, it is suggested that an economy can attempt to restructure itself to absorb the loss of the embargoed material. Again the Nixon strategy contained not only energy saving activities by individuals, industries and government, but also plans for increased mining coal and more emphasis on nuclear generated electricity. In sum, just as one state aims for influence based on another's vulnerability, in defence a state attempts to cut down on the need for specific goods from specific sources, even if the policies do not work so well—as in the Nixon administration's actions.

VI. OUTCOME

The ramification of sanctions revolves round the crucial question: What is the 'outcome' of sanctions? the outcome is related to 'effectiveness' which has been judged on the basis of many criteria: the degree of international support; the economic impact of the action; political changes in or by receiver, desired by the sender. Apart from the direct relationship between sender and receiver, sometimes the warning is meant for the third country: When League imposed sanctions on Italy for its aggression, it was also the signal for Germany; when US imposed sanctions on Cuba, the additional target was Soviet Union; when Soviet Union imposed sanctions on Albania, the ultimate target was China. The purpose to repeat the referred cases is to show that if sanctions do not change the policy of the receiver state, the effect on the other targets may also be reduced and the credibility of the sender using sanctions is lowered.

Even if one remains concerned with the sender-receiver relationship it is difficult to determine sender's real motives. What the sender nation claims publicly might be its bargaining position and thus, if the final outcome appears less than successful from the sender's perspectives, it might have actually achieved what it really intended. In the wake of Pokharan-II tests, the US pressurized India to sign CTBT and NPT and on her refusal, imposed sanctions. Since despite sanctions, India adhered not to sign these treaties, the sanctions may be considered a failure. But who knows that India's assurance of limited deterrence along with the stoppage of further testing would have been the real undeclared motives of the USA, and public declaration would have been merely a bargaining position. The presumption is that, being satisfied on this account, along with required political changes in relationship, particularly in the wake of terrorist attack of September 11, the US initiated relaxation and finally lifted completely that sanctions, which were imposed on India after Pokharan-II.

Since we can never know the real objectives of the sender, we can never determine, precisely, the success. As such the question of success may be judged from the sender's actions. If sender were satisfied with the political changes forced upon the receiver, it would naturally cease to apply sanctions. If sanctions continue, it means that the sender still feels a need to inflict punishment: In Cuba and Iraq, sanctions are not terminated as such they are considered unsuccessful. If sanctions are terminated, it does not necessarily mean that the success has been achieved. For instance the sender could admit that sanctions have failed and may decide to re-establish normal relations with the receiver, just as sanctions against Yugoslavia. Italy, despite sanctions, occupied Ethiopia and just after two months League terminated its actions.

It is typical of sanctions debates that they tend to focus on only one side and then mainly on the sender side. But the success and failure can actually be explained from both sides—sender and receiver—of the conflict and that a clear understanding of the outcome would have to incorporate the two perspectives. Moreover, the two additional plausible explanations—the relationship between sender and receiver and the reactions of other actors in the international system, the environment must also be taken into consideration in order to determine as accurately as possible the outcome of sanctions. Peter Wallensteen has mentioned all these four aspects—the sender oriented explanation; the receiver oriented explanation; the relation oriented explanation; and the environmental oriented explanation—which are, briefly, discussed below:[39]

(A) **Sender-Oriented Explanation.** Motives and power are the essential component of sender-oriented explanation.

(i) *Motives*: The sender may have varied motives: first, a sender may be interested in bringing about a solution and imposing sanctions may be merely a symbolic gesture, just as, League's action against Italy; second, the salience of issue may be at stake in which the senders shall be more interested in the successful conclusion of the conflict. For instance, in the case of Cuba, the United States pointed to the danger of communism; in the case of Yugoslavia, the Soviet Union found the deviation from Marxism-Leninism to be the issue. In all these cases, broader concerns have been involved, making the matter relevant to all those sharing the sender's value. In this way the issue is more salient and fundamental. Third, the sender government may find itself involved in internal or international conflicts that "over-shadow" the dispute with the receiver. The sender would then be less interested in the outcome of sanctions. For instance, at the time the sanctions were imposed on the

Soviet Union, Japanese aggression in China and international financial crisis seemed to have captured most of the British attention. With regard to sanctions against Yugoslavia, the Soviet Union was simultaneously involved in Berlin blockade and German question. Similarly at the time of sanctions against Cuba, the United States was heavily involved in conflict with the Soviet Union over the U-2 and over unfolding Congo crisis. The analysis of the motives of the senders in three different ways show that motives do not strongly determine the outcome of sanctions.

(ii) *Power*: Big powers are frequent initiators. Some time a group of small powers, non-controversial within and any extra alternative without, may initiate sanctions as Arab countries' sanctions against Israel. A general trait of all the sanctions is that they have been imposed on countries that have not been economically significant to the sender.

To sum up: The sender oriented explanations shed light on the origin of sanctions; they do not count for the outcome of sanctions.

(B) Receiver-Oriented Explanation. Trade dependence, political effect and issue of contention are the main ingredients of the receiver-oriented explanation.

(i) *Trade Defence*: The receivers are usually trade dependent on the sender before the imposition of sanctions. But it is significant to note that several highly dependent states such as Cuba and Albania successfully withstood the pressure whereas a less dependent state like the Soviet Union yielded to the sender. The possible explanations are as follows: First, the sender have not always cut-off all trade either because of deliberate policy or because all transactions simply cannot be immediately halted. Second, the receiver has been able to find new trading partners. Third, most sanctions are initially slow to implement; there will always be the states which, for economic or other reasons, are not willing immediately to comply or join the sanction effort, and trade with the receiver might become lucrative. Fourth, larger advanced states like the Soviet Union, having greater volume of trade has had to bear greater trade reduction and thus yielded comparing to smaller or developing state like Cuba with either single commodity trade or limited volume of trade, finding third party trade transactions.

There is no relationship between actual reduction of trade and the outcome of sanctions. In fact the economic impact was probably greater in unsuccessful case of Yagoslavia, Albania and Iraq recently than in the successful case of the Soviet Union.

The longer impact does not necessary make the economic condition worse. To the contrary, the investigation suggest that the impact is reduced over time; the technique for circumventing sanctions improve; the political and economic conditions change which can be exploited by the receiver; and as a consequence sanctions become weaker. The Iran and Iraq cases are pointer to this situation. In other words, the first years of sanctions are the most important, providing the receiver government with the most problems and giving rise to the most serious political challenges. However, even in this crucial period, there is no co-relation between the serious immediate impact on trade and outcome. The reason is that the aid and projects, already in the pipeline, are not usually covered by sanctions in retrospect and as such remains outside the impact of sanctions. This provides a lease of life to receiving nations even in the most important first year of sanctions. That is why even countries experiencing sharp reduction in the first year have not complied with the wishes of the sender.

(ii) *Political Effect*: The low cohesive states are more vulnerable to pressure than the high cohesive ones. The conflicting relationship, before the imposition of sanctions generates support for the receiver government on the basis of which it improves its position. Thus by the time sanctions are imposed they are least likely to have the desired effect. Galtung's "adaptive potential, particularly its socio-psychological aspect" are exemplified in all cases of economic sanctions. A conscious policy of receiver government is to make the hardship, following the imposition of sanctions, appear as suffering for the good cause. If at the same time economic impact can be reduced, the government is in a good position during the first period of sanctions—which is also the most important one. Further more, the government can acquire increased legitimacy to take measures of controlling the economy, that would normally not have been allowed, such as withholding publication of crucial statistics; controlling the trade, the balance of payment and the involvement in investment programmes; operating in clandestine economic transactions and restricting the freedom of the mass media. Most importantly, political opposition can legitimately be defined as "unpatriotic" and suppressed by all kinds of measures. Mass arrests were carried out in Yugoslavia, Cuba, Iraq, South Africa, Portugal, Rhodesia, etc. This means that, in general, the opposition will have a much more difficult time operating immediately after the imposition of sanctions. National loyalties will restrict its scope of action as will the police measures taken by the government. Ultimately it could mean expelling existing opposition from the country. Thus the immediate effect of the sanctions is to improve the position of the government and to worsen the condition of the opposition, contrary to the sender's expectation.

But the improved position of the receiving government has a paradoxical effect. On one hand it increases the option available to that government; on the other hand, it reduces those very options. A stronger government will be able to strike a deal with the sender government. As it is in control and opposition is reduced, it can work out arrangements that cannot be seriously questioned; on the other hand, the government's position might rest on its strong desire to withstand all outside pressure and exerting into deal with the sender might erode its support basis. However, either way the receiver government will be in a very strong bargaining position *vis à vis* the sender, since it can argue that its options are limited (but not non-existent). The sender in other words, will loose some of its leverage on the receiver through the sanctions. What it can do is to use the lifting of sanctions as a reward for compliance, but the punishment already inflicted certainly does not make such rewards highly attractive. All this of course assume that the receiver government is, at the same time, capable of maintaining its own power position beside coping with the economic problems created by the sanctions.

(iii) *Issue of Contention*: The sender demands changes in the receiver's policies as a condition to lifting the sanctions. From receiver's point of view the significance of the demanded concession will be measured against the damage inflicted by the sanctions. If the damage appears to be smaller than the concession, demanded, the receiver will resist. Specific changes—trade concession or tariff modification—are least significant whereas general changes—demanding amendment in the constitution or resignation of government—are more significant. This means that more significant issues, the more likely a settlement, whereas the more general the issue, the more likely a continued struggle.

When fundamental changes are demanded, the receiver government, which is responsible for the existing political structure and derives its own power from it, have every reason to resist because it is not merely the question of damage, it is a threat to the very survival of the regime. Where the issues are specific which do not affect the normal functioning of the government, negotiations can be carried out between the conflicting parties. The receiver government has the choice and, in fact, concessions are offered. It suggests that the more fundamental the issue the more unlikely it is that sanctions will be successful.

The receiver's strategy is to interpret the sanctions as directed against the independence of the state or against the people as a whole. This means that the issues are perceived to be fundamental than they would objectively have appeared. As a matter of fact, a very general feature of the sanction literature is the complaint by the sender that the receiver has not understood its intentions correctly. Certainly the receiver will see the conflict only from its perspective. North Korea interpreted the US sanctions as an attack on its political structure despite US clarification that it had no intention to change the regime. It is, of course, not unexpected that someone exposed to punishment from another party would fail to see the situation from the punisher's angle rather than its own. Thus the strategy of the receiver puts the sender in a dilemma: If it lifts the sanction, it weakens its own power position; if it persists to continue the sanctions, the sanctions itself would be ineffective.

(C) Relation-Oriented Explanation. The relations between sender and receiver involve the question of inter-dependence and conflict escalation on the outcome of sanctions.

(i) *Inter-dependence*: Sanctions group themselves into three major, distinct categories—economic, military and diplomatic—which have a differentiated impact on the sender-receiver relationship. In respect to South Africa, Israel and Portugal there was very little economic, military and diplomatic contact between the parties and sanctions were basically taking place between smaller states. In respect to Italy and Soviet Union, some diplomatic and trade contact but no military collaboration existed. In respect to Yugoslavia, Cuba, Dominican Republic, Albania and Rhodesia, the contact between sender and receiver was very intense prior to the imposition of sanctions. Since the senders were the major powers, the relationship was, in essence, "colonial" and the conflict had a distinct element of smaller states objecting to major power policies. Furthermore in these cases senders have been internally divided over how to deal with the opposition from the smaller countries.

Indeed there is a particular dynamics of inter-dependence: there will, most likely, be groups inside the sender who know something about the receiver and in one way or the other, regard its policies with sympathy and understanding. At the same time, however, the activities of the receiver might antagonize other groups also with links to the receiver, and consequently the dialogue is created within the sender how to perceive the receiver's present policies. However, in the cases of little interaction, a consensus can, probably, be more easily established within the sender about the optimal course of action.

This would also suggest that the repercussions within the receiver would vary. In cases, in which the receivers are highly dependent on the sender, the internal conflict would be sharper, particularly in cases of "colonial" character. Indeed it might be the aim of the sender to play on such cleavages within the receiver. However, this rarely is successful. An additional explanation is that within the receiver the sanctions shift power away from the sender-dependent group to sender-independent ones. Thus, groups particularly favourable to the sender are those with a vested interest in continued trade, contact and cooperate. Examples of such groups are pro-Soviet loyalists in the cases of Yugoslavia and Albania, drawing their power from a continued presence in the country or business involved international transactions, such as trade or tourism in the cases of Cuba, the Dominican Republic or Rhodesia. These groups are, however, the first victims once the sanctions have been imposed, making it difficult for them to continue economic or political cooperation with the sender. They are forced either to leave the country, to engage in clandestine activities or to participate in the country's effort to adapt to the sanctions. Interestingly enough, leaders of the most recalcitrant receiver governments have often built their power on groups independent of interaction with the sender. Thus Tito could draw support from peasants or workers rather than party bureaucrats, and Castro similarly did not rely on the American hotel interests or plantation owners. Ian Smith's support basis was primarily white farmers not intellectuals, merchants or Africans.

(ii) *Conflict Escalation*: Some argue that a threat of sanctions would be more successful than the actual implemented sanctions. But the threat of League of Nations against Italy, and of combined Arab nations against Israel could not deter the receiver to change its behaviour. It is often noticed that in trying to read the intention of the sender for a prospective sanctions, the receiver may resort to adaptation or evasion but it will not be deterred.

Sanctions used in symmetric relations (major powers *vs.* other major powers or smaller states *vs.* other smaller states) have, in the case of big powers imposing them, been the highest level of pressure and in case of smaller states imposing them, an initial level of action. In the former situation sanctions could be expected to lead to negotiation and settlement, in the latter, to escalation of military violence.

(D) Environment of Conflicting Parties. The co-senders, the cohesion among them and the effects on trade pattern are the key elements with which the environment of sanctions is constituted.

(i) *Co-senders*: When the issue is more specific, the international support is less necessary and is probably not readily forthcoming. Only in respect to such issues, which are deemed to be of universal and fundamental significance, the co-senders and as such the broadest possible international support is required. International organizations play an important role in implementing or broadening the international support for sanctions. World organizations—League of Nations or United Nations—against Italy, Rhodesia, South Africa and

Iraq (arms embargo); regional organizations—OAS against Cuba and Dominican Republic, OUS against Portugal and South Africa, and Arab League against Israel were involved. Such organized international support is, however, not decisive for the outcome of sanctions.

(ii) *Cohesion*: The cohesive part of sanction does not only bring the deviant state back into line but also aims at increasing the 'cohesion' within the big powers zone of influence. The Soviet sanctions against Albania were also aimed at reducing the impact of China on Eastern Europe or among international communist parties. Similarly, the American sanctions against Cuba and Dominican Republic were partly designed to set the limits of permissible political orientations and counter the influence of "Castroism" in Central and South America. The British action against Rhodesia served, in fact, to maintain cohesion within the Commonwealth, thus preserving British influence. The big powers, by temporarily sacrificing one dependent country hoped to consolidate or enhance their influence over those remaining.

Similarly the sanctions imposed by the smaller states were meant to enhance unity among otherwise quarrelling states. Pan-Africanism or Pan-Arabism, both diluted by the daily pursuit of particularistic interests could at least require joint action against a state clearly antagonistic to these group principles —South Africa and Portugal (racial discrimination) or Israel (occupation of Arab land). Participating in sanctions becomes a way of demonstrating allegiance to the group.

(iii) *Effects on Trade Pattern*: The international environment contributes, both ways, to the effect of sanctions on trade pattern; it helps to impose sanctions as well as to sabotage it. In most of the cases the second effect appears to be more powerful of the two as receivers has had little difficulty in developing alternative suppliers or markets. Sometimes major powers have little interest in participating in sanctions or actually expect to benefit from actively sabotaging them. Thus, the West supported Israel, Yugoslavia, Portugal and South Africa in the face of the Arab, Soviet and African sanctions respectively. The Soviet replaced the United States as Cuba's main trading partner and China replaced the Soviet Union as Albania's. Sometimes neighbouring countries find it economically and politically very difficult to participate in the sanctions.

Sanctions have not only provided an opportunity for rival powers to export, but have actually driven the receiver to the opposite camp. The West rapidly became a most important source for military equipment, assistance and collaboration in the case of Israel as well as of Yugoslavia (even joining the NATO linked Balkan Pact). Cuba became military dependent on the Soviet Union following the abortive invasion in 1961 (even to the point where it became a tempting launching pad for Soviet medium-range missiles in 1962). Also by 1967, close military cooperation had been established between the Rhodesian and South African armed forces. Thus sanctions set in motion the forces that have re-shaped international relations.

Two exceptional points are worth noting: First, the relative political isolation of a country is very significant to the outcome of sanctions. Countries that are, at the outset, politically isolated will be more willing to make specific concessions, as Soviet Union chose to yield to the British demand, avoiding a worsening of its own situation. Also such isolation will serve to undermine a government, in particular one already weakened by internal resistance.

Second, given sufficient isolation, it does not seem necessary to reduce all trade. Neither British nor United States did so. In some cases, however, the main sender consciously eliminated almost all elements of trade with the receiver without apparent success. This suggests that graduated sanctions are more efficient because they have additional leverage: The sender can inflict added damage after the first wave of sanction's effort has been absorbed. Also by not eliminating all trade, the sender might be able to play a more intelligent game, using the divergent interests existing on the receiver side. Big broadside sanctions would certainly create more immediate damage but would also convince all groups within the receiver nation that sender does not really care about any of them. Furthermore, these two points act in conjunction with each other. If isolation is not forthcoming, the sanctions can be undermined, fairly and quickly by the receiver.

Wallensteen's four-fold explanations of the outcome of sanctions lead him to point out that three important lessons emerge:[40] (i) Economic sanctions can be successful, but only under pre-existing restrictive conditions; (ii) Economic sanctions supplement rather than replace military action and (iii) Successful economic sanctions would not change the global distribution of power.

VII. ASSESSMENT

Sanctions paradox, discussed kaleidoscopically, reveal that either the 'ineffectiveness' of sanctions is spontaneously more pronounced or its 'effectiveness' is, at the best, incidental, speculative, derivative, imperceptible, assumed and implied, partial with side effect, 'flaunt in words and flout in fact,' short of intended objectives, leaky in implementation and slow in results.

The paradox is that sanctions punish more the initiator than the receiver; are more effective among allies but not among adversaries; are, occasionally, 'blessing in disguise' for the receiver and sometimes 'counter-productive' for the initiator; reward the 'vulnerable and coerced' receiver but punish the 'potent and coercive' initiator in one way or the other. The irony is that they hit the 'receiver' and hurt the 'initiator,'

If sanctions are of purely economic nature and exert sufficient economic pressure, they may encourage "Smuggling;" if they are of the admixture of economic and military coercion which is prolonged and based on the discrimination of the military capability of advanced nations and lack of such capability among smaller ones, then the compulsion of such asymmetrical situation make, virtually, the 'Guerrilla' warfare and even 'Terrorist' activities appear a more effective means to foil the sanction effect.

Despite such deficiencies and implied consequences, if sanctions are used, the reason is that they have the capability of making the international relations less brutal. Seldom they seem preferable to genuine dialogue across conflicting lines. But the question is that if their utility is so rare and exceptional, why do they so 'frequently' used? The reason is that the 'ineffectiveness' of sanctions has reduced the danger of the implications of imposing the sanction.

REFERENCES

1. Miroslav Nincic and Peter Wallensteen, "Economic Coercion and Foreign Policy" in Miroslav Nincic and Peter Wallensteen, (eds.), *Dilemma of Economic Coercion: Sanctions in World Politics,* Praeger, 1983, pp. 3-8.
2. *Ibid.*, p. 8.
3. *Ibid.*
4. John Galtung, "On The Effect of International Economic Sanctions," in *Dilemma of Economic Coercion: Sanctions in World Politics. Ibid.*, p. 19.
5. *Ibid.*, p. 20.
6. *Ibid.*, pp. 20-21.
7. *Ibid.*, pp. 22-23.
8. *Ibid.*, 23.
9. *Ibid.*, p. 24.
10. James Barber, "Economic Sanctions as a Policy Instrument", *International Affairs.* Vol. 55, 1979, pp. 368-70.
11. *Ibid.*, p. 370.
12. *Ibid.*, pp. 370-73.
13. *Ibid.*, pp. 373-79.
14. *Ibid.*, p. 380.
15. *Ibid.*, pp. 382-83.
16. *Ibid.*, p. 384.
17. For details of the reverse impact see "Economic Coercion and Foreign Policy," *op. cit.*, pp. 8-11.
18. *Ibid.*, pp. 2-3.
19. Schlesinger, "Fragmentation and Hubris." The National Interest, 49, 1997, p. 8. Quoted in Daneil Drezner, *The Sanctions Paradox: Economic Statecraft and International Relations,* Cambridge University Press, UK, 1999, p. 7.
20. Hufbauer, Garg, Jafferey Scot and Kimberly Elliot, *Economic Sanctions Reconsidered: History of Current Policy,* 2nd ed., Institute for International Economics, Washington, 1997. Quoted in *Ibid.*
21. Hass, Richard, "Sanctioning Madness," *Foreign Affairs,* 76 (6): 1997, p. 76.
22. See Nye, "Soft Power," *Foreign Policy* 80. 1996, p. 158 quoted in Drezner, *op. cit.*, p. 9. Also see Robert O Keohane and Joseph S. Nye, *Power and Inter-Dependence,* Scott, Foresman and Company, Boston, London, 1989, p. 16.
23. "Economic Coercion and Foreign Policy," *op. cit.*, pp. 11-15.
24. Franklin L. Levin, "Asphyxiation or Oxygen? The Sanctions Dilemma," *Foreign Policy.* Fall, Carnegie Endowment for International, 1996 (With the Complements of the American Center Library), pp. 139-43.

25. *Hindustan Times*, May 17, 1998.
26. *Ibid.*
27. *Ibid.*
28. Franklin L. Levin, *op. cit.*, pp. 143-47.
29. East Timor, a 192nd nation, attained independence on May 19, 2002. Xanana Gusmao is the First President of East Timor, *Hindustan Times*, May 27, 2002.
30. Franklin L. Levin, *op. cit.*, pp. 147-48.
31. *Ibid.*, pp. 148-52.
32. *Ibid.*, Quoted, p. 152.
33. *Ibid.*, p. 153.
34. Galtung, *op. cit.*, pp. 31-35.
35. *Ibid.*, p. 26.
36. *Ibid.*, pp. 26-29.
37. *Ibid.*, p. 35.
38. See Bruce Russett and Harvey Starr, *World Politics: The Menu For Choice,* W.H. Freeman and Company. San-Francisco, 1981, pp. 181-82.
39. Peter Wallensteen, "Economic Sanctions: Ten Modern Cases and Three Important Lessons" in *Dilemma of Economic Coercion: Sanctions in World Politics, op. cit.*, pp. 92-125.
40. *Ibid.*, pp. 125-28.

3

Theories of Sanctions

I. SURVEY

The review of the existing literature on sanctions confirms and the confluence of domestic and international factors leads to the same conclusion: Economic sanctions rarely work. Sanctions are initiated because other options are not feasible and the sender regime wishes to placate domestic pressure to take action. But domestic politics within the target country will defy the sanctions; unless they attract significant multilateral cooperation and hurt target elites as much as the population, they will not force acquiescence. Since these conditions are difficult to achieve, economic pressure will rarely be the causal mechanism for target concessions. Costly sanctions may more likely to act as a signal of stronger measures and convince the target to back-down, provided the sender state is prepared to take such risk and does not regard the 'costly sanctions' as self-inflicted punishment. It is very difficult to create the impression that despite being burdensome, the sender state should not consider its sanctions as 'counter-productive' and despite being less burdened, the target state must consider itself as being punished. As such economic sanctions in most of the situations are ineffective.

Galtung attributes this lack of success to socio-psychological endogenous responses while Green emphasizes that the success depends totally on exogenous sources for energy and other crucial commodities. But Drezner observes that sanctions are more effective than the literature claims. There are many successful cases in which the military force or multilateral cooperation were not involved and the sanctions were not even costly to the sender. This evidence hardly suggest that sanctions always work, but it calls into doubt the hypothesis that they always fail.

The rationale of domestic and international factors, contributing to the ineffectiveness of sanctions, has already been discussed in the preceding chapter. But Drezner claims that sanctions, contrary to common belief, are more effective. In this respect his critical assessment of the existing literature is significant, because inherent in it is the justification of his own argument. He points out:[1] Most of the studies assumed that the objectives of economic sanctions were to return to the *status quo* that prevailed prior to the act of aggression which caused the initiation of sanctions. In fact the aim of sanctions have been consistently less ambitious. It is wrong to compare the sanction's outcome with the *status quo-ante* to determine the success of coercive event. He visualizes many alternatives: Hypothetically, the outcome may be achieved even without applying the coercion in the first place; if sanctions are imposed and target state does not change its policies at all, then the events should be judged a failure; if there is some compromise, however, and the value of concession outweighs the sender's cost of coercion, then the episode counts as partial success. The degree of success also depends upon the type of demand: A moderate degree of success in accomplishing a difficult task may seem more impressive than a high degree of success in accomplishing an easy task. Thus, the level of difficulty would determine the quantum of success. Drezner observes that these nuances are overlooked in the simple dichotomy of success/failure mode in the existing literature.

The sanctions literature exaggerates the absolute affect of domestic politics on economic coercion. But it is quite possible that the effect of domestic politics of sender and target states may cancel each other out. Or the opposing effects of sanctions within the target country's ruling coalition may lead to the overall insignificance of domestic politics.

Almost all the arguments use an inductive approach; theories about the sanctions are developed only after an examination of case studies and the concern is not with the theory but with explaining the specific events. In the existing literature, there is the tendency to underestimate the main causal effects on the universe of events and overestimate the effects that are unique to the extreme set of cases.

Since dispute between adversaries are noisier than coercion attempts between allies, the best-known cases are likely to look like failures. By developing arguments inductively from a biased set of observations, the existing theories can at best explain a sub-set of data on economic coercion. There has been plenty of attention devoted to the UN sanctioning of Iraq. There has been much less scholarly literature on the US economic coercion of Israel. This does not mean that the existing explanations are incorrect. They do suggest the empirical evidence marshaled for their arguments is insignificant. Both imposers and targets of economic coercion incorporate expectation of future conflicts as well as the short-run opportunity costs of coercion into their behaviour. This situation has paradoxical effects: Adversaries will impose sanctions frequently but rarely secure concessions. Allies will be reluctant to use coercion, but once sanctions are used they can result in significant concessions. Ironically, the most favourable distribution of pay-offs is likely to result when imposer cares the least about its reputation or the distribution gains. Thus according to Drezner the conflict expectation is the real criteria on which the success and failure of sanctions can suitably be judged.

Drezner pretends that comparing to domestic and systemic approaches (Endogenous and Exogenous models), on which most of the existing literature is based, the 'Conflict Expectation Model' seems to be comprehensive and inclusive. Thus these three approaches, identified as Endogenous Model, Exogenous Model and Conflict Expectation Model, are examined below:

II. ENDOGENOUS MODEL

The thrust of Galtung's argumentation is endogenous in character. He says:[2] The target society like "Organism" reacts when hit and hurt in such a way as to try to undo the damage and to restore the *status quo-ante.* In so doing the target state may, even partially, be strengthened because of the hidden forces that are activated. The sending nations not only may fail to achieve their goals but also may even contribute to exactly the opposite of what they hoped for.

Sanctions against 'collectivities' will always effect to just together with unjust since it is based on the philosophy of collective guilt. It represents a dichotomy (isomorphism) between inter-personal and international relations. What works at the individual level does not necessarily work at the level of interaction between nations. Prisoners often feel precisely that[3] "only a part of me did wrong, and only a short time—and here all of me is imprisoned, and for a long time."

However, there is in practice a 'billiard-ball' conception of man as an undifferentiated whole. Biology protects this billiard ball from differentiated imprisonment; much as the norm of national integrity protects the national billiard ball. In both cases imagination must be exercised to find more differentiated forms of punishment.[4]

It does not imply that there are no conditions under which economic sanctions will work. Galtung illustrates the possible conditions as follows:[5] Due to the structure of internal economy of the target nation as well as to its trade structure, the damage wrought or anticipated may appear so frightening to the re-unification of its goal that capitulation or compromise may be the result. Although there may be short-term adaptation, the long term effect may nevertheless be capitulation or compromise out of boredom, fatigue and desire to return to more normal conditions and ways of life.

It is argued that sanctions have failed because they were not universal; some countries did not anticipate or were found some other ways of circumventing the sanctions such as smuggling or use of third parties etc. Galtung accepts that this argumentation has some validity but points out that there are important reasons to believe that this validity is limited:[6] A country may continue to run on its internal resources and these resources—economic, social, moral and political—may be strengthened rather than weakened. A feeling that the rest of the world is 'ganging up' on one may serve as a very effective and hardening stimulus, supporting paranoid and psychopathic tendencies as well as salutary forces. Such tendencies help, at least to start with, to create social and political integration rather than disintegration, though often may be conditioned and circumscribed. In short, the stimulus to endogenous factors rather than the arguments, generally given, are the effective reasons for the ineffectiveness of the sanctions.

Then it is argued that even if economic sanctions do not make a receiving nations comply, they may nevertheless serve functions that are useful in the eyes of the sending nations. When military actions is impossible and when doing nothing is seen as tantamount to complicity, then something has to be done to express morality, something that at least serve as a clear signal to every one that what the receiving state has done is disapproved of. If sanctions do not serve instrumental purposes, they can at least have expressive functions.

Galtung opines[7] that this judgment leads to suspicion that economic sanctions may serve the purpose of expressing moral disapproval best when they are of symbolic nature and value deprivation is kept low. In his estimation, this purpose is served still better if the senders deprive themselves of as much or even more value as receivers are deprived of. But which case is more effective: When only the senders are hurt or when the receivers are hurt? This dilemma has not been resolved so far.

It is further argued that the counter measures—broadening the basis of production for exports and supplies of their imports—consequent to a declared policy in favour of the application of economic sanctions are consistent with economic policy pursued by many nations today, but are based on other reasons. As such this consistency will facilitate their implementation, which will in turn further the acceptance of economic sanctions.

But Galtung argues[8] that these consequences do not appear to be consistent with a view of inter-dependent international structure as more resistant against violent conflict than a structure very low in inter-dependence. One may, in fact, run the risk of buying a (dubious) non-military coercive measure at the expense of an even more dangerous international structure than that we already have.

Galtung raises a query: If we exclude military actions on moral grounds and economic sanctions on pragmatic grounds, what is left? Answer to this question may possibly be found in his proposed following combination:[9]

1. Negative, collective and external sanctions (Sanctions);
2. Positive, collective and external sanctions (Reward);
3. Positive, external but individual sanctions (Unilateral Sanctions);
4. External and individual but positive sanctions (Unilateral Reward);
5. Internal sanctions.

A priori value of these alternative techniques is, at least, as positive as that of economic sanctions, the world's experiences in this century considered. Thus the field is open for both research and new policy measures and it seems safe to predict that the rest of this century will witness much experimentation in this field. It is only to be hoped that such experimentation will not completely be unguided by good theory and good data—as well as by a constructive and positive orientation in the international affairs.[10]

Out of theoretical formulation and critical assessment of the prevalent trends, the main ingredients of Galtung's endogenous model can be summarised as follows:[11]

> The endogenous model is based on domestic politics approach, which focuses on the politics within the sender and target countries. The decision to initiate sanctions is caused by the domestic pressure within the sender country. The outcome of sanctions effort will most likely be a failure because of the domestic politics within the target country. If the target country's behaviour violates international norms, citizens in the sender country feel compelled to 'do something.' On one hand the cost of military intervention shall be too high. On the other hand doing nothing creates the image of a weak leader. The lack of options leaves the sender's regime to go for an economic sanction as an imperfect substitute for forceful action. Economic sanctions can deflect domestic pressure and register the sender regime's disapproval of the target's actions without going to war. The sanctions themselves might be ineffective but their implementation allows the foreign policy leader to avoid accusation of do-nothing leadership.

Many authors have proposed all or part of this rationale. From such perspective, economic sanctions serve as a steam to relieve government from the pressure of their populace. In this explanation, sanctions are symbol; their effectiveness is of a secondary concern.

Domestic level (endogenous) explanation provide three factors working against the utility of economic coercion: Target country may not be convinced at all; domestic group line up behind the government in reaction to an external threat; the target government may prefer to be sanctioned because in the long run it may hurt the trade and economy of the sender and it may permit the target regime to strengthen state control over economy and re-adjust the impact of sanction policies away from its most powerful supporters—for instance UN aid to Iraq has freed up funds for Saddam Hussein to reward its inner elites.

For economic coercion to work, target elites must suffer as much as target population. Case studies of Uganda have shown that the sanctions to remove Idi Amin became more effective when Great Britain halted the export of luxury goods, which hurt the army elites; or in case of Haiti, when Clinton administration prevented the Haitian armed forces from acquiring oil or weapons on the global market. The half-hearted motivation of sender governments combined with backlash effects within the target country make it extremely difficult for economic sanction to generate concessions.

Another possibility of success is when the target government is domestically unstable. It may lack the means to convert a sanction dispute into political support. Such a government would be more to acquiesce so as to hold on to power or be removed in favour of those who prefer accommodation.

III. EXOGENOUS MODEL

Galtung's theory, according to Green,[12] down grades the external political factors that play a dominant role in virtually all economic sanctions. They are dependent upon the economic system that usually contributes to their ultimate failure. These seeming paradox result from the complex nature of international economic relations. However, these sanctions originate within the economic system and while not denying that "organism" have a certain self-maintaining potential, we must also recognize that no degree of self-re-enforcement will produce needed commodities such as food and fuel which might be denied to target state without which society cannot exist.

Impediments to the ability of economic sanctions to induce compliance may best be understood through consideration of the following factors:[13] First, when the price of compliance, demanded by the sender, outweighs the price of suffering economic sanctions, such compliance by the target state will not be induced. Second, comprehensive universal sanctions could achieve their goals because virtually no state can successfully enter into a period of sustained autarky (autarchy) yet. Third, the possibility of universal sanctions occurring is very remote. The degree of global coordination needed for such an undertaking could probably never be achieved. Thus, sanctions must be viewed against actual historical experience in which all sanctions have been partial in scope and functional in character. We have yet to see universal sanctions anywhere or at any time. The concept of universal sanctions is a theoretical concept rather than an empirically achievable notion. Fourth, particularistic economic sanctions can be successfully circumvented by the acquisition of exogenous, third party, trading partners. The character of the international economic system makes such a strategy feasible and effective. Fifth, whereas exogenous counter strategies might lead to desirable endogenous outcome (such as national unity), the obverse is not likely to hold true. In the face of sustained economic sanctions, political integration could not revitalize a rapidly failing economy although a revitalized economy might help to rejuvenate or stimulate the growth of national unity. The amount of time in which adaptation and self-re-enforcement could successfully stave off disintegration, and the political disintegration that would ultimately follow, at some point, is apt to be relatively short.

Green argues[14] that Galtung's formulation on the value of endogenous counter-strategies support, partially, the Cuban case: Standing up to American giant help make Castro look like a hero. But it is also true that had the alternative aid not available from Soviet bloc to Cuba, it would have collapsed, notwithstanding the endogenous counter strategies. (But how would Green react today when, after the collapse of Soviet Union, such aid is not available, and yet Cuba exists very much!). The Israeli dependence on the United States and the eagerly demand of Israeli military goods in non-US markets such as Latin America and Asia, has minimized the vulnerability of Israel to Arab boycott which would otherwise have much more effective. Arab states ignore their own sanctions and black list when Coca-Cola did business in Israel and Pepsi Cola in Arab states or when Japan exported Subaru cars to Israel and Toyota to Arab states. They preferred to turn blind eyes. Arab states failed to deny to themselves economically attractive products. Lufthansa and Air France served both Israel and Arab states because rejection would have isolated Arabs.

Economic coercions are ineffective as a means of inducing compliance. Galtung attributes this lack of success to social-psychological, endogenous responses. But Green points out that case studies of Cuba, Israel and Rhodesia manifest the primary importance of political and economic strategies of an international nature. Galtung emphasizes that 'organism subjected to stress change.' While not refuting his claim, Green asserts that the accurate and realistic pattern which emerges in three cases are as follows:[15]

In each of the three cases, the net costs of complying with wishes of sender state were clearly outweighed by the risk of attempting to endure economic sanctions. Compliance in each case would have necessitated a virtual dismantlement of the target's political, social and ideological system. Thus, elite in each case had only one realistic option, resistance.

In order to successfully resist, each target was compelled to seek alternative markets. Cuba, Israel and Rhodesia were totally dependent on exogenous sources for energy and to varying degrees on a variety of other crucial commodities. By ignoring such economic factors, Galtung underestimates the material basis upon which all modern states depend. Certainly domestic unity is important, yet it does not put food into our mouth or fuel into automobile. Economic sanctions can effectively be neglected only by economic measures. The importance of self-re-enforcement mechanism has, in each case, been subordinated to the far more crucial necessity of protecting the economy. There is definite pattern to the evasion. In each case we find one major evader, the Soviet Union for Cuba, the United States for Israel and South Africa for Rhodesia. In each of these instances the 'significant evader' intervened for essentially political and strategic reasons. The aid was offered not out of altruism, but from a pragmatic and logical calculation that it would advance the evader's own interest: Soviet Union helped Cuba in order to gain foothold in the Western hemisphere; the United States aided Israel to improve its footing in the Middle-East; and South Africa came to Rhodesia's support in order to protect a kindred yet rapidly endangered form of white colonialism that reflected its own political system. Certain moral and ideological factors also motivated the assistance.

In addition to the politically motivated 'significant evaders,' each case received aid from a variety of smaller, economically stimulated evaders. These may either be private business concerns or individual states seeking profitable trade relations. In each case, there were many actors who felt that 'some one else's' political considerations should not interfere with their own search for profit. Even in Rhodesian case, apparent supporters of the United Nations' sanctions eventually abandoned the sanctions in order to pursue their financial interests.

Another factor that emerges from the three cases is the irrelevance of a sanctions scope. Irrespective of their magnitude, from unilateral to multilateral to almost universal, each sanction was evaded with equal success which incidentally tells that wherever there is seller there is also a buyer and *vice versa*.

National integration is indeed a desirable goal and after attending to material needs, a ruling elite must concentrate on maintaining national unity and political integration. But self-re-enforcement cannot grow food, although when there is food, people can be, even in the face of an implacable foe, unified and integrated.

Thus the exogenous approach emphasizes[16] that without a high degree of international cooperation, sanctions are useless. In the absence of such cooperation, the target state may always find the alternative: US grain embargo on USSR neutralized when Argentina started the supply.

Economic sanctions are ineffective as a coercive tool but may be useful as signals. Their value as a signal comes not from the damage inflicted on the target but the cost to the sender. Costly methods of conveying efforts need to be convinced of the sender's commitment. Costly sanctions by a Great Power can convince other states to join in the sanctioning effort; the high cost acts as a signal of the Great Power's seriousness of intent. Thus costly signal of sanctions helps to send a credible signal to other possible senders as well as the target.

The inevitable conclusion is that unilateral economic sanctions, cannot work, on their own. They are only effective if they act as signal that stronger measures, like multilateral embargoes or military intervention, will be taken in future. As such the sanctions success is actually the product of an implicit military threat. Sanctions, therefore, are not a true cause of concession, but merely an observable signal of military power. The Haitian leadership acquiesced when they were told by American negotiators that the US 82nd Air Borne Division was on its way. Sanctions may have assisted in return of Aristide as President, but the chief cause was the threat of force.

Thus, the hypothesis derived from signaling explanations is as follows: If the sender incurs significant costs in its sanctions attempt, the credible signal is more likely to produce concession. If the sanctions fail to work, then economic coercion will only work if it is associated with companion policies that genuinely produce concessions. Multilateral cooperation in the sanctions effort is expected to generate concessions. Also, if there are threats of military or quasi-military intervention in the dispute, the target is more likely to acquiesce for obvious reasons, even though the economic coercion is not the cause.

IV. CONFLICT EXPECTATION MODEL

We have seen that the Endogenous and Exogenous Models contradict in approaches but compliment in findings. But the 'Conflict Expectation Model' differs in both respects. Hence a detailed examination is required.

Evolution. Drezner,[17] while developing the hypothesis of his model, points out that the two cases—Israel and Iraq—suggest several puzzles that need to be addressed. The US administration refused to grant $ 10 billion in loan guarantees until Israel froze the building of all new settlements in the territories of West Bank and Gaza in 1991. Why did unilateral US pressure on Israel succeed where multilateral UN pressure on Iraq failed? The Iraqi case had all the attributes traditionally associated with the successful sanctions: the target incurred significant economic damage; the sanctions effort was backed by an international institution; all major trading partners cooperated with the UN resolutions; and the threat of military force behind the sanctions effort was clearly signaled. Yet sanctions failed to achieve their goals without the additional use of force. By contrast, the Israeli case involved unilateral sanctions that imposed smaller though still significant costs on the target and no threat of military force. Unlike the Iraqi case, Congress was reluctant to threaten economic coercion and in taking action, President Bush incurred the wrath of the American/ Israel Public Affairs Committee, one of the most powerful foreign policy lobbies in the United States. Despite all this, coercion was still successful.

Why did the United States choose to use economic coercion as its preferred policy options? It could have done nothing; it could have tried traditional diplomacy; it could have offered economic inducement; it could have responded with immediate military intervention. Indeed in the Iraqi case, the United States eventually showed a preference to use force instead of relying on economic coercion. In the Israeli case, it could have offered a carrot as it had done in the past. How do senders choose among their policy options in an international crisis? Under what conditions will a sender attempt economic coercion?

The answer to such queries, according to Drezner,[18] lies in taking into account the opportunity costs of deadlock and expectation of future conflict, which determines the behaviour of senders and targets. Sanctions alter the allocation of benefits, by imposing costs on both the sender and target countries. Nation-states care about this redistribution if they think it will harm their bargaining position in future conflicts. As such the short run concern for relative gains and reputation varies with the expectation of future threats or conflicts in the bilateral relationship between the sender and target. The expectation of future conflict has a contradictory effect on economic sanctions:

Senders will be eager to coerce adversaries and reluctant to coerce allies. While the anticipation of future disputes might make the sender prefer a coercive strategy, it also reduces its ability to obtain concessions. The target's conflict expectation determines the magnitude of concessions. Facing an adversarial sender, the target will be worried about the long-run implications of acquiescing. Because the target expects frequent conflicts, it will be concerned about any concessions in the present undercutting its bargaining position in future interactions. The sender might exploit the material and reputation effects from these concessions in later conflicts. When the concern for the relative gains is prominent, a concession represents a gain for the coercionist and a loss for the coerced. When reputation is important, acquiescence bolsters the sender's credibility as a tough negotiator while weakening target's reputation. With allies this concern is less prominent because the target anticipates fewer zero-sum conflicts. Target will concede more to allies than adversaries. Ironically, the sender will obtain the most favourable distribution of payoffs when it cares the least about the relative distribution of gains.

Between adversaries, senders will be more willing to sanction, even if the target's costs of deadlock are only slightly greater than the sender's own costs. Despite these preferences, it will not be able to extract significant concessions from the coercive attempt. Because the target is also concerned with the future implications of backing down, any concession is a double blow; not only does it loose in the short run, it grants the sender greater leverage in the future disputes. While the presence of conflict expectations might make the sanctioning state prefer deadlock, it also makes acquiescence less palatable to the sanctioned state. Thus, between adversaries sanctions are frequently costly to the sender and produce only marginal concessions.

Between allies, the sender will be unwilling to threaten economic sanctions unless gap in the costs of sanction-imposition is large. The target's costs of deadlock must be significant and the sender's own costs must be small for the sender to prefer a coercion attempt. Once this threshold is met, however, economic sanctions must be fruitful. Because the target does not anticipate many future conflicts, it will care less about the material and reputational implications of conceding, and more about the immediate costs and benefits. It will concede to avoid the costs of deadlock. Thus between allies sanctions are less costly to the sender, with more productive results. Drezner has articulated this hypothesis into "Conflict Expectation Model" which has been illustrated below.

Illustration.[19] Conflict Expectation Model predicts that, as sender's costs of deadlock increase, economic sanction is both less likely and less fruitful. As the target's costs increase, sanctions are more probable and more profitable. The model further shows that conflict expectations have a contradictory effect on the dynamics of economic sanctions. On the one hand, an adversarial relationship will make the initiation of coercion attempt more likely. On the other hand, it limits the usefulness of the attempt. Between adversaries, economic pressure should be common but of marginal use. Between allies, economic pressure should be less frequent but also more successful.

The expectation of future conflicts limits the usefulness of both carrot and stick in negotiating with adversaries. Only under a narrow set of conditions will the sender be willing to use economic inducements with adversaries. Take the US economic diplomacy in two instances: South Korea's efforts to acquire nuclear weapons in the mid-1970s and the North Korea's efforts to acquire nuclear weapons in the early 1990s. Both countries face equal costs of not acquiescing to US pressure. Because North Korea anticipated far more future disputes than South Korea, it was worried about the material and reputation implications of acquiescing. It would not concede without the carrot. This result suggests that without willingness to use brute force, even great powers are constrained in their ability to influence an adversary's behaviour.

States, while facing a conflict, are either worried that the concession at present can be used later to threaten their security and as such concerned for 'relative gains' or prefer to have a reputation for 'tough bargaining.' And the importance for either concerns increases as the likelihood of repeated conflict increases. The care about relative gains arises either from the possibility of future military conflict or from the possibility that a small concession in the present could lead to the long-run disintegration of state's position on a particular issue. The issue could be the control of a disputed piece of territory, access to raw material, weapon's non-proliferation or the constraints on controlling a restive population. Whatever the prominent issue areas, foreign policy leaders will care about relative gains if they expect that an equal distribution of gains in the present will lead to reduced benefit in future conflicts.

Thus imposition of sanctions and effort of resisting and if possible neutralizing the impact of imposed sanctions depend not so much upon the reputation of tough negotiations but upon the fact that the concession made in present can be translated into future leverage.

When sanctions are imposed, economic leverage is used to extract political concession. A successful sanction episode results in an explicit transfer of political assets from the target to the sender. States will be concerned about relative gains due to the possibility of today's concession becoming tomorrow's leverage. A variety of demand can be used in this fashion. A great power may use the economic coercion to secure military basing rights, and those bases are used in a later coercion episode to threaten targeted country's territory. A demand for greater liberalization within the target regime might permit the sender country to exploit domestic divisions in a later dispute. The importance of transfer increases as the likelihood of future conflict increases. When a country makes a political concession to a potential aggressor, the decision to acquiesce has a greater probability of coming back to haunt the country in future.

Concessions that transfer information, institutional access or asset specific investments alter the local distribution of power in a way that other power resources cannot, without political externalities. For example, in the US dispute with North Korea over its weapon programme, the North Koreans were extremely reluctant to allow inspections of certain installations. From their public statements, the North Korean leadership believed this concession would have provided the United States with strategic military information that could not have been obtained elsewhere. The United States could have acquired this information through more forceful means (as it did in Iraq's case) but the repercussions from this sort of power projection would have affected the entire region. This concession was the transfer of asset-specific resources that North Korea perceived as hurting them in future conflicts, despite the differences in power at the aggregate level.

While the states may keep the aggregate distribution of power in mind, they will be more concerned about the local co-relation of forces and policy levers. For example, while United States holds an overwhelming military and economic advantage over North Korea in terms of aggregate power, that advantage rapidly diminishes when looking only at the military balance of power on the Korean peninsula. Over the long run, the United States could focus more of its power to deal with North Korea, but this would take time and draw resources from other foreign policy concerns.

Thus, the importance of relative transfers depends on the expectation of future conflict. If the concession is significant, but the number of expected disputes in bilateral relations is small, the relative distribution of pay-off will matter less. A high expected probability of future confrontations and threats from another states will lead to an enhanced concern for relative gains in the bilateral dealings with that state.

Conflict expectation also affects, to certain extent, the concern of state over their bargaining reputation. For example, if the country has the history of acquiescing in the face of deadlock, the other country will have the incentive to act tough in crisis, so as to obtain a better outcome. By contrast, if that country has history of refusing to yield even if that action is costly, the other foreign policy leader will take that history into account in later rounds of negotiations.

Furthermore, reputations are inter-dependent; one state's boost in reputation will come at the expense of the reputation of the other. In a crisis whichever side backs down is perceived to have lost credibility. At the same time, the side that triumphed will find its credibility enhanced. Therefore the leaders must be concerned that backing down in the present will raise the other state's expectations of success in later episodes. A state will care about the distribution of payoffs in the present because this will alter its perceived reputation in other states. The reputational incentive will be much stronger when states expect a greater number of potential conflicts; they will be more willing to sacrifice current gains for a larger pay-offs in the future.

The expectation of future conflict varies with the dyad: For example, during the cold war, the United States clearly expected more zero-sum dispute with Soviet Union than with West Germany. At present India can anticipate a greater number of disagreements with Pakistan than with Bangladesh. For the foreseeable future, the United States is more concerned with the possible North Korean nuclear programme than probable Israeli nuclear programme. The US is more concerned to India's nuclear programme to either China or Pakistan via China. In each of the cases where more future conflict is expected, one or both states perceive a significant threat from the other. In relationships where threat perception is high, so is the expectation of future zero-sum conflict.

A logical extension of this argument is that the concern for relative gains and reputation is inversely co-related with the degree of alignment. Allies will anticipate few disputes, and careless about relative gains and reputation. Adversaries will anticipate frequent threats of conflict, and therefore care a great deal about relative gain and reputation.

Apart from relative gains and reputation, the deadlock and stalemate are another issue areas of the model. The issues are intimately related to opportunity cost, which the coercion generates. Such an opportunity cost must be low for the sender and high for the target. If the two countries are allies, the gap in the opportunity costs of deadlock needs to be larger for the sender so that it may still satisfy the coercion condition. Among the adversaries, if the coercion condition is not satisfied, the sender will not threaten sanctions as it runs the risk of backing down in the end. However, if the coercion condition is satisfied, the next step is to determine the range of concession values for which targets prefers acquiescence to deadlock. The target's choice between the two depends on the magnitude of sender's demanded concessions. The sender will maximize its utility by demanding as large a concession as possible. The concession size is constrained, however, if target prefers a stalemate to backing down. The sender needs to calculate the range of values of demand in a way that the target should prefer acquiescence to deadlock. And in the calculation a decrease in conflict expectation increases optimum possible concession in demand.

Senders are usually great powers and it is frequently assumed that their preferences and power guide international events. This is true only in their ability to increase the costs to target without incurring significant costs to themselves. The concession function shows that the target state's preferences also affect the outcome. While target's preferences do not affect whether economic sanctions are threatened, they do affect the size of the concessions if the coercion conditions are satisfied. If the sender's demands exceed the optimum possible concession, target will prefer to stand firm and go to deadlock. Thus, in crafting its demand, sender must be sensitive to target's preferences. Its power is expressed in this model through the ability to make target incur significant opportunity costs. This influences the demand size. But power, however, is still constrained by target's preferences.

Seen from the target country's perspective, it is not at all surprising that it would acquiesce to a larger demand if it were less concerned about future dispute. Acquiescence implies a transfer; the sender gains and the target looses. By contrast both countries suffer losses in deadlock outcome. A stalemate outcome is not as damaging from conflict expectation perspective because sender does not acquire what target looses; it suffers some costs as well. If the concern for relative gain and reputation are significant, target will acquiesce only to smaller demands to avoid deadlock. As conflict expectations fade, target is less concerned with how much its acquiescence in the present will affect bargaining in future dispute. Acquiescing to sender's demand looks preferable to the alternative of deadlock. As the target country's preference function moves from distributional to egoistic concerns, its grudge about conceding wanes, so the sender country can ask for more.

The target's concessions will increase when the difference between target's and sender's opportunity cost of deadlock increases. The target's concession will also increase when target and sender are closely aligned with each other. The greater the concern for relative gains and bilateral reputation, the more likely that sender will employ economic sanctions. At the same time, however, the optimum possible concession decreases, because the target country is more resistant to transferring concessions to the sender. The condition, which makes the sender wish to threaten coercion in the first place, also makes the target more reluctant to concede to large demands.

The assumption that the source of economic coercion attempt is a single policy conflict between target and sender and that policy disagreement is independent of the long-term alignment between the two actors is not always true. For example, since the early 1960s, the United States has used the economic pressure against Cuba because of latter country's switch in political alignment following Fiedel Castro's rise to power. United States economically coerced Cuba because it anticipated more conflict with Cuba led by Castro than by Batista. Similarly the United States had fewer conflicts with Iran ruled by Shah than with Iran ruled by Khomeini. In these cases sender might be motivated to attempt coercion because of a shift in target's entire foreign policy.

Sometimes it is not the shift in target's foreign policy but a change in sender's perception about the target country, which brings about alteration in its behaviour from coercion to inducement or *vice versa*. For example, after the collapse of Soviet Union, USA's perception about India changed, despite the fact that there has not been any significant shift in India's foreign policy. This shift changed both state's conflict expectations, affecting the utility of sanctions strategy. If target radically re-structured its foreign affairs so as to oppose sender's policies, their relation would naturally become antagonistic, such as Iran. If sender's perception change due to absence of the rival power, supposed to legitimize the foreign policy of a target country, the sender and target relationship shall become accommodating after the collapse of that rival power even if there is no structured change in target's foreign policy, such as India. Under the pressure of circumstances, even the feeling of the expectation of future conflict may wane and process of realignment may start as is characterized in lifting of the sanctions and achieving the cooperation between US and India recently, in the context of opposing terrorism. The differentiated quantum of concession in the process of realignment may still be hurdle in developing fully the Indo-US relations but it has weakened the possibility of deadlock.

In another situation, if target realigns against sender during the coercion dispute, the target's concession would be smaller. A decision by the target to balance against the sender implies a greater expectation of conflict and therefore more concern for relative gains and reputation effect. This makes it more likely that sender will prefer deadlock to *status quo* and thus makes a sanction event more likely. On the other hand, the increase in distributional concern also makes acquiescence a less appealing outcome to target. Sender must reduce its demand to make it more agreeable for target. Balancing behaviour only reinforces the effect of conflict expectations; the result is more events of economic coercion, but fewer concessions made.

It is assumed that demand is a continuous variable and can be calibrated to any value. This is not always true. The sanctions against South Africa were not lifted during early 1990 despite numerous steps by the South African government to end white minority government. The strong norm against apartheid made it difficult for any of the sender countries to settle for any thing less than complete abolition. Nelson Mandela, in his first speech upon release from prison, emphasized that sanctions should be maintained until apartheid was completely dismantled. Norms concerning nuclear non-proliferation and human rights can also make demands non-negotiable.

Sanctions will be imposed for a longer duration when the two countries are adversaries. It is logical that if sender and target share heightened conflict expectations, the likelihood of a deadlock outcome increases. If sender and target are adversaries, sender is more likely to coerce, but it will also be forced to ask for a small concession. By contrast, if sender sanctions an ally, the odds are better that it can extract a concession big enough to satisfy even a non-negotiable demand. A greater concern for relative gains and damage to reputation will constrain the magnitude of targets concession; this, combined with an inflexible demand, leads to deadlock.

There is another reason why deadlock is more likely between adversaries. Demands can become immutable through public diplomacy. If the sender country articulates the firmness of its demand in the public domain, the reputation-cost of any compromise increases. By contrast, if sender and target negotiate behind closed doors, without stating their position publicly, the price of compromising is less. Publicity leads to bigger audiences, and thus to higher stakes in the battle for reputation. If public negotiation can lead to inflexible demands, then conflict between adversaries are more likely to produce lumpy demands. Allies have multiple channels of communications with each other, and those channels are more routines and less public. This lowers the transaction costs of negotiation. Adversaries often lack these routine channels, and have an incentive to keep information private. This raises the costs of bargaining and makes it more difficult to keep negotiations private. Negotiations become a public spectacle, making demand inflexible and ensuring, thus, the situation of deadlock.

If the sender offers carrot (economic inducement rather economic coercion) the following is likely to be observed: (1) The demand is non-negotiable; (2) The carrot is very lucrative for the target; (3) The carrot is virtually costless for the sender. Just as the concern for relative gains and reputation makes target more reluctant to acquiesce, it makes sender more reluctant to offer the carrot. Because it anticipates future conflict, the sender is reluctant to surrender its own resources and strengthen the target at the same time. Given the right set of conditions, the sender will prefer the trade-off option even if the target is an adversary. This outcome is more likely if the demand is non-negotiable and the carrot is cheap to the sender but valued by the target. If the demand is non-negotiable, then sender's alternative to carrot is deadlock rather than acquiescence. If the carrot is cheap to the sender but lucrative to the target, the utility of carrot option increases.

The inclusion of carrot option in the coercion game does not affect the earlier results or hypotheses. Even if the sender can use carrot instead of sanctions, their use will largely be restricted to circumstances where the sender cannot use economic coercion as a rational threat. When both options are possible, the sender will choose to use carrot instead of the stick only under a narrow set of conditions. Those conditions are at the most stringent in dealing with adversaries.

These dynamics of economic coercion is an attempt to extract political transfers, and those transfers may undercut bargaining positions in future conflicts. Given this the sender country will decide to threaten coercion if it prefers a stalemate; it will prefer a long-term economic sanctions instead of backing down from a threat and accepting the *status quo*. The sender will prefer a deadlock if the target's opportunity costs of deadlock are sufficiently greater than its own costs and there is some expectation of future conflict. If the sender faces an adversarial target, it will prefer a deadlock even if the target's costs are only marginally greater than its own. If the target is an ally, then the gap in costs must be extremely high for the sender country to attempt to coerce. As the concern about the relative pay-off declines, the gap in costs must be greater for the sender to threaten sanctions.

As conflict expectations increase, the target will be more resistant to concessions because the sender will benefit from whatever losses it incurs. The sender must reduce its demand in order for the target to prefer acquiescence. Conflict expectation has a contradictory effect on the game. If the bilateral relationship is amicable, then the sender will be less eager to attempt coercion. Yet if it still prefers sanctions, it will obtain more significant concessions from the target. An increase in the sender's costs makes economic sanctions less viable and less profitable. The gap in cost has a consistent effect on the outcome, while alignment has a contradictory effect.

If the country tries to engage in balancing behaviour at any point during the coercive attempt, the basic models predictions are intensified. Balancing against the threat will increase conflict expectation on both sides; this will encourage the coercion attempt but also reduce the expected concession. If for normative reasons the demand has an all-or-nothing character, one would expect to see sustained deadlock between adversaries more often than between allies. Finally, the introduction of a carrot option to the coercion game does not seriously affect the use of economic coercion. Economic inducements will be used primarily when the sender is unable to threaten sanctions. When both options are available, the carrot will be chosen under a very selective set of condition.

Thus, national preferences are partially motivated by conflict expectations. There are two effects of this expectations: First, state will have some concern for relative gains because concessions made in the present can be used against nation-state in future. Second, countries are concerned that conceding in the present will damage their reputation in future interactions. Both these concerns vary with the expectation of future conflict. The state will care more about relative gains and reputation effects when their perception of threat is palpable. Because states balance against their threats, conflict expectation will be greatest between adversaries. Disputes will also be anticipated between allies, but to a lesser degree. The sender will rationally threaten sanctions if there is some concern about relative gains and reputation effects. Even if conflict expectation is minimal, there can exist a set of circumstances under which sender would prefer deadlock. This would happen, if the difference between the relative opportunity costs were significant, or if the price of sanctions to the sender were small. This does not imply that the existence of conflict expectations automatically leads to sanctions. If sender's opportunity costs were greater, then it would prefer to back-down even if it viewed the relationship with the target as strictly conflicting; it would be worse off in deadlock. The coercion condition represents a blending of short run and long run concerns. Foreign policy leaders must balance the short-run costs and benefits with the repercussions that present action will have in future clashes.

Unless states are perfect allies or perfect adversaries, it is a world of mixed motives. Even if sender is facing an allied target, there could still exist a set of circumstances in which threatening sanctions is the rational course of action. Likewise, even if target is adversary, sender might still prefer not to disrupt exchange.

Evaluation. In international relations, facts are slippery, quantitative data are inexact, and qualitative data can be interpreted in multiple ways. As such testing and evaluation has become a difficult process.

The existing sanction-data show that the initiation rate of economic coercion attempt is higher; sanctions are not always fruitful but there is significant variation in the outcome; evidence rejects the alternative hypotheses that sanctions are caused by either domestic pressure or the absence of feasible alternatives; it supports the model prediction that the sender's and target's expected opportunity costs and conflict expectations play an important role; sanctions outcome explanations reject the claim that sanctions success can be explained by variables such as aggregate power, the threat of military force or the presence of multilateral cooperation; domestic forces within the target country appear to have some effect. The evidence leads support to the 'conflict expectation model.'

As for as sanctions initiation is concerned, the studies find that sanctions are more likely when target nations act in ways contrary to sender's interests. For instance James Blessing concludes:[20] "In the vast majority of 126 cases, aid was suspended by the executive branch more directly in response to recipient behaviour, rather than in response to overt Congressional pressure.... The United States have been more apt to suspend aid to those countries in which it had a high interest and was less apt to suspend aid to those states in which it had low interest." Blessing finds:[21] "Economic coercion is more likely to be threatened if the target's opportunity costs are high, but the alliance variables was found to have no significant effect." Drezner says:[22] "This may have been a result of co-relation between high aid levels and alignment." In the same way Drury's[23] result strongly support the hypothesis that senders are more likely to sanction targets when conflict expectations are high. Drezner, by quoting these empirical studies, points out[24] that these results are consistent with the basic assumptions made in the model. Thus, in sanctions initiation threatening interest has been the main cause.

But it is difficult to point out the 'sanctions outcome' because of the involvement of varied variables: the target's regime type, the cost of the aid disruption, the alliance relationship between the target and the sender, the level of private investment in the target country etc. It is difficult to examine which independent variables have significant explanatory power. If the target's response to economic coercion were driven by domestic weakness, then one would expect to see authoritarian governments being less likely to concede. If conflict expectation drives the target's response, then the target's costs and the presence of an alliance should be positively co-related with a successful outcome. The target's cost, as noted earlier, should be positively, and sender's cost should be negatively, co-related with sanctions success. The prior relationship variable is the best measure of conflict expectations. Since it takes higher value if the two countries are close allies and a lower value if they are adversaries, it should be positively co-related with the successful outcome.

Drezner quotes Martin[25] who, according to him, provides compelling statistical evidence that greater is the sender's costs of coercion, the more international cooperation the sender obtains in sanctioning the target. The evidence indicates that although higher costs to the sender lead to enhanced multilateral cooperation, they are negatively co-related with a successful outcome. How can both claims be correct? Martin points out that primary sender's costs can act as a signal to attract multilateral cooperation but that this does not lead to a greater number of concessions.

It is argued that sanctions are merely a stalking horse for the threat of military force. Balance of power trends the predicted direction but no significant effect on the outcome of economic coercion. That is why economic coercion is less likely to succeed if the sender is significantly more powerful than the target. Thus, the argument that the sanctions success can be explained by military force or relative capacity has absolutely no empirical support.

Of the other independent variables, two appear to have some significance: First, if the target receives third party support, then sanctions success is less likely. Second, the measure of the target country's over-all economic health and political stability appear to be significant. Sanctions are more likely to succeed if the target country is in a 'distressed' situation.

In conclusion, the statistical studies of sanctions outcomes support the conflict expectations model and reject other system level explanations. The target's opportunity costs of deadlock, the sender's opportunity costs of deadlock and the prior relationship between the two countries trend in the predicted directions. These results are particularly encouraging. On the other hand, variables that measure the aggregate balance of power, the use of companion military policies and the presence of multilateral cooperation perform badly. They are either statistically significant or trend away from the predicted direction. This suggests that economic coercion is not a stalking horse for military threats or relative capabilities. Of the control variables, only the, target's domestic stability and third party assistance to the target appear to have any explanatory power.[26]

In addition to conform his model with the statistical studies of sanctions outcome, Drezner has deliberately selected such cases which, *prima facie*, defy his model so as to testify that in what respect and up to what extent the model is valid and relevant or the cases has not followed its basic tenets.[27]

The Grain Embargo. In the wake of Soviet invasion of Afghanistan, the United States halted the export of 17 million metric tons of grain to the USSR. But two weeks after the US decision, Argentina, refusing to participate in the embargo, signed a long-term grain with the Soviet Union, guaranteeing export for five years. Other countries, such as Australia, Canada, and European Union followed. As a result Soviet Union was able to import a record amount of 31 million metric tons.

This shows how difficult it is to apply unilateral sanctions on an easily substitutable commodity. Naturally the Soviet Union refused to leave Afghanistan. Fulfilling his campaign pledge President Reagan lifted the embargo three months after taking office.

The consensus on this episode, as referred earlier, is that the grain embargo is an example of how sanctions can hurt the sender more than the target. As mentioned earlier: 'Economically sanctions can hurt the target country less than the implementing country. When the United States imposed a grain embargo on the Soviet Union in 1980, the Soviet easily found other suppliers, but the United States found no alternative buyers.' Or 'indeed the costs to the United States were so significant that after the declaration of martial law in Poland, the Reagan administration refrained from implementing the embargo again because of the prohibitive costs to the US government.' This case is often cited as evidence that in responding to crisis situations in the public glare, policy-makers take impulsive and costly actions that fail to work.

However, the advocate of the model seems speculative when he emphasizes that the Carter administration was willing to incur significant costs when it believed the Soviets would suffer more, because of the heightened expectation of future conflict. At the same time the consistency of model's prediction is presumed to be justified, on the ground that the Soviet Union did offer, even if only token, concession in response. But this consistency is too glaring to be taken as the creditable part of theory.

The Pipe Line Sanctions. In the late 1970, in an effort to diversify their energy imports away from OPEC countries, Western European Nations began negotiations with the Soviet Union to secure natural gas imports from Siberia. To Western Europe it meant a guaranteed source of energy free from OPEC and the prize of lucrative Pipe Line contracts to generate jobs during a crippling recession. USA resisted this arrangement on the ground that at least 30% gas dependency on Soviet energy would leave its NATO allies vulnerable to communist economic coercion. The Declaration of Martial Law in Poland gave the United States an excuse to exhort the allies to sanction the Soviet Union which include a ban on oil and gas equipment export. The Western European allies refrained from those sanctions, because they would have affected the Pipe Line.

US put diplomatic pressure, which yielded nothing. Reagan announced on June 18 that the United States was extending the ban on oil firms and foreign firms that were using US technology. The ban was retroactive, applying to technology licences that were already granted. Penalties included ten years prison sentences for executives, a fine of $ 100,000 for each infraction, and denial of trading privileges with the United States. In essence these measures threatened European firms with heavy sanctions unless the American demands met.

In response, all of the allies rejected the extra-territorial and retroactive nature of sanctions. European community issued protest against the sanctions; West German Chancellor Helmet Schmidt affirmed: 'The Pipe Line will be built;' the French Foreign Minister described relation with the United States as a 'progressive divorce;' and even UK invoked the Protection of Trading Interests Act to ensure that the embargo would be overridden.

Despite such reaction from the allies, USA barred the French firm, which had shipped compressors to USSR from importing US goods and services and imposed penalties against firms in Italy, UK and West Germany for delivering on their contracts. All of the states refused to concede. Since the USA was reluctant to take action costly to itself, it undercut its credibility with Western Europe. USA found itself increasingly isolated.

At last USA backed down. On November 13, Reagan announced that all sanctions against Western Europe would be lifted because an agreement had been reached on export to the Soviet Union. United States claimed that the European had compromised their positions. Empirically this is dubious proposition. In six months after the incident, European firms signed more than $ 1.5 billion in new contracts with the Soviets. Gas imports from Siberia were curtailed but mostly because of a slackening of demand and a drop in oil prices. Thus the Pipe Line control was the least effective and was most costly controls in US history. There is no doubt that the United States acquiesced completely on this issue.

The economic and political fall out from the episode was considerable. Economically, the sanctions made US firms appear to be unsafe trading partners. As a German Official commented: "There is a doubt, a lack of trust, a feeling against the United States, that is the worst thing to come out of this affair." After the episode, the US firms encountered greater difficulties trying to export to European companies fearful of a future embargo. Foreign direct investment in European community also became a sensitive issue. The strains on the NATO alliance were also considerable.

This episode seems to completely falsify the conflict expectation model. First, the United States decided to coerce its allies despite the lack of conflict expectation and high cost of sanctions to itself. Second, the Western European countries refuse to acquiesce despite the significant opportunity costs of deadlock and minimal expectation of future conflict with the United States. The Pipe Line sanction case is an example of off-the-equilibrium behaviour. The problematic part of this case is the US decision to apply sanctions against Western Europe. According to the Model, that option should not have to be taken. After that mistake was made, however, the choices of the sender and targets were rational. The allies correctly perceived that United States preferred the *status quo* to a stalemate. The United States compared the possible outcomes and rationally chose to back-down.

Why did the US decide to apply the sanctions in the first place? There are two reasons: First, The US sanctions were directed against firms, not countries. The coercion of firms is usually easier than the coercion of nation-state. It was presumed that European firms would comply with the sanctions unless their governments prohibited them from doing so. Faced with the choice of the Soviet market or US technology, they would give in to American demands in spite of the sales and jobs they would loose. By originally targeting firms rather than countries, the US policy makers believed that they had circumvented the coercion condition. The Reagan administration did not err in thinking that firms preferred to acquiesce; it erred in believing that the allied governments would not transform the situation into an inter-state dispute.

The second reason for the decision was the lack of the unity within the US foreign policy regime. The Reagan administration was divided into two camps on the Pipe Line issue: The hard liners believed that any friction within NATO was worth the benefit of reduced commerce with the USSR. In other words, they thought of the Soviet Union and not Western Europe as the Target and were willing to incur significant political costs to employ sanctions. The other faction believed that the Pipe Line was a bad idea, but that the time for stopping it has long since passed. Any sanctions against Western Europe would produce nothing but discord between the allies. This faction correctly perceived that the NATO allies disagreed with the US on this issue. The US did not prefer deadlock to the *status quo*.

Thus the conflict expectation model would not have predicted that the United States would have attempted economic coercion against the European allies. However, no other theory of economic statecraft seems capable of explaining it either. The model does predict that the European states would stand firm on the issue because they have every reason to believe that the United States would prefer the *status quo* and quickly back down. Once the Reagan administration realized that the allies were standing firm, the high cost of coercion and minimal expectation of future conflict made the *status quo* preferable to a stalemate. This case represents an outcome that is off the equilibrium path, but nevertheless consistent with the conflict expectation model.

Economic Sanctions and Human Rights. Public pressure led to the addition of human rights as relevant issue of foreign policy. However, in deciding which countries to coerce, the United States incorporated issues of opportunity costs and conflict expectations into its decisions-making calculus. It refrained from sanctioning allies where no other conflicts were expected such as Western Europe, Israel etc; it maintained human rights sanctions where it anticipated other conflicts in areas like nuclear proliferation and commodities trade such as Brazil, Argentina and South Korea; it avoided sanctions where economies were small enough for economic coercion to have an appreciable impact and the coercion condition could be satisfied such as El Salvador, Haiti, Guatemala, Nicaragua, Paraguay and Uruguay; in addition to different categories of allies, it imposed or threaten to impose human rights sanctions against adversaries like Soviet Union, China, Vietnam, Cambodia, Laos, Angola, Mozambique, Cuba etc. Thus there was a great willingness to threaten sanctions against troublesome allies and adversaries.

All of the states believed that human rights issue had a political as well as moral dimension. The extent of the concessions varied with the expectation of future conflict. Allies that anticipated fewer conflicts were more willing to concede than adversaries. Furthermore, contrary to the conventional wisdom, allied targets generally did not use the sanctions as an excuse for rallying public support. There is no question that domestic politics within the United States can explain the prominence of the human rights issue, but the evidence indicates that the conflict expectation model can explain the overall pattern of economic statecraft.

Although the broad lines of the above three cases revealed that cost and alignment cannot explain all the variations, however, a closer look reveals that the model is consistent with the details in each case. In the case of 'Grain Embargo,' the US policy-makers believed that sanctions would impose greater costs on the Soviet Union than the United States. Because of the heightened conflict expectations, there was the willingness to incur considerable costs, provided the target incurred even greater costs. The 'Pipe Line Sanctions' reveal that if one side makes a strategic miscalculation, the conflict expectation model can still predict each side's behaviour. The 'Human Rights Sanctions' show that although public opinion can bring issues to forefront of the foreign policy arena, opportunity costs and conflict expectations govern implementation and outcome of statecraft. Thus the 'Model' generates a clear understanding of each of these cases, even though they were chosen because of their suitability to alternative explanation.

The plausibility probe of economic coercion reveals that the blanket claim of ineffectiveness is false; the details support the 'Conflict Expectation Model' although this support, as Drezner realizes, is at best preliminary; the sender's and target's opportunity costs and the expectation of future conflict trends are in the predicted direction; neither military power nor military threats affect the outcome of sanctions attempt; the level of cooperation is not co-related with either the rate of success or the significance of the demand; high sender costs cannot effectively signal resolve and they cannot lead to a successful outcome; and high sender costs are found to be negatively co-related with sanction success.

V. APPRAISAL

Drezner's "Conflict Expectation Model" presents a very penetrating analysis of sanctions. Such a scientific study naturally fertilizes ideas and evokes queries for seeking clarifications. First, the model has been examined in the context of the universe of sanctions.[28] Second the model itself has been critically assessed.

Conflict expectation is presumed to be an exogenous factor to the statecraft game. It is possible, however, that conflict expectation is endogenous to sanctions disputes. But as a consequence, the conflict expectation model largely avoids the relationship between economic and military coercion. It is emphasized that economic coercion is viable alternative to the use of force in political disputes and does not act merely as a signal for military statecraft. That does not exhaust the set of possible relationships between forms of statecraft however. Economic statecraft needs to be judged in relations to other means of influence. This model avoids linking the causes of economic coercion with the causes of war. The subsequent studies will need to pay attention to this dynamics.

The statistics of cold war phenomenon still dominate; the post cold war statistics are insufficient. The mind-set of actors cannot be probed. These are the extraneous constraints on the model. As a consequence the theory and evidence are incomplete. The model does not describe every interaction of the bargaining process. It does not explain all the variation in the occurrence or outcome of sanctions episode. The alternative explanations play some role in the adjudication of coercion disputes. But this model is a significant step in explaining the dynamics of economic sanctions.

All else being equal, China, North Korea or Cuba will not make the same concessions to the United States as Japan, South Korea or El Salvador. The first group of countries views the United States as a threat, and are reluctant to make concessions that they believe will be exploited in the future. Diplomacy and rhetoric can alter these perceptions only at the margin.

Over the long run, the model, developed, shows that the engagement *vs.* containment debate is sterile and unproductive. An on-going argument in policy circles is whether it is better to compel other states to change their policies through increased trade and exchange or through a long term trade boycott. In theory the engagement option works in two ways: First, by increasing interdependence, engagement makes it costly for the target regime to adopt policies that conflict with the sender. Second, increased trade fosters a powerful domestic bloc within the target country that undercuts the regime's grip on power. In theory the containment option works by punishing the target so that it has the incentive to change its existing policies.

In the United States this debate has lasted for at least thirty years. In 1970s, the argument was about the Soviet Union; in 1980s, the debate was about Cuba and South Africa; in 1990s, the controversy surrounded US economic policies towards

China and the group of the so-called rogue states—Iran, Iraq, Libya, Cuba and North Korea.

What all of these states are in common is that they anticipate frequent conflicts with the United States over a broad array of policies. The Theory and evidence suggest that neither strategy will be particularly successful in the long run. The containment option will generate few concessions from adversaries, even if the target's opportunity costs of containment are high. None of the outlaw states has made any concession to the United States because of economic pressure.

The engagement option seems to be more attractive. Increased trade would increase the target's costs of any coercion attempt. There is the additional argument that the increased trade undercuts the target regime's domestic base by creating a new internal group that prefers acquiescing to the sender. Furthermore, the North Korean case shows that economic inducement can lead to acquiescence in the present and enhanced leverage for the future.

The close look at these arguments suggests that the engagement option is only marginally superior to containment option. First, the benefits of engagements appear only when the sender is willing to threaten the disruption of economic exchange. Adversaries anticipate the probability of future conflict and will act to minimize their trade vulnerabilities. Unless conflict expectations change, this threat will not produce many more concessions. Even if trade level to rise, increasing an adversarial target's costs of coercion increases concession size by only a marginal amount.

Second, domestic politics stand-point cuts both ways: an engagement strategy can lead to a less responsive target. Assume that increased trade generates a faction in the target's ruling coalition but prefers accommodating the sender. The regime could react in several ways. It could indeed shift its policies in line with sender's preferences, reflecting the shift in the medium preferences of the ruling coalition. However, a second possibility would be to increase cleavages within the old ruling coalition, leading to the formation of a new, narrow coalition by removing the accommodation-faction. A new coalition would include previously excluded hard-line elements, leading to a more aggressive stance towards the sender. An engagement strategy has just as much potential to backfire as a containment strategy.

The case study of the US-DPRK conflict highlights the success of the carrot option, but it also reveals that the United States choose the carrot because non-proliferation policy was non-negotiable and the cost of the carrot was cheap. The Clinton administration considered economic and military coercion before reluctantly agreeing to the carrot. One policy analysts commented during the crisis, 'all policy options stink.' That, in a nutshell, describes the problem of the engagement/ containment dilemma. This debate inevitably deals with adversaries. Due to the heightened conflict expectations, no policy option will produce significant concessions and therefore all of them will be frustrating. In dealing with adversaries, neither option will reap what its supporters claim.

Economic coercion between adversaries is likely to be more public, more costly to the sanctioning state and less successful at forcing concessions. This is because adversaries anticipate frequent conflicts with each other and will care more about relative gains and reputation, making sanctions more likely but less profitable. Economic coercion between allies, although rare, is considerably more effective. States will be understandably reluctant to coerce allies. Once they do, however, the absence of conflict expectations will make the sanctioned country more willing to concede.

Therefore in observing the entire range of coercive episodes, one sees a majority of noisy sanctions disputes between adversaries with limited success, and minority of quiet sanctions disputes between allies, with greater success. Contrary to the standard explanation of sanctions, which fails to see the entire picture, the spectrum of 'Conflict Expectation Model' seems to be inclusive and comprehensive, though not as perfect as it should be. This turns our attention towards the critical evaluation of Model itself.

Sanctions are unilateral, multilateral, institutional (UN), and of military and/or economic initiative. Conflict Expectation Model explains predominantly, the unilateral economic sanctions alone and as such do not cover the entire spectrum of sanctions.

The model illustrates the implications of the varied behaviour of sender *vs.* target countries, but remains deficient in assessing or analyzing the phenomenon of sanctions.

Drenzer reviews: The existing literature on Sanctions underestimates the causal effects on the universe of events and overestimates the effects that are unique to set of cases; theories about sanctions are developed after the examination of case studies and the concern is not with the theory but in explaining the specific events (pp. 66-67). But the question is: How far his own theory, modeled on the case studies of North Korea and South Korea, is free from such Inductive Approach and in what way it is not the victim of his criticism of the existing sanction literature?

The Model, at the "axle" of 'conflict expectation', revolves round the relative gains, bargaining reputation, opportunity costs, concessions, back-down, deadlock, stalemate etc. in the context of senders and targets as an allies and adversaries along with an extraneous factors such as domestic factional disputes and balance of power. Each variable is compared with the rest and analyzed in the context of sender's and target's perception of conflict expectation along with differentiated impacts upon adversaries and allies. In an attempt to comprehend and explain the varied and numerous interlinking variables of the situation, which characterize the dynamics of economic coercion, the 'model' has itself become complex and repetitive leaving the impression that everything or anything can be proved or rejected. Such diversities and inter-linking complexities of numerous variables may easily be computed but cannot, so quickly, be comprehended by human mind. Thus, contrary to the norm that 'an elegant theory must conform to the inelegant fact' the 'model' itself has become somewhat inelegant. Great theories pre-empt the situations, occurrences and events. In the case of sanctions, the situations, the occurrences and the events still pre-empt the model so far developed.

The 'model' advocates the sender's case alone in terms of its initiative in inflicting damage or getting benefit; it treats target as a 'reactive entity.' It means on the side of imposer, the model is "original" and on the side of target it is merely "responsive" as if the target can only "react" but is unable to "initiate;" all the initiative of the target states are coloured as "responsive" to the behaviour of imposing state. When in the interactive process whatever sender is doing is "initiative" and whatever target is doing is "responsive," the model becomes somewhat lop-sided because target's "initiative" and sender's "responses" remains either missing or weak. The 'model' creates another impression: If the real objective or intention behind sanctions is to enhance the sender's national interests, all the arguments and interpretations of the consequences of target state seems to be merely a camouflage because it is the only objective behind it which can alone be regarded as 'effective.'

Thus, 'counter sanctions,' imposed—directly or indirectly, consciously or unconsciously—by the target state, is not covered under this model. In the grain embargo case, when USSR found other suppliers of grain while the USA failed to get buyers of its own grain, it was not just the 'consequential failure' resulting in 'back-down;' it was virtually a reverse sanction imposed on the United States by USSR.

Sometimes the change of events and circumstances thwart the objective and change the position. In the Gas Pipe Line case, the curtailment of Soviet gas import was not the result of the US claim that Western Europe had compromised their position; it was actually due to slackening of demand and a drop in oil price. This altered the position so much so that it led to the reduction in the import and export independently of the initiator's own emphasis. The model is deficient to sustain the impact of such counter sanctions, though explains the rationality of sender's failure.

The Conflict Expectation Model discusses elaborately the minute details, explains, rationally, the quantum of success and failure and analyses, scientifically, impartially and neutrally, the initiation, the procedure and the implementation phases of sanctions. No doubt, the model is procedurally improved, analytically scientific and empirically rational, but in terms of outcome, it is almost identical with less scientifically proved inferences of other theories. As such it seems to be strong on 'initiative' but weak on 'outcome.'

Sanctions imposed on allies are rare; sanctions imposed

on adversaries are frequent. The "privy" success among the allies and the "prominent" failure among the adversaries is the common conclusion. Any attempt to include the cases of allies so as to increase the ratio of success in order to refute the general belief that 'sanctions are blanket failure' is neither quantitatively nor qualitatively a balanced judgment.

Another such deliberate attempt is worth noting: Under the model, the success is determined on the basis of primary objective, secondary objective and tertiary objective, irrespective of what was initially aimed at. Success is also judged on the basis of correct initiation, established procedure and predictable outcome. Even if, on all these grounds, success is no more visible, the resulting high costs of sender is interpreted as ensuring international cooperation or aim is declared as warning others, thus serving as deterrent or satisfying the domestic public opinion that target's behaviour is disapproved of. Such diversification represents a hidden desire to retain the flexible situation in order to cover up any possible oddities of the initiator. Such expanding jurisdiction ensures, no doubt, 'effectiveness' in any context, but, in fact, contains the element of 'pre-conceived' notion in the name of scientific justification.

The dynamism of gains and loss within the economic system is not sanctions by itself unless attached with political gains and goals. Similarly, the bombing of an economic installation is an, 'economic war-fare,' not sanction. If any theory, in a zeal of proving the effectiveness of sanctions, tempts to include "intra-dynamism" of economic system or "intermingled" military and economic goals, cannot justify its assessment because the gain and loss within the economic system or intermingled military and economic goals shall be broad-based and as such the 'effectiveness' cannot exclusively be associated with sanctions alone. The Model, despite all the precautions, is not completely free from such pitfalls.

Finally, how can this model be suitable if sender and target are neither perfect allies nor perfect adversaries, but represent somewhat the admixture of both the qualities? For instance, in the wake of Pokharan tests, the US imposed sanctions on India with great fanfare, which is the sign of adversaries. But at the same time the process of secret talks, behind the camera between Talbot and Jaswant Singh started which indicated the qualities of allies. Where and how can the Indo-US relations concerning sanctions behaviour, be placed for analysis within the framework of this model?

However, the Conflict Expectation Model familiarizes with the phenomenon of the dynamics of economic sanctions and provides some plausible answers to the basic questions: When will countries threaten economic coercion? When will the targeted countries concede? How large will their concessions be? After all the model's canvas is large, the variables are numerous, the interlinking process is complex, and the investigation, according to estimation of Drezner himself, is preliminary. Precision of content and contour is further required otherwise any one, waddling through this model at this stage, runs the risk of 'sinking in rather swimming out.'

REFERENCES

1. Daneil Drezner, *The Sanctions Paradox: Economic Statecraft and International Relations,* Cambridge University Press, U.K., 1999, pp. 18-24.
2. Johan Galtung, "On the Effect of International Economic Sanctions" in Miroslav Nincic and Peter Wallensteen (eds.), *Dilemma of Economic Coercion in World Politics,* Praeger, 1983, p. 46.
3. *Ibid.*
4. *Ibid.*, p. 47.
5. *Ibid.*
6. *Ibid.*, pp. 47-48.
7. *Ibid.*, p. 49.
8. *Ibid.*, p. 50.
9. *Ibid.* pp. 51-22
10. *Ibid.*, p. 53.
11. See Drezner's comment on the existing literature on sanctions. *Ibid.*, pp. 12-15.
12. Jerrold D. Green, "Strategies For Evading Economic Sanctions" in Miroslav Nincic and Peter Wallensteen (eds.), *Ibid.*, p. 64.
13. *Ibid.*, pp. 64-65.
14. *Ibid.*
15. *Ibid.*, pp. 81-83.
16. See Drezner's comment on existing literature on sanctions, *op. cit.*, pp. 15-17.

17. See Drezner, *op. cit.*, pp. 1-4.
18. *Ibid.*, pp. 4-6.
19. See the details of the theory, *Ibid.*, pp. 27-55.
20. James Blessing, "The Suspension of Foreign Aid: A Macro Analysis," *Polity* 13, 1981, p. 33, quoted by Drezner, *Ibid.*, p. 63.
21. James Blessing, *Ibid.*, pp. 528-29, quoted by Drezner, *Ibid.*, p. 67.
22. Drezner, *Ibid.*
23. *Ibid.*, pp. 67-68.
24. *Ibid.*, p. 67.
25. *Ibid.*, p. 72.
26. *Ibid.*, p. 73.
27. *Ibid.*, pp. 74-100.
28. For "Universe of Sanctions" See *Ibid.*, pp. 311-21.

4

South Korea and North Korea

Under the impact of cold war, like East and West Germany or North and South Yemen, Korea was also divided into two halves—the South Korea, which came under the influence of the West and the North Korea, which came under communist rule. When the United States used economic coercion to stop South Korea, its ally, from going nuclear in 1975 and to freeze nuclear programme of North Korea, its adversary, in 1994, the Korean peninsula turned unique in assessing the implications of sanctions in respect to target-ally and target-adversary simultaneously. The proximity of space and the identity of the culture between the two target states in a differentiated position of ally and adversary is not only an ideal position for comparative study but also the best case-study which Drezner himself selected to testify and justify his Conflict Expectation Model.

I. SOUTH KOREA

(a) Evolution

Under Nixon Doctrine, the USA and South Korea agreed[1] to a withdrawal of the division, a redeployment of US troops away from the demilitarized zone, and a US appropriation of $ 1.5 billion for military aid. Despite the agreement, the South Korean reaction was far from sanguine. Doubts were lurking that if North Korean leader miscalculates, will America abandon its security or come to defend South Korea? So the South Korean President Park Chung Hee made the decision that his country needed a nuclear deterrent.

In 1970, he set up the Weapons Exploitation Committee, which was, in the words of US House Investigation Committee,[2] "a covert *ad hoc* government committee, responsible to the Blue House (the South Korean White House) for weapon procurement and production." In the early 1970s this committee voted unanimously to develop nuclear weapons.

There are three pre-requisites for a viable nuclear programme:[3] a sufficient level of technical knowledge, a delivery vehicle such as missile, and a suitable amount of fissile plutonium or highly enriched uranium. Seoul actively pursued all three requirements in the early 1970s. It was relatively successful in acquiring both the knowledge and missile technology. In addition to training its own personnel, the Republic of Korea (ROK), government made a discreet effort to recruit ethnic Koreans in the United States with nuclear, chemical and engineering expertise. By 1976, South Korean had a sufficient cadre of trained personnel. Seoul entered negotiations with Israel in 1972 to purchase its Gabriel surface-to-surface missile. The United States, after trying to dissuade the South Koreans, eventually assisted them in the development of a Nike-Hercules variant. Seoul's first successful missile test came in September 1978.

Acquiring the fissile material proved more difficult.[4] One way to procure it was to convert the radioactive waste products from a civilian nuclear reactor. South Korea already had an active nuclear energy programme and USA was building a light water reactor, scheduled for completion in 1978. Although the nuclear fuel for the plant was not weapon grade, the radioactive waste generated by the reactor contained weapon grade plutonium. In order to extract it from the waste, however, a reprocessing facility was necessary. In 1972, the South Korean initiated negotiations with the French government for the purchase of the plant. Negotiations were also initiated with Belgium to purchase a mixed-oxide reprocessing laboratory.

The United States paid little attention to these efforts until India announced its peaceful nuclear explosion in April 1974.[5] India had created its fissile material by using its Canadian research reactor and reprocessing plant. The US intelligence Committee looked at other states to see if they were taking similar step. South Korea's pattern of acquisitions fitted the Indian approach. The last piece of technology was the re-processing plant. Belgium cut off negotiations following the

Indian explosion, but negotiations with France continued. The United States reacted to the ROK-French negotiations by placing pressure on both sides to cancel any transfer. The French rebuffed the American request, stating that the decision to cancel the agreement was up to South Korea. The same month the US Secretary of State Henry Kissinger, repeatedly, threatened to cancel the US security commitment to Korea if the ROK weapon programme continued.

By the summer 1975, the deal with France had been signed.[6] Although the contract included IAEA safeguard but the United States doubted South Korea's commitment to it. With the reprocessing plant, the Seoul would have had all the ingredients for nuclear weapons on its soil. As a result of intensive US-South Korean consultations about the issue from November 1975 to January 1976, the South Korean abandoned their nuclear weapon programme.

What transpired behind the negotiations is not clear. As process-tracing is impossible due to lack of information, congruence procedure throws some lights:[7] US threatened to halt all trade and exchange involving Seoul's civilian nuclear energy programme and military procurement if the processing plant was not cancelled; to jeopardize availability of best technology and largest financial capability which only US could offer, as well as vital partnership with US, not only in nuclear and scientific areas but in broad political and security areas; to halt loans worth $ 275 million and loan guarantees worth $ 227 million from the Import-Export Bank; to withhold export licences and block the purchase of a second Westinghouse reactor; to persuade the Canadian to suspend their own reactor deal with Seoul unless the processing plant was cancelled.

In March 1975,[8] Congress had frozen a $ 79 million loan and a $ 157 million loan guarantee to finance an additional Westinghouse plant unless the South Koreans ratified the NPT. Although the ROK had signed the treaty in 1968 but parliament had not ratified it till 1975. The President of the Export and Import Bank, while retreating Congress's message, informed the South Korean government in March that 'the availability of a reprocessing facility in Korea could be considered to create a potential for nuclear proliferation which could become an impediment to our final approval of this loan.' After Congress made its threat, the South Korean parliament promptly approved the Non-Proliferation Treaty, and in June the House and the Senate approved the financing.

Furthermore, economic sanctions would have found legitimacy in treaty.[9] The accord between the two countries on nuclear matters restricted the Koreans from reprocessing any US supplied uranium without Washington's permission. The agreement allowed the United States to revoke export licences if the fuel was reprocessed, which gave it a clear legal mechanism to impose sanctions. The Ford administration made it clear to Congress in the fall of 1975 that it was willing to take such action if necessary.

Following the ROK decision, analysts praised the threat of economic coercion as a useful tool for non-proliferation. The US office of Technology Assessment wrote:[10] "Recent American pressure upon South Korea to forego acquisition of a reprocessing plant illustrates that sanctions can be effective, at least in a situation where the target state is highly vulnerable." Stephen Mayer Comments:[11] "The threat of an economic cut off was particularly potent. By playing on an special dependence of South Korea, the United States was able to produce a rapid change in the incentives and disincentives perceived by the South Korean government." Albert Wohlstetter notes:[12] "The effectiveness of the levers at our disposal can be illustrated by the extreme sensitivity of various programmes in the non-weapon states of the third world (where the impending spread is now most threatening) to simple alterations in the terms of financing. Korea for example, has drastically cut back its nuclear programme in response to a slight hardening in Canadian and American financial terms."

(b) Evaluation

The factors for the USA's success of economic coercion of South Korean back-down are to be probed. Three factors explain why economic coercion succeeded:[13] South Korea's high opportunity costs of deadlock; USA's low opportunity costs of deadlock; and the absence of serious conflict expectations between the two countries.

To properly understand Seoul's opportunity costs of deadlock, it is necessary to comprehend the expected importance of nuclear power to the country in 1975 as well as the inability of the Korean nuclear programme to substitute away from US suppliers. As early as 1967, a ROK Government Commission had determined that the growth in energy demand would soon outstrip its indigenous coal supply. From 1967 to 1976, the demand for electric energy was expected to increase six-fold and Seoul would be forced to increase oil import by 50% in order to meet those needs. The 1973 energy shock had reduced ROK reserves to just two weeks of oil. To reduce its oil dependence, the Council for Promotion of Nuclear Power Generation decided in 1968 to order two medium sized reactors. South Korea plans included an expansion to its nuclear sector to forty-five plants by the year 2000, which was expected to provide Korea with over 60% of its electricity by the end of the millennium.

Given the structure of the international nuclear industry at the time, the South Korean had the little choice but to depend on the Americans for plant construction and fuel supply. Three of the four bids for constructing the ROK's first plant came from American firms. When the United States threatened sanctions in 1975, that plant was still under construction, and the contracts had been signed with Westinghouse to build another reactor. The purchase of nuclear facilities also implied that the Koreans would have to rely almost exclusively on the United States for fuel. The reactor types required low enriched uranium. The US market power was significant enough to impose costs on the South Koreans if they had tried to purchase their fuel elsewhere. The threat to suspend all trade in nuclear material would have completely devastated ROK plans for energy autonomy.

The contrast between the asset-specific nature of the nuclear industry and the more flexible market in missile technology is particularly illuminating. As noted, when South Korea wanted to acquire ground-to-ground missiles, the United States refused to supply them and threatened to disrupt its military aid programme. The Koreans were able to get the same technology from the Israelis. Washington, realizing the Seoul would not have to acquiesce, eventually provided the technology itself.

Because the missile technology was widely available, US export controls and limited sanctions were insufficient to prevent the South Korean from acquiring what they wanted. The threat to disrupt the nuclear programme was more potent, because Seoul was hard-pressed to find a substitute that could absorb its expected demand.

If implemented, the economic costs to the United States of sanctions would have been mild; the specific US threat was to cut off loans and loan guarantees. In the wake of growing nuclear energy, Westinghouse would have had little difficulty in making up the expected loss in lost sales to Korea by finding other customers. Overall US costs were minimal.

Finally, conflict expectation between South Korea and the United States were extremely low. The Koreans were concerned about the extent of the US commitment, but at no time did they consider balancing against the United States. Of the five states with interest in the region—USA, Soviet Union, China, Japan and North Korea, the United States represented the lowest perceived threat to ROK security.

The United States anticipated few conflicts with South Korea. This made it difficult for Washington to satisfy the coercion condition on other issues. Only the proliferation issue sparked any concern for relative gains. Kissinger, in a cable to the US embassy in Seoul, mentioned three US concerns:[14] "Any Korean effort to establish nuclear capability would have ... major destabilizing effect in area; North Korea and possibly Japan would have responded by acquiring their own weapons; and this impact will be complicated by fact that ROK nuclear weapon effort has been in part reflection of lessened ROK government's confidence in US security commitment and consequent desire on ROK's part to reduce its military dependence on US." Because their expectation of serious political conflict was minimal, there was little reason for either side to think of dispute in relative terms.

Thus, the South Korea's high opportunity costs of deadlock; the USA's low opportunity costs of deadlock and the absence of conflict expectation between the two enabled the USA to impose successfully the economic sanctions.

As to the question why did the South Korean back-down,

three plausible alternatives were discerned:[15] First, the ROK leadership could have decided to delay their plans for weapons development and cave in temporarily to appease the Americans. Thus economic coercion did not really succeed. Second, the United States may have persuaded France to cancel its contract with South Korea. So international cooperation explains the successful attempt. Third, the US could have offered up carrot in the form of an extended nuclear umbrella or increased aid to the South Korean military. It was the carrot that created the concession, not the stick. Each of these possibilities is considered in turn.

First possibility, the coercion attempt was not successful: It is said that if Seoul focused on the non-nuclear aspects of weapons, such as the engineering and delivery components, and then covertly procured the fissile plutonium, it could have acquired weapons without threatening its civilian energy programme. Washington would have had a more difficult time tracing this approach, since there would be no pattern of acquisition to trace. It would have been the cost-effective approach; the reprocessing facility was never viable solely for the purpose of recycling nuclear fuel.

There is some evidence to support this explanation. Just six months after the reprocessing plant was dropped, the US officials, including the Secretary of Defence, voiced concern about the Korean restarting their programme. The South Korean Foreign Minister threatened to play the nuclear card and the Carter administration considered withdrawing American troops from Korea. In May 1977, he commented:[16] "Weapons might be developed, if and when the US tactical nuclear weapons had withdrawn." A month later, he refined the conditions:[17] "If nuclear weapons are required for national safety and the people's survival, or if under special conditions international treaties are not observed." In 1978, two research reports from Koreyo and Hanyang universities recommended[18] the development of a small-scale nuclear deterrent. That same year, ROK officials allegedly approached the French about the reprocessing plant again. Anonymous US officials maintained[19] that Seoul tried to acquire heavy water facilities until 1980.

This causal explanation is impossible to falsify. If South Korean succeeded in a covert effort to acquire plutonium, no one could have detected it. However, this explanation is still suspected. First, having nuclear weapons is useless if the information is completely private. Successful deterrence rests upon the premise that one's opponent knows the price of attacking. If Seoul tried to acquire weapons, it would be in a tricky position of wanting to covertly inform the North Koreans without tipping off the Americans. Such a delicate distribution of information would be difficult to sustain.

Second, neither the United States nor the IAEA officially detected any serious ROK effort to develop nuclear weapons after 1976. In 1985, the Canadian rebuffed a ROK proposal for a joint programme involving the separation of weapon-grade plutonium, which would have indicated an effort to restart its programme. Beyond that nothing happened. Peter Hayes concludes:[20] "There is no hard evidence that the South Korea is welching on its 1975 bilateral agreement with the United States to forego nuclear weapons." Following the January 1976 decision, no Non-Proliferation analyst included the South Koreans as a potential nuclear power.

Another flaw in this explanation is South Korea's reaction to the US decision to withdraw its tactical nuclear weapons in the late 1991. Despite an easing of tensions elsewhere on the globe, the North Koreans were still extremely belligerent, and as will be seen, developing their own nuclear weapons programme. With the collapse of the Soviet Union, Seoul had its greatest opportunity to obtain the plutonium it needed through illicit means. Instead, the South Korean reaction was to propose to Pyongyang that Korean peninsula be a nuclear free zone. The ROK President, Roh Tae Woo, suggested an open inspection of nuclear facilities, including US military bases to ensure that the North Koreans were not pursuing their own nuclear programme. Thus, if the South Koreans continued to pursue alternative nuclear plans, they had abandoned those plans by 1991.

Finally the specific American demand was to cancel the reprocessing plant agreement with France, which the South Koreans did. Clearly, Seoul's preferred option in 1976 was to manufacture the plutonium from its civilian reactors. By cancelling the reprocessing plant, the Koreans were forced to eliminate their preferred choice of a domestic ability to produce plutonium. It is possible that after 1976 Seoul made covert attempt to acquire the fissile material, but one could argue that it was in response to a new threat, specifically Carter's troop withdrawal decision. Furthermore, it is equally possible that the United States used covert economic pressure in those later instances to block the South Koreans.

Second possibility, the US succeeded as a result of international cooperation: The Indian nuclear test in 1974 alerted all of the states exporting nuclear technology to the dangers of developing states exploiting their civilian nuclear programme to develop nuclear weapons. This threat was serious enough to cause those countries to meet twice in London during 1975 to craft an agreed set of rules governing nuclear export. It was during this time that the French and the Koreans were finalizing the deal on the processing plant. It is likely that the United States pressured France at these meetings to cancel the contract. Some of the direct evidence supports this explanation. South Korean statement that strong pressure the United States placed on both South Korea and France, Kratzer's praise, in the testimony, of the French stance on non-proliferation or French President's statement that Paris has already decided not to sell the facility to South Korea are some of the evidences in support of explanation. If this were true, then the apparent success of US economic coercion would be a mirage; the South Koreans caved in only because they knew that France would not honour its contract.

This explanation is weak on both evidence and logic. First, take the evidence. The French and Americans were split at the July meeting in London. The United States believed that export controls were the best policy to halt the spread of weapons. France argued that legal commitments to obey IAEA safeguards were sufficient. The French IAEA representative wrote of his country's position:[21] "France remained opposed to any form of nuclear embargo aimed at putting pressure on the energy policy of a country which refuses to submit full fuel cycle to safeguards." Furthermore, there are six months gap between July meeting in London and Kratzer's announcement that South Korea had cancelled its purchase. If the French actually behaved then the cancellation should have been sooner. Kratzer[22] in response to senate's question, 'was this terminated at the request of South Koreans or did the French call off this deal?,' answered: "The South Korean government reached its own decision that the cancellation of this plant was in its best interest. It decided not to produce."

Logically, France was engaged in a bitter commercial rivalry with the United States to supply nuclear technology to developing countries. By May 1976, the United States had exported[23] sixty nuclear reactors; fifty-seven of them came from the financial assistance from the Federal government. France had repeatedly accused the United States of using the proliferation issue as a way of maintaining its nuclear monopoly on the industry. In the mid 1970s US non-proliferation policy was suspect. After the May 1974 explosion of India's nuclear device, the Canadian, who had supplied reactors and technical support, suspended all nuclear exchange with India. The United States continued to supply nuclear fuel. Only a month after the Indian explosion, the Nixon administration offered to sell both Israel and Egypt 600-mega-watt reactors. IAEA safeguards were guaranteed, but the timing of the proposal cast doubt on US non-proliferation policy. Five months after the Indian test, Secretary of State, Henry Kissinger[24] made a speech in India indicating that the United States was not bothered by New Delhi's actions. In 1976, one analyst wrote:[25] "It is the present US policy not to allow the export of reprocessing or enrichment plants, but there is concern in the nuclear industry that the continued refusal to do so may put Americans at a commercial disadvantage." It appeared that non-proliferation was not a high property for the United States until the South Koreans episode. It is unlikely that France would have switched its policy because of moral suasion.

One more episode discounts this hypothesis. If the French had decided to halt exports to South Korea because of suspected nuclear proliferation, then the policy should have been implemented against all potential nuclear states. It was not. At the same time the South Korean plant was scrubbed, France and Pakistan also agreed to build a reprocessing plant. The United States and Canada reacted strongly to the agreement, with Canada halting all exports of uranium and heavy water for Pakistan's Canadian-built plant. Despite the identical patterns of combined Canadian-American diplomatic pressure, neither the French nor the Pakistanis yielded on the project.

Third possibility, it was the carrot not the stick: The South Koreans only decided to acquire nuclear weapons when the Nixon Doctrine was announced. Statements from the ROK President and Foreign Minister indicated that the nuclear option would be pursued contingent on the withdrawal of troops and tactical nuclear weapons. It is possible that South Korea agreed to cancel its weapons programme because the United States extended iron clad security guarantees, eliminating the need for nuclear weapons, as well as increased level of military aid. US Secretary of Defence declared that United States would defend South Korea with nuclear weapons if necessary. This could have convinced the South Koreans that there was no need to develop the nuclear weapons. Security guarantees might not have been enough. While the two countries were in negotiations about the reprocessing plant, the South Koreans requested $ 1.5 billion in loans from the US government for a new force improvement programme. The United States might have decided to link the aid request to the cancellation of the reprocessing plant.

It suggests that the United States really used carrot to alter ROK policy. It also highlights an interesting question: What incentives would the Koreans have to maintain their extremely, close alignment with the United States after they have just been coerced by their ally? Intuition suggests that the United States must have used the carrot to appease the South Koreans, not the stick; otherwise the South Koreans would have pursued other allies.

Despite this intuition, the case of economic and security inducement is weak. First, the original motivation for the weapon programme was suspicion about US intention. The Nixon Doctrine had already given the perception that the United States did not consider South Korea to be a strategic interest. The fall of South Vietnam in April 1975 further weakened the US reputation in Asia despite statements from Ford, Kissinger and Schlesinger reaffirming the Mutual Security Treaty. The US was in the process of pulling out of Thailand at the same time it was reassuring Seoul. South Koreans had also been frustrated by US docility towards North Koreans aggression. It observed mild US reaction to such North Korean provocation as to guerrilla attack on the Blue House, 1968; to the seizure of USS Pueblo, just two days later; to the shooting down of an EC-121 reconnaissance plane in April 1969; to the repeated provocations at the DMZ; to the discoveries of the North Korean tunnel crossing the DMZ into South Korean territory; and to the heightened rhetoric of North Korean President Kim-Il-Sung after the fall of Saigon.

Secretary of State threatened to withdraw all security arrangement; Secretary of Defence threatened a review of the entire spectrum of its relations with the ROK. Seen in this context, Schlesinger's statements, which are usually interpreted to mean a nuclear guarantee, were in fact more qualified. He believed in conventional deterrence not the nuclear one. "Using fire power to save Seoul" did not include nuclear weapons. At one of the press conference he clarified:[26] "That is stretching the presumption a little too far. If there were the danger of catastrophic defeat which I do not expect in view of the force balance, I think that the President would then have to consider the situation."

However, such statements surely introduced some element of uncertainty. It is possible that private consultations conveyed a firmer message. Kissinger threatened to withdraw the security assurance, why did Schlesinger strengthen the commitment in the summer? While Kissinger's March threat failed to move South Korea, the December threat, which emphasized the economic dimension, did succeed in getting the South Korea to acquiesce? Theoretically the security threat does not work. The original motivation for the South Korean nuclear programme was uncertainty regarding US security assurance. Since a wavering security commitment from the United States caused the initiation of the weapon programme, why would an additional flip-flop have caused it to stop? Why would United States have believed that such a threat would have worked?

In the 1976 presidential race Ford faced a tough primary fight. In one poll published in 1975, only 14 per cent favoured US military involvement if North Korea attacked South Korea. Of the elites polled, the figure was 19 per cent. Other polls taken during the same time also suggested a strong isolationist streak with regard to Asia. These figures suggest that no security guarantee would have been worth much at the time of the coercion event.

The possibility of increased military aid is more intriguing because, if true, it would show that the United States extracted more concessions with the carrot than stick. The direct evidence of this argument is not strong however. First, a key element of the December 1975 ROK aid request was to have the ability to co-produce the M-60 tank as well as fighter and interceptor aircraft. The United States refused these requests, fearing it would destabilize the balance of power in the region. It also refused to sell F-16 aircraft and advanced rocket technology. South Korea did not receive offer of increasing its conventional production of arms in exchange for halting its nuclear plans.

It is still possible that Korea received more aid in exchange for not buying the reprocessing plant. If the offer of military aid convinced Seoul to drop its nuclear programme, then the US contribution to the Korean defence budget should have risen after 1976. Starting in 1963, there was a slow decrease in the US contribution. The pattern did not change after 1976. This shows that the timing of the statement was not designed to increase the attractiveness of the aid carrot.

A state department official described the US bargaining strategy as follows:[27] "We simply made the negative clear to them, that if they went forward with the reprocessing plant, Congress would insist on the termination of further military credit sales. And they understood this." The *New York Times* reported:[28] "Seoul officials say: Strong pressure forced cancellation of plans to purchase a French nuclear plant." What comes through in these statements is that both the Koreans and Americans perceived the *status quo* as involving some sort of US assistance. Any threat to disrupt their aid was perceived as coercive policy.

A review of 1975-76 episode shows that the South Koreans backed down because of US threats to disrupt exchange in the nuclear technology and military arms sector. In both sectors, the Koreans were extremely dependent on American suppliers, and would have incurred significant costs if the threat had been executed. The United States would have suffered minimal costs if the threat had been carried out. Alternative explanations, such as the use of economic incentives or necessity of international cooperation, do not have much empirical support.

II. NORTH KOREA

(a) Evolution

The end of cold war put extraordinary economic and political pressure on the Democratic People's Republic of Korea (DPRK), providing the incentive to develop nuclear weapons.[29] The economic pressure came from the collapse of North Korea's trading relationship with Russia and China. Both countries stopped trading on the concessionary terms and insisted on hard currency payment. Despite the North Korean ideology of 'Juche' or self-reliance, Pyongyang relied on energy and grain import from both China and Russia in order to fuel its economy and feed its population. The shift to hard currency and the resulting drop in energy imports caused the North Korean economy to shrink in the early 1990s.

Diplomatically, the DPRK also suffered serious reversals. The USSR and China, both established diplomatic relations with South Korea in 1990 and 1992 respectably. As a reaction, the North Korea threatened to develop nuclear weapons. The fate of its closed ally East Germany did nothing to alleviate the DPRK leadership; it did not want to be absorbed by the ROK.

As its incentives increased, the DPRK nuclear programme accelerated. By 1991, North Korea had both the incentive and the means to acquire nuclear weapons. The United States, after consulting with Seoul, decided to remove North Korea's incentive to build the weapons through a two-pronged approach: First, Washington would offer negative security guarantees, *i.e.*, a pledge not to attack DPRK, in the hopes of reducing North Korean insecurity. Second, Washington also urged the other great powers in the region to pressure Pyongyang into fully implementing the NPT. Both the Russian and Chinese have successfully pressured Pyongyang in the past. In 1975, Beijing vetoed a North Korean proposal to invade South Korea. In 1985, the Soviet held up signing a new trade agreement to pressure the DPRK into signing the NPT.

The diplomatic manoeuvring started in late 1991. In October President Bush announced the withdrawal of US nuclear weapons from ROK. Weeks later, South Korean President Roh Tae Woo proposed making the peninsula a nuclear free zone. Both Seoul and Washington offered to open up US military bases for North Korean inspection. In the same month, China put pressure on North Korean President Kim-Il-Sung to cut a deal with Seoul during his October 1991 visit to Beijing. The combined diplomatic assault appeared to work. Kim convened a politburo meeting immediately after the Beijing visit to switch to a more accommodating policy towards South Korea and the United States.

The Koreans (ROK & DPRK) signed two historical joint declarations in December 1991. The first agreement was a general pledge towards reconciliation and non-aggression; the second agreement dealt specially with nuclear matters. Both countries pledged not to test, manufacture, produce, receive, possess, store, deploy or use nuclear weapons. The agreement also included a section promising not to possess nuclear reprocessing and uranium enrichment facilities. In January 1992, Pyongyang signed a safeguards agreement with the IAEA. On paper at least, North Korea had agreed not to pursue any weapons programme.

But the ROK-DPRK deal was never implemented, as a result of renewed friction between the two countries. The IAEA also encountered problems. US intelligence, supplied to the IAEA, indicated that in 1989, the North Korea had extracted enough plutonium from the research reactor to manufacture one or two atomic weapons. The extracted plutonium was stored in the reprocessing facility. North Korea did not list that plant on its declared list of facilities open to inspection. In February 1993 the IAEA inspection of the declared facilities partially confirmed US allegation. The IAEA then requested special inspections of the suspected plutonium sites. The North Koreans refused, and shocked everyone by announcing in March 1993 that they would withdraw from the NPT in three months. No country had ever attempted to pull out of the treaty. If it withdrew, it would have been impossible to stop any future DPRK weapon programme.

The immediate US response was: Sanctions would be the result if North Korea continued on its present path. Despite this initial reaction, the US adopted conciliatory approach. There were good reasons for this. The USA had no trade to interrupt with North Korea; unilateral sanctions would have meaningless. If economic coercion was to be effective, it needs international cooperation. While China, Russia, Japan and South Korea all preferred the North Koreans not to have nuclear weapons, they also preferred an attempt at negotiations rather than an immediate rush to sanctions. After consultation with Seoul and Tokyo, the Clinton administration agreed to direct talks with the North Koreans to resolve the impasse.

In June 1993, barely a week before the North Koreans were to withdraw from the NPT, the American and the North Korean delegations met. The talks were fruitful enough for Pyongyang to "suspend" its declaration and permit continued IAEA inspection of its declared facilities but not the special inspection that triggered the crisis. It also pledged to restart working level contacts with South Korea. In return, the United States reiterated its pledge not to attack North Korea and to hold further talk.

In further negotiations, North Korea repeatedly signaled that it was willing to accept a "package deal," the North Koreans would stop work on the reprocessing plant and its gas-graphite reactors in return for the construction of light-water reactors of commensurate size. Since Pyongyang was unable to pay for the reactors, they were essentially asking for a carrot.

The United States was resistant to the carrot option for two reasons: First, the DPRK had not returned to the negotiation table with Seoul and the ROK government was paranoid about any cooperation between Washington and Pyongyang. Second, there was considerable reluctance about the cost of the carrot, which was in the billions. By March 1994, the IAEA informed the UN Security Council that if the North Korean tried to extract more plutonium from their research reactor, it would go unobserved by the IAEA. Before the third round of talks were to be held, IAEA inspectors were unable to examine all of the declared facilities. The United States in response halted negotiations. The North Koreans reacted by breaking off parallel negotiations with the ROK by declaring in outburst: "Seoul is not far from here. Should war erupts, Seoul will become a sea of fire."

Following the cessation of talks, the UN Security Council requested the North Korean regime to resume cooperating with the IAEA inspectors and gave them a deadline of six weeks to do so. This statement was not diplomatically strong as a resolution but was noteworthy because China, largely agreed to the US language, participated in the drafting and was willing to approve a document that threatened sanctions at a later date. Before the six weeks deadline, the DPRK informed the IAEA that it would extract spent fuel rods from research reactor and would permit its inspectors to observe the process. But before the third round of US-DPRK negotiations could start, another crisis erupted. North Korea refused to allow the IAEA to examine the fuel rods at the research reactor to see if prior extractions had occurred. On June 10, the IAEA threatened to cut off all nuclear assistance and withdraw all of its inspectors. DPRK, intransigent, caused the United States to push harder for the sanctions option in the Security Council. Pyongyang withdrew from the IAEA and reiterated that the implementation of the sanctions were equivalent to war. A day later, the United States, South Korea and Japan issued a joint pledge to impose sanctions regardless of Security Council's decision. Washington also took steps to reinforce its troops in the South Korea with an additional 10,000 men, more sophisticated weaponry and ships prepared to enforce a naval embargo.

North Korea, though publicly reiterated that sanctions would mean war, but privately indicated to Washington through different channels including Jimmy Carter, who had direct access to the Clinton administration, that it is willing to accept a package deal; it would eliminate its existing nuclear programme in exchange for modern light-water reactors and diplomatic relations with the United States. After receiving written confirmation on June 22, the United States suspended its sanctions efforts at the United Nations and went back to the negotiating table. Despite the death of Kim-Il-Sung, less than a month later, US-DPRK negotiations continued into the fall, and sanctions were not imposed.

In October 1994, a Framework Agreement was signed between the two countries. The agreement was consisted of a series of reciprocal actions that could be broken off at any time if the other side failed to cooperate. In sequence it worked as follows:[30]

(1) North Korea remains in the NPT, freezes all activity in its existing nuclear facilities, and suspends construction of its 50 M.W. and 200 M.W. reactors. The IAEA monitors this halt.

(2) The United States supplies heavy oil in lieu of the lost energy from the reactors. The Korean Peninsula Energy Development Organization (KEDO), a consortium of Japan, South Korea and the United States, contracts out for a light water reactor. Trade and investment barriers between the United States and North Korea are reduced.

(3) The IAEA resumes routine inspections of non-frozen activities.

(4) Construction of first light-water reactor commences.

(5) Before the delivery of key nuclear components of the reactor, North Korea complies fully with IAEA safeguards. This includes allowing special inspections of the reprocessing plant.

(6) The components are delivered.

(7) North Korean ships its spent fuel to the United States and start to dismantle its existing facilities.

(8) The first reactor is finished; heavy oil shipments cease.

(9) All existing DPRK facilities are dismantled.

(10) The second light-water reactor is built.

The agreement of 1994 was not based on trust; it forced North Korea to make a concession for every incentive. Nevertheless, the DPRK benefits enormously from this arrangement. The cost of the Framework Agreement was estimated at $ 5 billion, by far the largest foreign investment in North Korea's history. Averaged out over the agreement's eight years, the deal injects capital investment equal to 2.8 per cent of its gross domestic product. The electrical power from the reactor boosts electricity output by 27.4 per cent.

(b) Evaluation

In the context of 'Conflict Expectation Model,' the question is: Given the adversarial relationship between the United States and North Korea, why did the former decide on economic inducements instead of implementing sanctions?

The threat of economic sanctions was unsuccessful in generating all the desired concessions for two reasons:[31] First, North Korea's expectations of future conflict were so extreme that it preferred stalemate to total acquiescence. Although Pyongyang was willing to make some concessions to avert sanctions, its expectations of future political conflicts made conceding doubly painful; it was afraid that the United States would exploit a favourable settlement in later interactions. Second, the United States could not compromise its demands due to the normative importance it placed on non-proliferation issues. Faced with the choice of economic inducements, military options or stalemate, it chose the former because of the costs association with the latter options. Thus the carrot was selected because Washington was unwilling to scale back its demands. Sanctions were insufficient to extract the required concessions and the costs of military option were far too high.

Despite the potential cost of sanctions, North Korea's over-riding concern for relative gains and reputation made it prefer deadlock rather than acquiescence to all of Washington's demands. DPRK expectation of future conflict dictated that the costs of stalemate were less than those of conceding to the United States. It treated the negotiations as a zero-sum game. The source of this concern was both the high degree of threat the country felt following its diplomatic isolation and its fear of losing its sovereignty through future conflicts with the United States and South Korea.

The North Korean regime was pre-occupied with the fate of East Germany, surprised by the fall of communism in Mongolia, isolated by South Korea's diplomacy and non-recognition by Japan and the United States when all the great powers recognized and traded with ROK. As South Korea's economy grew in size, an assumption developed among region's players that North would eventually be absorbed. The underlying emotion behind the foreign policy of North Korea was fear—fear of encirclement, fear of invasion, and fear of foreign influences directed its actions. With a high security dilemma and indistinguishable offensive and defensive deployments, North Korea was facing an acute threat perception.

The consistent resistance to 'special inspection' by the official DPRK press and Kim-Il-Sung's statement:[32] "What they want us to be is a man without defence secret just as a naked man. We cannot accept that. We would rather accept a war" confirm DPRK fear and coincides with two facts:[33] First, during its existence, North Korea has been the subject of no less than seven nuclear threats from the United States. Second, in 1992, the Bush administration officials told reporters that to answer the nuclear question, they would need a[34] "mandate to roam North Korea's heavily guarded military sites." This fits very well with DPRK characterization of the inspections as a fishing expedition for US intelligence.

Pyongyang was concerned that conceding on the nuclear issue would give the United States greater leverage in future disputes. North Korea believed that the United States would be able to exploit concession in the present in any militarized dispute down the road. Because Pyongyang's expectations of future conflict with Seoul and Washington were obviously high, it had to think of any concession in terms of relative gains and reputation.

Once this substantive preference becomes clear, North Korea's actions make more sense. Scot Snyder comments:[35] It is but natural that "when faced with demand from the United States, contrary to its principle of sovereignty and self-reliance, the DPRK would choose to take exactly the opposite action—even if that action appeared to damage North Korean national interests—rather than be seen as capitulating on its core principle:" North Korea perceived as Bracken notes[36] that "its immediate strategic isolation would lead to greater economic isolation and opportunities for international intervention in Korean affairs:" "The pressure to open suspect nuclear facilities to inspection by IAEA was surely be seen by Pyongyang as only the first move to open up North Korean state."

Thus the North Koreans were vitally concern about the distribution of gains. They worried that any concessions about the inspections would give the United States additional leverage in the future. Pyongyang believed that the transfer of intelligence information and the general opening of the DPRK to outside influences, would weaken the regime's bargaining position in future conflicts. It was willing to suffer the formidable costs of deadlock rather than acquiesce to all of the US demands.

Despite such extreme concern, North Korea was willing to make some concession in exchange for avoiding deadlock. DPRK negotiators divided the proliferation issue into two separate categories:[37] Complying with IAEA safeguards against the development of weapons in the future, and agreeing to special inspections to trace past nuclear efforts. During 1993 stand off, both the US and South Korean negotiators indicated that unless Pyongyang backed down, sanctions will be implemented. Pyongyang then agreed to suspend its withdrawal from the NPT and permitted IAEA inspections of its declared facilities. Washington agreed not to attack Pyongyang, but this was 're-cycled' carrot; the United States conceded nothing new. But at the same time USA could not compel North Korea to concede to special inspection either. In agreeing for inspection of declared facilities, DPRK did not either concede to any new inspection.

The chief benefit to North Korea was the delay of sanctions. It would agree to a small portion of the IAEA and US demands, thus putting off sanctions and prolonging the nuclear dispute while leaving the most important issues on the table. Thus, North Korea found some way to re-engage the United States. It is argued that if the option of economic sanctions had been pursued sooner, it is possible that the North Korea would have been forthcoming as well.[38]

Here a bit of contradiction in the analysis appear, perhaps as a result of aspiration dominating the fact. It is already pointed out that the USA has no leverage in North Korea; its imposition of unilateral economic sanctions are meaningless unless attains international cooperation, which is not only easily forthcoming but takes its own time. As such the aspiration of sooner imposition of economic sanctions was misplaced. In fact, DPRK's strategy of 'partial acceptance and re-engaging the United States' is the result of USA's inability of directly and unilaterally imposing sanctions effectively.

It is argued that threat of US sanctions led the DPRK to be more accommodating after the June crisis. But such accommodation was not one-sided as is emphasized. For example, the DPRK offer in June to freeze its nuclear programme left unclear whether reprocessing was included. The United States insisted on a total freeze before the sanctions drive was called off. The North Koreans quickly agreed to the US specific terms. Even if it is presumed that the specific term, which DPRK agreed, include 'reprocessing' as well, it is still unclear whether the USA succeeded in 'fishing expedition' of the past investigation, which the special inspection aimed at. It means that if the sender is accommodating by conceding 'special inspection,' the target is accommodating by conceding 'reprocessing.' Even if it is a "pressure," which is no doubt a fact, it resulted into somewhat "balancing," not one-sided surrender.

Even in this apparent balancing the inherent domination, no doubt, exists.[39] June 1994 threat of economic coercion did modify the package deal between the two countries in favour of the United States. As US position became more belligerent, North Korea increased the number of private messages that it was ready to cut a deal. In the final agreement normalization and special inspections were not explicitly linked but it was made clear to the North Koreans that South Korea would build the light-water reactor. The asset specific nature of the nuclear reactor made this change a significant concession because it created a North Korean dependency on South Korean technology.

US leverage was constrained by the DPRK's expectations of future conflict. The threat of economic coercion was capable of producing a certain number of concessions. Pyongyang would have been willing to acquiesce if the United States had reduced its demand to allowing the IAEA to maintain safeguards on all of its declared nuclear facilities, preventing any future proliferation effort. By contrast, the DPRK preferred deadlock, and even war, to making the additional concession of permitting the United States to investigate previous efforts to develop nuclear weapons. Only with the proffering of the carrot was North Korea prepared to agree to all Washington's demands. It is doubtful whether 'all of Washington's demands' include investigating the previous efforts!

It is still to be investigated: Why did the economic coercion fail? Two explanations are provided: First, sanctions would have imposed minimal costs on the DPRK. This was the result of either autarkic nature of North Korean's economy or the inability of the United States to generate the necessary international cooperation. Second, the North Korean leadership was irrational and therefore was incapable of responding to cost-benefit analysis. These alternatives are discussed in turn:[40]

(i) *Opportunity Costs*: An economy, built on the ideology of Juche or self-reliance, would at least theoretically, appear to be invulnerable to sanctions. However, despite the DPRK's claim about self-reliance, it was practically dependent upon foreign trade and exchange. The cut-off of Soviet aid and trade credits caused the North Korean economy to shrink drastically during the early 1990s. Trade levels also decreased as more countries insisted on hard currency payments. In December 1993 even the DPRK worker's Party Central Committee blamed its economic down turn on 'the collapse of socialist countries and the socialist markets of the world.' At the same meeting, the party announced its new economic plan in which top priority would be given to foreign trade. In such situation, most commentators agreed that United Nation's sanctions could have imposed serious damage to the DPRK economy.

Another possible explanation is that the United States could not generate the necessary international cooperation to have any bite. These sanctions would have been ineffective without Chinese cooperation. By 1994, China was Pyongyang's largest trade partner, with 34 per cent of its total trade, exported oil, rice and corn, the figure had claimed to 43 per cent. If Chinese failed to participate in the sanctions effort, the disruption would have not been costly enough to force acquiescence. Chinese position even at its height of crisis was not clear whether it would veto or ignore sanctions. In addition to Chinese recalcitrance, the United States was having difficulty getting even Japan and South Korea on board.

It is clear that China wanted North Korea to abandon its weapon programme and adhere to the NPT. As such China abstained rather than veto against the IAEA sanctions. With the June 14 pledge by the United States, Japan and South Korea to impose sanctions regardless of Security Council's veto, the Chinese veto held less influence. Rather than be seen as 'obstructionist,' it was entirely possible the Beijing would have abstained. It appears consistent with Don Oberdorfer's claim that[41] "Chinese diplomats in Beijing and Pyongyang told North Korea that although it opposed sanctions, the strength of international opinion would prevent a veto."

At the absolute minimum, the United States, Japan and South Korea were pledged to attempt economic coercion. This leads to second point: Economic sanctions would have hurt the DPRK elite regardless of Chinese participation. It is generally believed that the "Court Economy" is both more efficient and more entrepreneurial. It is responsible for military exports to Iran, Syria and Libya, as well as a textile industry that generates considerable exports revenue from Japan and South Korea. Russian analysts estimated that the court economy is responsible for 15 per cent of DPRK industrial production, and up to 40 per cent of its export revenue. The Court Economy would have been more vulnerable to economic coercion regardless of Chinese participation. It relied heavily upon capital inflows from Japan and South Korea; $ 600 million annually hard currency transfers from Japan and $ 200 million worth of goods from South Korea have been estimated. Sanctions would have disrupted this exchange. It would have also frustrated the court economy oil-for-arms trade with Iran and Libya. By the mid 1990s the DPRK military was selling roughly $ 500 million in ballistic missile technology to Middle Eastern customers. It is highly unlikely that China would have been willing to allow the DPRK to transport these goods across their territory during an embargo. Beside the obvious reputation-costs, such a move would have required China to assist North Korea in eroding its own share of the international textile and arms market. Beijing's behaviour during the episode suggests that while it did not whole-heartedly favour sanctions, it would not have blindly supported Pyongyang at its own expense.

Applying to most conservative estimate to Japanese transfers and exports, sanctions applied by Japan alone would have been the equivalent of 3.6 per cent of North Korea's G.D.P. Adding in exports to South Korea, the figure jumps to 4.5 per cent; a cut off of missile sales would have increased the amount to almost 7 per cent. Relative to the sanctions episodes described in HSE data, this is a sizable sum. It is larger than South Korea's estimated costs of coercion in 1975.

The second fact to consider is the political calculus behind the court economy. The military elite was the most powerful interest group in North Korea. The second economy was setup largely to service the interests of that elite. Bureaucratically, its finances were organized separately from the civilian sector. Its demands were fulfilled before resources were committed to the official economy. Even in times of economic crisis, that sector remained in operation. This was consistent with the effort of Kim-Il-Sung and his successor son, Kim-Jog-II to provide the army with access to consumer goods and opportunities for hard currency, as well as their concerns about losing power. High-ranking defectors claimed that the younger Kim relied on handouts of high priced luxury goods to ensure this fealty. The organization of DPRK military seemed designed less to fight a war than thwart anyone group from overthrowing the Kims. If the leadership was willing to sacrifice military efficiency to protect itself, it indicates the strong concern of a coup.

Sanctions would have threatened the court economy most of all, eliminating access to hard currency and luxury goods. Economic sanctions would have crippled the upper echelons of the North Korean government and promoted instability within the target regime. One of the arguments in the sanctions literature is that acquiescence becomes more likely when the economic sanctions hurt the country's elite and lead to domestic political instability. Economic coercion, even without Chinese help, would have devastated the DPRK elite.

(ii) *Irrationality*: The chronology of consistent pattern behaviour shows that DPRK was willing to make concession when faced with pressure from either the Soviet Union or China. In 1985, North Korea signed the NPT in response to Soviet pressure; in 1991, it agreed to negotiations with South Korea in response to Chinese pressure. Why would a decision-maker, divorced from reality, accede, consistently, to allied pressure but resist similar pressure from adversaries?

Second, the chronology also shows a consistent pattern of offering minor concessions just before sanctions were about to be implemented. This pattern is particularly regular for an irrational actor though consistent with an aggressive bargaining strategy. Finally, even after the death of Kim-II-Sung in

July 1994, the pattern of tough bargaining, the DPRK inflexibility and the concession at the last minute continued as before.

Overall, the pattern of DPRK behaviour highlights the difference between subjective and instrumental rationality. Subjective rationality claims that all actors have the same ordering of preferences; instrumental rationality argues that given a set of preferences, actors will act strategically to maximize those preferences. From an American perspective, it is easy to accuse the DPRK regime of being subjectively irrational. In its fifty years existence North Korea has repeatedly violated several international norms, including terrorism and state sponsored assassination. It has continued operating a Stalinist economy despite the collapse of communism as a viable system. Violating the norm of non-proliferation was merely the latest action that was in conflict with US preferences. Clearly the United States and North Korea do not value the same things. Given what is important to the DPRK elite—staying in power, maintaining sovereignty—however, the regime acted in a manner consistent with instrumental rationality. Scott Snyder concurs:[42] "Rational self-interest in the North Korean context was measured overwhelmingly by political and ideological considerations; from the outside North Korean choices appeared irrational and self-defeating." Once conflict expectations are factored in, it is easy to understand why Pyongyang would have cared so much about its reputation and the relative distribution of gains.

Despite all such alternative explanations the carrot was the ultimate choice. The Clinton administration was well aware of the damage the sanction would have inflicted on North Korea even if China were not a participant. The North Koreans were also made fully aware that sanctions would be implemented without the Security Council's approval. Despite this knowledge, the United States acceded to negotiations because it needed the cooperation of Japan and South Korea and wanted the cooperation of China. All three countries wanted to see an attempt at dialogue before sanctions were implemented.

The United States was willing to negotiate, but it viewed these negotiations as away to satisfy its allies' qualms about sanctions, and to brandish the possibility of sanctions as the outcome if the North Korea failed to concede. Washington's strategy during the first round was of 'showing the stick first and holding the carrot in reserve.' Most of these carrots, furthermore, were nothing new. They consisted mostly of negative security assurances, which had been made in previous negotiations. Even after North Korea suspended withdrawal from the NPT, the United States retained a belligerent tone. On a visit to Seoul in July 1993, President Clinton warned Pyongyang that[43] "if North Korea developed nuclear weapons, it would be the end of their country." Defence secretary told Japanese officials that negotiations would likely fail, and the result would be a sanctions attempt. Even after Carter's message in mid June that North Koreans were ready to accept a package deal, the Secretary of State Warren Christopher met with Russian Foreign Minister Andrei Kozyrev to hammer out the exact sequencing of UN sanctions. It was not until President Clinton received a written communication from North Korea confirming Carter's statement that the sanctions machinery halted.[44]

Even though the United States was willing to coerce but decided to offer carrot instead. Why? In a situation where two states are adversaries, the expectation of frequent conflicts constrains the ability of the sender to make too large a demand. This concern for relative gain placed a severe constrain on what the United States could demand, despite the DPRK's costs of deadlock. If the demand has an all-or-nothing quality, then economic coercion in itself is insufficient to obtain the necessary concessions. Pyongyang was willing to compromise on reduced concessions to avert sanctions but would not acquiesce to all of the US demands. In this instance the United States could not compromise its demands because of the importance it attached to the norm of non-proliferation. Forced to choose between a sustained deadlock, a military strike and economic inducements, Washington chose the carrot because of conditions unique to this case.

The United States consistently pursued two goals, a non-nuclear Korean Peninsula and a strong international non-proliferation regime. Why was the United States adamant about its position? The reasons were as follows:[45] Inspection following the Gulf War revealed that the standard IAEA inspections had failed to uncover Iraq's massive programme. It weakened the

IAEA's reputation and made North Korea's programme a test case of US commitment to non-proliferation. The renewal of NPT was in 1995 and several developing countries expressed reservation about its extension. The break-up of the Soviet Union created three nuclear states; Kazakistan and Ukrain were reluctant to transfer their weapons to Russia. The collapse of Soviet nuclear infrastructure greatly reduced the barriers to acquiring the necessary atomic material and technical expertise. With the end of cold war, non-proliferation became highly priority for the United States. It was at this juncture that the North Korean crisis emerged. In view of its long-standing support for the integrity of the IAEA and NPT regime to American policy-makers, it was imperative that the DPRK programme be completely eliminated, to demonstrate US preferences on the issue. As such for its absolute position it was not enough to guarantee that the North Koreans would not be able to make nuclear weapons in the future; the US had to ensure that all the previous attempts were exposed.

The threat of sanctions was sufficient to coerce North Korea into making some concessions. But it preferred deadlock to acquiescence given US demands; indeed there was evidence to suggest it preferred war. Secretary Perry's testimony in January 1995 reveals the Clinton administration's thinking on the issue[46] "While the United States and the international community were preferred to resort to sanctions if all other diplomatic remedies had failed, the outcome of a sanction regime would have been highly unpredictable. Certainly sanctions would have heightened tensions on the peninsula and would have obligated the United States and South Korea to take measures to prepare for military hostilities, especially in the light of North Korean assertions that sanctions were tantamount to war. In general our past experience shows that the North Korea does not usually respond well to such blunt applications of pressure and, given the North's need to nurture its national pride, it is unlikely that the North Korea would have acquiesced to US demands after sanctions had been imposed."

Sanctions were insufficient to extract the necessary concessions from the DPRK, and by June 1994 US policy-makers were aware of it. This left the United States with three options:[47] military action, economic inducement or stalemate. The costs of war were exorbitant; the USA was never willing to go to war over a possible NPT violation, even when violator was considered a "rouge" state. North Korea's declaration that imposition of sanctions means declaration of war had increased the costs and risk to United States. It would not stop North Korea to reprocess its spent fuel and extract plutonium. The prospects of Chinese intervention added uncertainty. Seoul would have to suffer some damage. The prospect and process of re-unification would be weakened.

When economic coercion was not sufficient and war incurred greater costs than the benefit of a nuclear free Korea, the only option left was to use economic inducements. Despite the lack of other options, the Clinton administration was reluctant to turn to carrot because there was sufficient opposition within the United States for bribe. But when Clinton called-off the sanctions campaign, the administration received serious criticism for its decision. These criticisms confirm the model's prediction that a sender country will be extremely reluctant to use the carrot with an adversarial target because it will weaken the sender's reputation for toughness. Despite these concerns, the Clinton administration opted for the carrot for three reasons:[48]

First, the deal went much further than adherence to the NPT, satisfying the non-negotiable demands of the United States. In agreeing to trade its gas-graphite reactors for light-water reactors, North Koreans lost two links in their ability to manufacture fissile plutonium. Light-water reactors need enriched fuel to operate; gas-graphite reactors can use natural uranium. Because the DPRK has no enrichment capability, it will have to import the fuel. This combined with destruction of the reprocessing facility, eliminated North Korea's proliferation potential. Testifying before Congress, Leonard Spector emphasized the totality of the arrangement:[49] "If this agreement is implemented, I would say that with the exception of involuntary de-nuclearisation that was imposed on Iraq after the 1991 Gulf war, there has never been an international agreement that goes so far to eliminate an emergent nuclear weapon capability."

Second, the primary sender paid a very low price for the inducement. When North Korea originally proposed the package deal in June 1993, the United States balked because of the large price tag involved. The carrot option was eventually feasible only because South Korea was willing to shoulder most of the costs. The annual US contribution to the Frame Work Agreement was estimated[50] to be between $ 20 and $ 30 million, far less than the $ 5 billion total. As carrots go, this was an extremely inexpensive one for the United States. Yet even these costs were contested within the country because of the reported South Korea's diversions of the heavy oil from the United States to power a steel plant.

Finally, the agreement gave the United States economic leverage over North Korea, which it never had before. That leverage was on display when North Korea tried to prevent a South Korean firm from building the light water reactors in early 1995. Ambassador Gallucci replied by observing that[51] "there would be no financing for any project other than a South Korean reactor." Pyongyang forced to choose between deadlock and accepting the carrot, conceded.

As the 'Framework Agreement' implemented, the United States and South Korea will have increased leverage over the North. The Economist Intelligent Unit noted:[52] "Externally, as Pyongyang becomes dependent for oil and grain on powers that it still treats as enemies, so the donors acquire the leverage to cut off the flow unless the North proves more accommodating on other matters." The need for low enrichment uranium will only increase the extent of North Korean dependence upon the member of Korean Energy Development Organization (KEDO). The dominant market share of the United States in enriched uranium will give it significant influence over the Korean Energy sector. Furthermore, the Framework Agreement assumes a lowering of trade and investment barrier between the two countries. If North Korea's pattern of trade with South Korea and Japan were any indication, the United States would acquire additional leverage. In this sense, the carrot can become a future stick. Of course the utility of such stick will remain dependent upon whether North Korea continues to anticipate frequent conflicts in its relation with the United States.

In conclusion, process-tracing of this episode shows that the United States rationally chose to offer economic inducements to the North Korean regime because it was the most attractive option, given the constraints of economic and military coercion. The Economic coercion of North Korea, even if limited to trade with Japan and South Korea, would have inflicted serious damage. Despite the high opportunity costs of deadlock, the DPRK regime was so concerned about the relative distribution of pay offs that it was willing to accept deadlock and go to war rather than completely acquiesce to the United States. Pyongyang was willing to make some concessions in the face of economic pressure, but it would not completely surrender. The United States was aware of the DPRK preferences, but could not compromise its demands. Washington's attachment with the NPT regime was too great. Faced with a choice of either brandishing the gun or offering the carrot, it chose later. It was less expensive and achieved the desired end.

III. APPRAISAL

Drezner has developed the 'Conflict Expectation Model' with the sole purpose of studying the cases of South Korea and North Korea as they provide unique opportunity to clarify the ally and adversary behaviour and, in turn, to justify his Model's predictions. The assessment of the comparative behaviour and differentiated predictions may be summarized as follows:

The United States used economic coercion to stop South Korea from going nuclear in 1975. In freezing North Korea's nuclear programme in 1994, Washington considered both economic sanctions and military action but ultimately decided to use economic inducements. The United States made the same demand of both the countries but differed in option. The close alignment between South Korea and the United States combined with the cost of disrupting Seoul's nuclear energy programme, proved to be sufficient leverage for Washington to extract a significant concession. In the North Korean case, although the United States first considered economic coercion, it was clear that the target's leadership viewed the situation in strictly conflictual terms. It was unwilling to make major concessions, despite the serious costs of a stalemate, because it feared the United States would exploit them in future interventions. Economic coercion by itself was capable of producing minor concession, but the United States could not compromise in its demands because of the strong norm of non-proliferation and the need to review the nuclear Non-Proliferation Treaty. Sanctions were insufficient to produce such a significant concessions. The United States had to choose between a military option and an economic inducement. Given the costs associated with all-out conflict and cost-free nature of carrot, it chooses the latter.

If the adversarial relation between USA and North Korea is converted into the argumentation of the model, the clarification of the situation and the prediction of the model can, in principle, be summarized as follows: The cost of military compellence (forcing an adversary to back-down without using force, such as land forces are used for compellence on Indo-Pak border) and economic inducements make economic coercion the preferred policy option for the sender, yet its usefulness is bounded. Because adversarial targets anticipate frequent conflicts, the sender will be constrained in its ability to make significant demands. If the sender is unable to compromise its demands, it will be forced to choose between military compellence and economic inducements from the target country. If the carrot is sufficiently cheap to the sender and lucrative to the target, the sender can successfully use carrots with adversaries.

Process-tracing and congruence procedures support this explanation: Why the United States was able to use economic coercion to force its ally, South Korea into abandoning its nuclear programme in 1976 but had to use economic inducements to convince its adversary, North Korea to abandon its programme eighteen years later. Although the target's potential damage from sanctions was greater in North Korean case, the concern for the distribution of gains was also greater. North Korea's security and sovereignty preferences made its interactions with the United States a zero-sum game. The extreme distributional concern made it unwilling to completely acquiesce in the face of economic pressure. The United States was incapable of modulating its demand and reluctantly decided that its best option was to use the threat of coercion combined with economic inducements to get what it wanted. The imposing cost of military intervention was also a factor. South Korea, by contrast, anticipated few conflicts with the United States and was thus willing to make concessions rather than suffer the short run costs of stalemate. Because its costs of coercion were minimal, the United States could satisfy the coercion conditions.

Thus the case histories of both the Koreas reveal that the threatened sanctions would have been painful to both the countries. Because South Korea did not perceive the United States as a threat, it was willing to make the concession. By contrast, North Korea's expectation of future conflicts were so high that it was unwilling to accede to all of the US demands without significant compensation. The United States could not compromise its demands because of the importance attached to the NPT regime and the norm of non-proliferation. Although economic coercion was capable of producing limited concessions, the United States had to offer carrots to secure its demands.

The episodes of both the Koreas have been discussed so far within the theoretical framework of 'Conflict Expectation Model'. The critical appraisal demands that these should be detached from this theoretical frame so as to deprive them of its glazing effect. Only then the substance of the cases itself may properly be judged.

One observation, already referred in principle earlier, clearly emerges out of the cases of both the Koreas. The South Korean episode shows a series of high-level talks between the United States and the Republic of Korea. When the decision was announced, it was done with little fanfare. No American and South Korean officials were willing to publicly confirm what exactly happen during the negotiations. This lack of public discourse eliminated some of the reputation-costs. Although South Korea was obviously displeased by the coercion, the level of public rancour was minimal. By contrast, the crisis between two adversaries, the USA and North Korea, resulted in more covert claims of coercive strategies. Much of the diplomacy in the North Korean episode was public. Both sides made inflammatory statements that occupied much of the private negotiations. The lack of the multiple negotiating channels forced the DPRK to rely on private intermediaries and third party countries to relay messages to Washington. Had the United States been willing to send a high level delegation to Pyongyang, the conflict could have been resolved much earlier. This shows yet again that it is easier to detect coercion events between adversaries than allies because adversarial targets are more likely to publicly claim that they are being pressured. Beside, the side effect of this situation on the 'Conflict Expectation Model' is significant: Since it is little known in South Korean case that what transpired, the Model is based on 'reasonable conjectures,' while in a publicly known North Korean case, it is based on factual ground.

The case studies reveal that military statecraft is useful only when regular force is used; threats alone are insufficient. The domestic politics approach has a more mixed record. It can explain when economic coercion is initiated. It fares somewhat better in explaining the outcome. While an unstable target regime can contribute to a successful sanctions episode, it is neither necessary nor sufficient. A weak target regime has a knife-edge property. It can lead to acquiescence, but it can also lead the regime to harden its position *vis à vis* the sender so as to bolster its domestic support. The conflict expectation model does no superior job of explaining both the initiation and the outcome of economic coercion.

The coercion of adversaries is far more public than the coercion of allies as we have seen in respect to North Korea and South Korea respectively. By focusing only on the pronounced publicity cases, most of the studies on sanctions came to the conclusion that sanctions were ineffective. In this respect, Drezner has the point that 'actually the universe of cases is more diversified than is usually suspected.' But still the fact remains that the cases of sanctions among the allies, apart from being 'privy' in nature which compels one to resort to congruence approach, causal explanation and 'plausible probe', as is seen with the South Korean case, are actually so few and far between that they come under the category of 'exceptions' and cannot, therefore, be counted as part of generality to judge the ratio of effectiveness and ineffectiveness.

In North Korea the negotiations of 1993 was damage control exercise without any break through. It remains unclear: On the part of North Korea how can the light-weight reactors serve the objective of reprocessing plant; or on the part of USA, what successfully replaced its special inspection demand. Contrary to Conflict Expectation Model, the sender instead of target paid the price while the target instead of the sender got the concession. But coinciding with the Model, the sender had to forego the Special Inspection, which triggered crisis (although the Model keeps it ambiguous under the umbrella of 'all the US demands') and initiated economic inducement, as objective was non-negotiable and the target had to forego the reprocessing plant and had to remain content with light water reactor. The economic inducement may be the part of sanctions provided that 'today's carrot is tomorrow's stick' is not only perceived by the target but also intended by the sender. No approach except this model could successfully illustrate the overt and covert behaviour in North Korean case. As a result, one, behind the cosmetic of carrot, could clearly see the reality of sanctions. But in terms of outcome, such extra efforts resulted in the impression of 'tailor-made' rather than spontaneous "effectiveness."

NOTE

This Chapter is drawn on Drezner's book: *The Sanctions Paradox*, which contains very good case study material on South Korea and North Korea. It provides the most comprehensive analysis of the sanction issues, rationalized under his 'Conflict Expectation Model.' The Model and the case studies together represent a powerful case to determine precisely the quantum of success and failure of sanctions.

REFERENCES

1. Daniel Drezner, *The Sanctions Paradox: Economic Statecraft and International Relations,* Cambridge University Press, UK, 1999, pp. 254-55.
2. *Ibid.*, p. 255.
3. *Ibid.*
4. *Ibid.*, pp. 255-56.
5. *Ibid.*, p. 256.
6. *Ibid.*, p. 257.
7. *Ibid.*, p. 258. (Such information has been gathered by newspaper reports and anonymous official statement).
8. *Ibid.*, pp. 258-59.
9. US Senate 1975, pp. 224-26, quoted: *Ibid.*, p. 259.
10. Office of Technology Assessment, 1977, p. 219, quoted, *Ibid.*, p. 259.
11. Meyer, 1984, p. 126, quoted, *Ibid.*, 259.
12. Wohlstetter, 1976, p. 168, quoted, *Ibid.*, p. 259.
13. *Ibid.*, pp. 259-63.

14. Quoted in Oberndorfer, *The Two Koreans: A Contemporary History,* Reading M.A.: Addison-Wesley, 1977, p. 70, quoted, *Ibid.*, p. 263.
15. *Ibid.*, pp. 264-75.
16. *Ibid.*, p. 265.
17. *Ibid.*
18. *Ibid.*
19. *Ibid.*
20. Hayes Peter, *Pacific Powerkeg: American Nuclear Dilemma in Korea,* Lexington Books, Toronto, 1990, pp. 209-10, quoted, *Ibid.* 265.
21. *Ibid.*, p. 268.
22. *Ibid.*
23. *Ibid.*
24. *Ibid.*
25. *Ibid.*
26. *Ibid.*, p. 272.
27. *Ibid.*, p. 274.
28. *Ibid.*, p. 275.
29. *Ibid.*, pp. 275-82.
30. *Ibid.*, p. 282; As quoted: For a copy of unclassified portion of agreement see Council on Foreign Relations, 1995, Appendix 1. The classified portion of Agreement is a two pages minute containing the exact time-table of the Special Inspections, Reiss, 1995, p. 276.
31. *Ibid.*, pp. 283-84.
32. *Ibid.*, pp. 284-85.
33. *Ibid.*, p. 286.
34. *Ibid.*
35. *Ibid.*
36. Bracken, Paul, "The North Korean Nuclear Programme as a Problem of State Survival" in Andrew Mack (ed.), *Asia Flash Point: Security and Korean Peninsula,* Allen & Unwin, Canberra, 1990, p. 91, quoted *Ibid.*, p. 286.
37. *Ibid.*, p. 287.
38. Mitchell Reiss, *Without the Bomb: The Politics of Nuclear Proliferation,* Columbia University Press, N.Y., 1988, p. 283, quoted, *Ibid.*, p. 287.
39. *Ibid.*, p. 288.
40. *Ibid.*, pp. 289-95.
41. Oberdorfer, Don, *op. cit.*, pp. 320-21, quoted *Ibid.*, p. 290.
42. Snyder, quoted from unpublished paper, 1995, p. 8, *Ibid.*, p. 295.
43. *Ibid.*, p. 296.
44. *Ibid.*
45. *Ibid.*, p. 297.

46. US Senate, 1995, p. 94, quoted. *Ibid.*, p. 298.
47. *Ibid.*, pp. 299-300.
48. *Ibid.*, p. 301.
49. US House, 1995, p. 44, quoted *Ibid.*, p. 301.
50. US House, 1995, p. 20, quoted *Ibid.*, p. 302.
51. US House, 1995, pp. 26-27, quoted *Ibid.*, p. 302.
52. Economic Intelligence Unit Country Report: South Korea and North Korea, 3rd quarter, 1995, p. 43, quoted, *Ibid.*, p. 302.

5

Iran and Iraq

The long-time US policy of Iran and Iraq, supporting one against the other—Iran until revolution in 1979, Iraq until its invasion of Kuwait in 1991—had not produced the desired result in the region. On one hand, the Iranian support for organizations committed to the violent rejection of Arab-Israel peace, the effort to acquire long-range missile capabilities and the complicity in international terrorist acts, and on the other hand, the quick recovery of Iraqi Air Force, the regular challenge to the American and British-propelled no-fly zones and the rumour of covert weapons of mass destruction (WMD) programme, despite regular UN inspections, had convinced the USA that its policy of "Dual Balancing" would not work. The Clinton administration decided that since both states were proving inimical to US interests, both should be opposed. Accordingly, in a speech delivered on May 13, 1993, Martin Indyk,[1] Director for Near East and South Asia at the National Security Council, unveiled the newly elected administration's policy toward Iran and Iraq. The policy, termed "Duel Containment," aimed at to weaken both countries through strict economic sanctions and diplomatic isolation.

From the beginning, Duel Containment was not evenly balanced. In his speech, Indyk[2] labeled the Iraqi regime "criminal," "beyond the pale of international society," and even "irredeemable." Speaking of Iran, however, he stated: "The Clinton administration is not opposed to Islamic Government in Iran, but it is firmly opposed to specific aspects of the Iranian regime's behaviour." In effect, therefore, the goals of the policy differed as between the two governments: to topple the one, but only to pressure the other to change some of its ways. Furthermore, the means were necessarily different, with UN sanctions already in place against Iraq and no support among the international community for similar action against Iran. The Clinton administration thus continued to act in a multilateral context *vis-à-vis* Iraq, but was forced to apply sanctions unilaterally in the case of Iran.

Thus the US policy of containing both Iran and Iraq and the imposition of sanctions in the context of 'dual containment' shall be separately discussed. Finally, the latest situation, the effectiveness of the policy and some prevalent suggestions for improvement shall be critically examined.

I. IRAN

(a) Evolution

Until the over-throw of Shah Mohammad Reza Pahlvi in 1979, the largest single arms transfer programme in the world was that between the United States and Iran. A Congressional staff report had assessed this bilateral arrangement as follows:[3] "Every one seemed to be basically pleased. The government of Iran was getting the equipment it wanted; the state department was happy because US-Iranian relations were good; Department of Defense was actively selling in accordance with policy; the contractors were pleased because they were making money." Thus at one point Iran had a larger tank arsenal than Britain and was allowed to obtain any US conventional weapon the Shah desired, evidently in return for the Shah's promise not to 'go nuclear.'[4]

Washington had lavished unlimited support upon Iran under Shah. Ultimately, however, even with the most advanced weapons in the world, the Shah and his army were unable to suppress a popular revolution, which swirled around Ayatollah Khomeini.[5]

As satisfactory as this relationship might have appeared at first blush, its implementation not only created friction between Iran and the United States but also served to strengthen the ultra conservative insurgent movement under the Ayatollah Khomeini. The revolutionary ideology stressed the need to return to the fundamental teachings of Islam and to reject negative Western influence. The power of an ideal—an Islamic political ideal—destroyed whatever political gains the United States might have anticipated by placing Iran in a position of military dependency.

The justification of an armed transfer programme such as that of Iran and of the United States often rests on the basis that a modernization of the military provides the needed impetus for further economic development. That is, the technical and administrative skill, taught to military trainees, are readily convertible to civilian enterprises. To a degree, there is indeed a spillover effect: The repairs to a tank can sometimes approximate those to a tractor. Nevertheless for many military skills there is no civilian counterpart. In the end, the weaponry in a state of operational readiness means that other areas of public policy will be neglected.

For the United States, the outcome of a close alliance with the Shah, as manifested in the arms transfers and other forms of penetration, had been equally serious. The establishment in 1979 of a new government under the Islamic Republican Party led to a cancellation of orders for arms, which signaled a cooling of relations between Washington and Tehran. In November of that year Revolutionary Guards stormed the United States Embassy compound in Iran. Thus, the policy of arms and influence followed so long in Iran had come to naught.[6]

On November 4, 1979, fifty-four Americans in the US embassy in Tehran were seized; the hostages were to be used to extract certain concessions from the US government. It was not until January 20, 1981, after 444 days in captivity, that the Iranian government finally released the American diplomatic personnel.[7]

The action of the Iranian government represented such a departure from the routinely honoured canons of state practice that observers at the time feverishly searched through history books to discover the last time such violation had occurred. There was a certain irony involved, too, since it was in Persia, in the land that is today called Iran that the principle of 'Diplomatic Immunity' first evolved a thousand years ago.[8]

One of the rules of diplomacy is: show some empathy and understanding towards other side's position. This position lies in-between two extreme of either caving in or to be self-righteous in defence of one's position. Fisher notes[9]: "How other parties feel about the choice we will be asking them to make is just as important to us as how we feel about it." Had the United States and Iran kept this rule in mind in their bargaining over the hostage issue in 1980, each might have been less inclined to behave as if God were on their side.

In response to the seizure and detention of American diplomatic and counsellor personnel in Tehran, President Carter sought in November 1979[10] to retaliate against the regime by first freezing Iranian assets in the United States and then calling upon allied governments to halt their trade with Iran. Although the major European industrial powers were initially supportive, one by one they resumed and eventually even expanded their commercial ties with Iran.

The reasons for the inefficacy of economic weapon against Iran were fourfold:[11] First, many governments and commercial organizations saw in the embargo only an opportunity to expand their trade with the target state. For example both Iran and Pakistan have railroads equipped largely with American rolling stock. When the United States halted the shipment of spare parts for train to Iran, the Pakistanis were eager to supply the needed materials at a price.

Second, if a country, subjected to an embargo, is experiencing the economic chaos associated with the revolutionary upheaval, the denial of trade has only a limited effect. In 1979, the Iranian gross national product fell as estimated 20 per cent. In view of economic depression, which had befallen the country, the American sponsored embargo was hardly critical.

Third, to be effective economic sanctions must block both imports and exports. In the case of Iran, the export, such as oil, remained in high demand. Iran, thus, continued to acquire the capital needed to attract blockade breakers.

Fourth, the collaborations of non-state actors such as multinational corporations are indispensable. In Iranian instance, many multinational banks declined to declare Tehran in default on its financial obligations and thereby mitigated the effect of the American sanctions.

In sum, the international economy is sufficiently complex;

it evades manipulation by any single centre of power or even combination thereof. While the economic weapon may appear deceptively simple, its application is complex and requires careful, extensive diplomatic preparation.

At present, Khatami's election has had an impact on Washington and generated a new curiosity about Iran, extending beyond Iran's war-making capabilities, and some interest in pursuing dialogue. But the main problem with the current effort at engagement through the 'critical dialogue,' pursued by many European states, is Congress's negative attitude towards Iran, which is still convinced that it is not critical. However, the change will take time and filter through the administration rather than Congress.

Moreover it is visualized that with the existing moderate regime in Iran and in the absence of any evidence to implicate Iran in Khobar Towers bombing,[12] it would be more difficult for the United States to convince Europe that sanctions are needed against Iran, as well as more difficult for vehement critic of Iran in the United States to push for sanctions against foreign companies that do business with Iran.

Though rhetoric from both sides—Iran and USA—has been toned down but one should not become too much optimistic about the implications of present regime in view of the fact that Rafsanjani's[13] plans were thwarted by conservatives in Iran; the Iranian government is not always able to deliver on its statements, and as such different expectations of policy results may be needed.

At the same time it is perceived that Khatami's election is a massive vote for change;[14] the regime emphasizes on rule of law; Rafsanjani's economic programme shall continue; Khatami's choice to head the Ministry of Culture, known for his liberal views, remained controversial; foreign policy concerns will remain much the same, focusing on the US presence in the Gulf and improving ties with Europe and Russia as well as with Saudi Arabia and the Arab Gulf states. The tactics of demoting and circumventing the United States while developing direct relations with Arab Gulf neighbours would probably not successful. Iran is only delaying the time when it would have to deal directly with the United States.

This rapprochement analysis is one-sided, seeing only the internal changes in the target regime, understanding its implications, finding ways and means how to exploit the internal situation to sender's interest, critically assessing the target's tactics of isolating the sender and wishfully pinning hopes that target will, some day, have to come to sender's terms. No analysis is available to show what way the USA has responded to these changes. If there is no accommodating response, the 'wait and watch' approach of the USA, not the circumventing tactics of Iran, shall be the cause of delay. As such the dream of rapprochement may shatter on the 'self-righteous attitude,' which is still considered beyond the pale of critical evaluation.

(b) Evaluation

The evolution, which represents the admixture of internal situation and justification of sanctions requirements, contains, inherently, the elements of differentiated policy prescriptions of US and Europe on sanctions in Iran. This requires detailed discussion.[15]

United States and Europe, broadly speaking, agree on the need to prevent Iran from achieving nuclear capabilities and engaging, allegedly, in terrorist activities as well as on the importance of promoting human rights and peace process in the region. But here similarity ends. The United States recognizes that European states have different views, making it difficult to forge a strange and cohesive European policy. The United States hoped that the German court decision on the Mykonos case[16] in April 1997, incriminating Iran, would serve an impetus for Europe to pursue a tougher common policy on Iran together with the United States. But this window of opportunity proved short-lived and there was no sustained effort to coordinate policy. In the eyes of the United States, Europe was soon back to putting trade and economic interests first.

Europe highlights the failure of US policies in the Gulf such as 'dual containment.' They particularly point out the high failure rate of economic embargoes, which both inflict harm on domestic population and are often ineffectual or even counter-productive. The US embargo has encouraged Iran to expand its regional ties; it has developed relations with Asia,

Russia, the Caucuses States and the Arab Gulf. It is noted that Iran is the largest purchaser of Russian manufactured goods in the world. Iran's economy is improving despite the embargo and given its new ties to the East, would not likely suffer much from an expanded embargo enforced by Europe. In view of such effect of US policy, which resulted in shifting Iran's perspective to the North and East, it is generally believed that the US allies should be permitted to play a more central role in facilitating some dialogue and influence with Iran.

The United States runs the risk of alienating its Western allies if it pursues a unilateral embargo of Iran or of pushing Iran closer to undesirable states like China if the embargo expands. Military spending cuts, resulting from the embargo, may also push Iran towards developing weapons of mass destruction, which are often said to provide 'more bang for the buck' relative to conventional weapons.

It is pointed out that the United States is already pursuing Europe's policy of critical dialogue with other so-called "rogue" states such as China, North Korea and Syria. The new administration in Iran is expected to be more responsive to a policy of critical dialogue, which is essential to make a contact with a foe just as all Western powers including USA had embassies in Moscow at the height of cold war. Any effort at such contact with Iran, while sanctions are still in place, will necessarily be hindered. Such efforts would be further complicated by a clash in the nature of contact desired by both sides. The United States and Iran may wish to keep things on an official, above board levei but the 'anti-Iran, anti-US' rhetoric prevent official from taking such risk. Effective contact in Iran, at least initially, needs to take advantage of more discreet channels.

The main reason behind US policy towards Iran is the hostage crisis of 1979 and America's special relationship with Israel. The active role in the current administration of those involved in the hostage crisis was seen as a real block in US policy towards Iran. Rivalries between US administration and Congress also contribute to an escalation of anti-Iran rhetoric, as both bodies try to cater to public opinion by appearing more vigorously anti-Iran.

Having tried a carrot-stick policy with Iraqi President Saddam Hussein throughout 1980s—thinking there could be a balance of power in the region, only to see Iraq occupying Kuwait in 1990—the United States was determined to be tougher. The hard line policy, notably 'dual containment' derives from the failure of the US in 1980 and an unwillingness to repeat the same mistake with Iran.

Apart from the economic coercion regarding the hostage issue, it is presumed that sanctions serve the purpose of dealing with the regional security situation arising out of Iran and curbing its nuclear weapon programme. Both are to be evaluated.

United States takes more seriously the Iranian military capabilities. Its intelligence emphasizes Iran's capability to close the Straits of Hormuz and catalogues the preparatory steps that could be used to place mines in the Straits and holding exercises judged provocative by he United States—even though Iran itself would be most hurt by the blocking of the oil lanes.

Most Europeans, on the other hand, do not consider Iran to be a military threat at present. Iran acted responsibly in some regional affairs, mediating civil wars in Tajikistan, Azerbaijan and Armenia and trying to adopt a fair policy on the Caspian. While some fear that Iran's desire for a role in Gulf security means that it expects the US presence to disappear completely, others believe that Iran would be satisfied with the reduction in the level of US forces in the Gulf in conjunction with some role for itself in Gulf security, such as in conducting joint exercises with GCC states. Europe is more optimistic on the future of Iran than the United States, given the recent election of the moderator Mohammad Khatami as President of Iranian Republic. On 'fundamentalism,' Europe, though wary of it, is aware of the need to live with it given the proximity of Southern Europe to the Maghreb states. Similarly on terrorism (and Iran's role in it), is attributed by Europe to the high presence of US soldiers in the region who proved to be a target in Khober Tower bombing. Additionally US threat perception of the region is coloured by its relationship with Israel.

Iran has legitimate reason to develop nuclear weapons.

During Iran-Iraq war, Iran saw its territory invaded and its army destroyed without getting any response from the United Nations. Rolling back of nuclear programme is not possible until regional issues are resolved. Iraq, Israel, China, India, Pakistan and four Central Asian Republics, disintegrated from erstwhile Soviet Union, surround Iran; they either possess or pursue nuclear programme. Any effective resolution of Iran's nuclear ambitions must take into consideration many elements that encourage Iran to become nuclear-weapon capable: Its experience with Iraq; US military presence in the region; its geographic location; and sense of encirclement. It would therefore need to be part of a concrete regional security arrangement that addresses these concerns. No doubt the long reach of ballistic missiles held by some states has made the task of defining the region for purposes of regional security more doubtful. The fact that Iran has appointed a former energy and oil minister, who was not notable for his organizational skill, to head Iran's atomic energy programme, indicates that the nuclear programme is not accorded high military priority. It is argued that if Iran's nuclear programme has stagnated, it shows that the restrictive sanction policies, rather than any independent internal decision to downgrade nuclear efforts, has discouraged the regime from putting still more money and effort into it.

In order to dissuade Iran from the nuclear path, few suggestions are forthcoming: First, help Iran develop gas, which alleviate Iran's need, as stated, for a nuclear reactor as a power source. Second, try US-North Korean model of aid in exchange for a nuclear roll back. Third, integrate Iran with the region; strong regional ties would necessarily pose less of a threat. All these suggestions lack sufficient political will in the United States to pursue such deals with Iran.

Iran-Libya Sanction Act (ILSA)[17] passed by the US Congress in August 1996, under which for the first time US sanctions extended to foreign companies, which make (a 20) million investment to develop petroleum sector in Iran. The aim of law is to force companies to choose to do business into either the United States or Iran. Under ILSA the US President may impose two, from a choice of six, sanctions on such companies. Possible sanctions include: denial of US export licence, restriction on imports to United States, ban on US procurement, and a prohibition on loans by US financial institutions.

Despite the passage of the bill since 1996, no sanctions have yet been imposed although three projects are being scrutinized:[18] an offshore platform project awarded to an Iranian company financed by Germany; the development of Balal oil field by Canadian and Indonesian companies; and a deal with Total to develop the South Pars natural gas field. It appears that pipeline project from Turkey and Turkmenistan via Iran will go ahead as US Secretary of State, Albright has said that the project will benefit Turkey and Turkmenistan. The pipeline was initially to carry only the Turkmen gas but is expected to include Iranian gas after two years. But it is unconceivable that Iran shall be able to export gas by 1999, given the high degree of mismanagement in the gas sector in Iran and heavy domestic demands.

No doubt ILSA has prevented investment but has not discouraged interest: Companies are actually cultivating contacts, preparing for the day when sanctions end. All the preconditions of US for changing its instance—such as Iran must end its support for international terrorism; reduce its confrontational arms build-up in the Gulf; stop acquiring or producing nuclear weapons or the means to deliver them—have been repeatedly given assurance by Iran.

It seems that the US position on sanctions against Iran is changing. The possible reasons behind this change are as follows:[19] Lobbying by the US business community and US oil companies in particular had weakened support on Capitol Hill for sanctions preventing US investment in Iran and posited that if Iran began to offer more attractive terms for investment, pressure from these groups to waive or lift sanctions would grow. Support for ILSA on Capitol Hill may also be waning because its chief advocate, senator Alfonse D' Amato,[20] who was fighting a difficult re-election campaign, did, in fact, loose in November. The Hamilton-Crane-Lugar bill, for example, which calls for careful security of potential losses and gains in adopting sanctions, has increased dialogue between administration and Congress on sanctions measures in general. The changing US view was also attributed to hard reality, namely that, since the waiver decision, the administration has admitted that it could not have won the argument and that many European companies are insulated from US sanctions.

It is pointed out that the US has been impressed by the Khatami administration and its diplomacy. This attributed the slight shift in the US view on sanctions to better US-Iranian relations. More cynically it is argued that better images of Iran may stem from events that have merely directed US attention away from Iran.[21] First, following the East African bombing, US attention turned on Saudi dissident Osama Bin Laden as terror suspect number one. Second, the Indian-Pakistani nuclear tests have made these two countries the main nuclear problem states. Third, the milder position that Iran—or at least some milder forces there—has taken on the Fatwa of Salman Rushdie, has removed some of the stigma attached to Iran. And lastly, the campaign against terrorism following the terrorist attack and destruction of WTC in New York on September 11, 2001 and US war against Taliban, Osama, and his Al Qaida, compelled US to reach understanding, though indirectly, with Iran with its approval to protect or return safely the US plane or soldiers if inadvertently be fallen in the Iranian territory in the wake of an air attack on Afghanistan.

The Bush administration assured Iran that[22] the US would respect its territorial integrity, including its air space. It requested Iran to go to the aid of any American who might be shot down or forced to land in Iranian territory or escaped into Iran. This US request was made through Swiss government, which officially represents US-Iranian interests in the absence of diplomatic relations between the two countries.

In response to this US request, Iran,[23] through Swiss government on October 8, sent a secret message to Bush administration agreeing to rescue any American military personnel in distress in its territory. The messages reflect what appears to be a significant shift in Iranian-American relations, with political ramifications extending far beyond the fate of American military personnel.

But the diplomatic maneuvering is extremely delicate: Iran is still listed by state development as the world's most active state supporter of terrorism. And yet the Bush administration, for the first time, has asked a federal judge to throw out a law-suit brought against Iran by the 52 Americans who were held hostage in 1979 and many of their relatives who were seeking damages from the Tehran government.[24]

Weeks before the September 11 attacks the Bush administration opened a full-scale inter-agency review of American policy towards Iran. Among the issues under discussions were how much Iran needed to build its conventional defensive military strength and whether American economic sanctions against Iran should be sustained. There is a growing consensus in the administration that the Clinton administration policy of 'dual containment,' which isolated and punished both Iran and Iraq, was unwise and that the United States could no longer have both as enemies. Defence Secretary H. Rumsfeld asked: "How did it happen that we are on the opposite side of both Iran and Iraq? It makes no sense."[25]

In a related development American and Iranian officials met face to face on October 7 in an obscure UN-sponsored forum in Geneva for the second time since September attacks to discuss the shape of future Afghan government. They added that the talks focused on ways to broaden the base of future Afghan government. The US, through UN World Food Programme, is shipping food aid overland from Iran to Afghanistan. A first consignment of wheat was delivered to Herat, Afghanistan on Wednesday.[26]

These developments manifest that as Iran becomes more acceptable in US eyes, the sanctions may be put to abeyance. But it is also emphasized that focus of US sanction might switch from the economic field to the military, particularly missiles, reflecting the tendency of the US Congress to adopt uncontroversial issues on which it can show an overwhelming majority.

The changing nature of US sanctions does not conform to the progress made in the Congress: The anti-Christian legislation exists; and ILSA is still the law of the land. Moreover, the Congress, except few, is neither progressive nor knowledgeable on foreign affairs and as such nor can be considered internationalists. The US Congress will only change its attitude towards Iran if the administration takes a strong leadership position.

The ramification of such latest development may have some far-reaching consequences but cannot be predicted, exactly, at the time of writing. As newspapers reported that USA accused Iran of giving shelter to Al Qaida fugitives to which Iran replied: How can Iran provide, knowingly, the shelter to our adversaries. If in accordance to your intelligence information, they were hidden, Iran would be eager to seek your help to get them out. This disarming diplomatic response exposes the prejudice of the USA, in the face of which it is difficult to say whether in the wake of recent development, its rapprochement approach is the 'stress-strategy' under pressure of circumstances or the 'sustaining one,' aiming at completing the normalization process.

But it can safely be predicted that these developments may soften the American attitude towards Iran as an unalterably hostile and intrinsic strategic threat in the Gulf. It may mitigate the view that Iran is out to harm the United States at nearly any cost while the United States is wary of anything that might strengthen the enemy state. At least the recent happening opened up the prospects, so far regarded as not possible, for a viable dialogue with the United States along with some sign of accommodating behaviour of the Iranian regime.

At the same time, it may boost up and activate another perception, so far lying low in the US administration: Iran is seen as a pragmatic regime moving out of revolution; devoting most of its attention to its severe economic problems; and practicing a restrained, cautious and largely nationalistic foreign policy. Even before the September 11 attack, perhaps under the influence of this perception, the Burton-Helms sanctions[27] against foreign investment in Iran had been disappeared even if on the ground that while insufficient to force Iran to change its external behaviour, it would enrage American allies.

It is hoped that the recent rapprochement between the USA and Iran would enable to overcome the US inability to reconcile these conflicting perspectives, which has so far 'bedeviled' the analysis and 'shifted' the creative policy formulation. And once this break-through in dilemma becomes feasible, the key conflict of interests and policy between United States and Iran would start receiving attention. The next step would be the realization on the part of the USA that it must deal with Iran rather than ignore it, since the potential pay offs are substantial and the alternative of unremitting hostility is dangerous and largely futile as a strategy for changing Iran's behaviour. Under the impact of sea changes in the region, as a result of varied responses to terrorist attack, the US exaggerated Iranian opposition is bound to subside along with the rise in the significance of peace process.

II. IRAQ

(a) Evolution

Eight years of war with Iran (1980-88) followed by Gulf war of 1990-91 had already left Iraq and Iraqi people exhausted. In the wake of Gulf war, after Iraq's invasion of Kuwait in August 1990, the UN imposed trade sanctions. The comprehensive trade embargo to inside Iraq to withdraw its troops from invaded Kuwait, has been renewed a number of times since then. Added to this, in what has been called 'the year's other war,' the United States and Britain aircraft continued to bomb targets in the North and South of the country everyday since the four day "Desert Fox" operation in December 1998.[28]

Iraq's compliance with the UN resolutions calling for the destruction of its unconventional weapons, imposed as a result of Iraq's defeat by the coalition in 1991, remained controversial. The UN team was not satisfied with Iraq's claims that its unconventional weapons had been destroyed. It was stressed that United Nations would need to retain significant monitoring and verification capabilities far into future even if sanctions were removed. Despite the June 1996 agreement that allowed the UN team full and unrestricted access to facilities anywhere in Iraq, concern was expressed that Iraq might balk in the future, as it had in the past, in the belief that Western demands would be satisfied only with the demise of Saddam Hussein. It was also considered that Iraq might decide to eject the UN Special Commission entirely. This would inevitably precipitate a major crisis involving the use of American force.[29]

An intriguing question was: why was Iraq prepared to play for such an inordinate political and economic price to retain a handful of prohibited weaponry? It is suggesed[30] that the political utility of these weapons to intimidate Iraq's neighbours is perhaps significant than their limited, but still relevant, military effectiveness. Iraq may also regard its unconventional arms as an important emblem of regional leadership and a guarantee that Iraq will be taken seriously as an important regional power. These devices may also be regarded as weapons of last resort in the event the United States should try to destroy the Iraqi regime. Finally Iraq has been optimistic, as the later events confirm, that the Security Council consensus on maintaining the sanctions would break down. The calculation would increase Iraq's incentive to hold out and hold onto its prohibited weapons.

As a consequence of these developments, the situation of a civilian population is increasingly desperate. Deteriorating living conditions, inflation and low salaries make people's everyday lives a continuing struggle, while food shortages and the lack of medicines and clean drinking water threaten their survival. As in war, it is civilians who are the prime victims of sanctions. Salaries are as low as US $ 2 a month; there is around 50 per cent unemployment. People have had to sell their belongings in order to survive: first their cars, then household appliances and even their books and furniture. Regular school attendance by children under 15 has fallen drastically since 1990 for "school does not give us money in order to live." And in schools themselves, pupils often have to squat at the floor for want of chairs and desks. Water pipes have not been repaired, and there are huge pools of stagnating water in the school-yard.[31]

Just a decade ago, Iraq boasted one of the most modern infrastructures and highest standard of living in the Middle East. The world's largest second oil producer, it had in recent decades used oil revenues for ambitious projects and development programmes as well as to build one of the most powerful armed forces in the Arab word. It had established a modern, complex health-care system, with giant hospitals built on the Western models and using the latest equipment. It had an extensive school and university system. By 1990, therefore, Iraq presented some of the features typical of a modern society: reliance on imported food (about 70 per cent calories in Iraq were imported in the 1980s), dependence on the imported technology and engineering skills, and interdependence of the different branches of the economy—accompanied by an attitude that 'the government will do it for you' and 'to replace is better than to repair.'[32]

No wonder, then, that Iraq's infrastructure should have proved so vulnerable to the effect of comprehensive trade sanctions, and with such devastating effect on the lives of civilians. The population, in particular doctors, technicians and teachers, are now exposed to third world problems, which they had never been prepared to deal with. Even if sanctions were lifted tomorrow, it would take years for the country to return to the same standard as before the Gulf war. Prospects for the better future are bleak, and an increasing number of Iraqis, specially the highly qualified, are trying to leave the country or have already done so. This brain drain exacerbates the situation for those staying behind, as it leads to a loss of skills, which are then not passed on to the next generation.[33]

In order to curb such devastating effect on the lives of civilian, the Security Council has set up numerous mechanisms for exemptions from sanctions regime, notably under UN Security Council resolutions—661 (1990), 687 (1991), 706 (1991), 712 (1991) and 986 (1995). Resolution No. 986 (oil for food) resolves some but not all the problems. The most far- reaching of these humanitarian exemptions, resolution 986 entered its fifth phase in March 1999. It has done much to alleviate the plight of civilian population, especially as regard food and medicines. Mal-nutrition rates have stabilized since the programme began to be implemented in 1997.[34]

Under the same resolution, India and Iraq agreed to swap wheat for oil. Both countries have agreed to consult the UN appointed Sanctions Committee before formalizing a deal. Iraq cannot directly sell its oil under the UN sanctions regime. First, agreements need the approval of a Committee of the Security Council members. The proceeds from such sales are put into an escrow account and after deduction of a fixed percentage toward war reparation, the remainder is administered for import of food and other essentials for the country. The Sanction Committee has not rejected any agreement based on food purchase by Iraq—the contracts blocked involve import of perceived dual items.[35]

However, it has not halted the collapse of the health system and the deterioration of water supplies, which together pose one of the gravest threats to the health and well-being of the civilian population. This resolution 986 also allows certain equipments to reach Iraq, for example pump for water treatment. This does not, however, solve all problems. The equipment needs to be properly installed and backed up by more general maintenance work on existing equipment and structures. The government often does not have the resources to pay for the contractors to install it. This has thus become one of the major tasks for humanitarian organizations in Iraq.[36]

The mixed result of "oil for food" resolution, the plight of the Iraqi civilian population and reaction of the world community led Britain, backed by the US, to propose recently, that[37] the United Nations lift the 11 year ban on international trade with Iraq. The long awaited UK-US proposal, if adopted by the Security Council, would prohibit only the sale of specific list of arms and weapon related items in Iraq. But the plan would require Iraq to let international inspections resume before any sanctions could be lifted and it would reject Iraqi demands to return to Baghdad the control over money Iraq earns from oil sales. The money would still be deposited into a UN supervised escrow account, to be drawn for import. Iraq has already said that "it would accept nothing short of an end to the embargo." The British official said: "The measures that we are proposing in effect will mean the end of sanctions on ordinary civilian imports in Iraq."

Though jointly sponsored, the US administration is reluctant to comment publicly on the plan, because of administration's critics among conservatives who believe Bush should increase pressure on President Saddam Hussein in the hope of bringing down his regime. But Bush administration's liking for the proposal can be realized by focusing on enforcing sanctions on military transfers and Powell's statement: "It simply does not work to try to block up the country, specially when so many other countries are willing to turn the other way. So it is time to try a different approach."[38]

Thus the UK-US wants to end sanctions on civilian goods entering Iraq but toughens enforcement of arms embargo. Russia and China were not ready to support it and Baghdad signaled its outright rejection. French officials were waiting to see the text of the British draft resolution. Russia, China and France have been Iraq's supporters on 15-Member Security Council and their support is critical to any overhaul of sanctions because each has veto power.[39]

Russia actually threatened to wield its veto in the United Nations to torpedo US and British plan to introduce anew 'Smart Sanctions' regime against Iraq. The Russian foreign ministry lodged a fresh protest after earlier detailing its objection on the proposal; the Foreign Minister linked the issues of continued US-British bombing and "no-fly-zone" over Iraq to the current sanctions negotiation in New York. The Russian Foreign Minister told Powell that Russia would be damaging its own commercial links with Baghdad if it gave the green light to the 'smart sanctions'. Moscow says that $ 5.5 billion of Iraqi oil supplies to Russian companies are at stake, and more than $ 2 billion in business contracts could suffer. Thus, commercial considerations appear to be partly behind the Russian threats to block the proposed resolution in the UN Security Council where Russia has the veto. But undeterred by the veto threat, Britain said that it would press a heed with refining its proposal.[40]

Against the background of the evolution in the context of sanctions, various scenarios are drawn on Iraq and Saddam Hussein's future: First, Saddam Hussein will remain in power for the next decade, more by default than his ability to revive Iraq while cracks in sanctions appear. It represents two major policy dilemmas: how to keep consensus within the coalition on enforcing sanctions, and how to prevent the erosion of contacts with Iraqi society in preparation for a post Saddam Hussein Iraq. The second scenario involved his potential replacement or overthrow. In this scenario, it is critical that a new Iraqi regime, faced with a near impossible economic situation, has the West's assurance of quick aid. The third scenario is the collapse of government, accompanied by a period of violence. The scenario presents the biggest policy challenge as Turkey, Syria and Iran would all be affected by the disintegration of Iraq. Iraq would not be able to re-establish control over Northern Iraq, which has now had experience of limited self-government.

(b) Evaluation

Sanctions on Iraq are not likely to last indefinitely as support for them is eroding from within the Security Council and coalition as well as within the regime. There is no post sanction policy due to perceptional differences among the partners of the coalition. The evaluation of the perception of each actors involved would clarify the existing situation of the sanctions regime in Iraq.

USA.[41] Both the US Presidency and the Congress have given themselves sweeping powers to impose sanctions on foreigners who offend America's ideas of what is proper. These measures range from unilateral bans on selected export or restrictions on entry into the US of 'undesirable' individuals to full-scale trade, travel, investment and diplomatic embargoes. In such latter cases, the US will routinely ask the UN Security Council to endorse its actions, ensuring the other UN members to follow its lead. Thanks to the enormous clout and its veto power, it usually gets its way.

When US disapprove of a foreign government's actions, policies or dialogues, it usually pursues one of the three options. It bombs; it punishes; or it persuades. Sometimes it does all the three together. American armed action of the kind seen in Iraq is relatively rare and is usually embarked upon as a last resort. If persuasion fails and a coercion of a foreign power or dictator is required, much more usual preferred tools is punishment by economic and diplomatic means—in other words sanctions. Iraq is the most notorious victim of all out US-led punitive sanctions. Although the most countries in the UN General Assembly no longer support the sanction regime as applied to Baghdad, it remains in place regardless.

However, the US policy towards Iraq is not sustainable over the long term. At the US insistence the United Nations has applied sanctions but they have not led to the over throw of Saddam Hussein nor eased regional fears of Iraqi intentions. When the US is asked: How long the United States should or can maintain these sanctions, the US turned on: how long the present Baghdad government lasts; how great the need for Iraqi oil; and how long UN support continues. Moreover, lifting of sanctions is not up to the United States alone since they are imposed by the United Nations.

There is a lack of post sanctions policy for Iraq. Isolation of Iraq is contributing to its undesirable behaviour. It is suggested that the United States should pursue a policy based on the centre or the periphery. In the case of the former, the United States should resign itself to dealing with Saddam or similar successor. Indeed the United States and all regional countries would probably prefer to deal with Baghdad government than a divided Iraq. This pursuit of centrist policy is generally favoured.

An alternative would be to promote a policy of strengthening the periphery, particularly the Kurdish zone in the North in hopes this will bring Saddam Hussein down. To this end the United States has tried to mediate peace between the major Kurdish factions. However US interest in the Kurds is basically humanitarian, not strategic. The Kurds have been in perpetual civil war and are unable to form a viable state in the North, even under UN protection. Eventually a successor government in Baghdad will try to re-incorporate Kurdish areas into the Iraqi state and when it does, will the United States abandon the Kurds? It is believed that the United States is prolonging the Kurdish tragedy by making promises to them that it cannot keep.

The sanctions Washington enforces against Baghdad look increasingly like a punishment seeking a crime. Even the US has given up on trying to over throw Saddam Hussein. Its secondary goal of ensuring Saddam never develops nuclear or chemical weapons are fraying at the edges. Washington continues with sanctions seemingly for lack of an alternative policy that it can sell domestically. The US needs to dilute its policy goals and broadly ensures that Saddam is not a threat to regional or international security. This goal has largely been accomplished. Iraq's nuclear and chemical weapons infrastructure has been more or less dismantled. Iraq, in part because of the social consequences of economic sanctions and Saddam's cynical manipulation of their effects, is in no position to threaten its neighbour for decades.

However, there is still enough bellicosity and unpredictability in Saddam's behaviour for there to be a case against completely lifting sanctions. Iraq has shown little contrition for invading and pillaging Kuwait. It continues to press its claim to the

Shiekhdom. Such medieval tendencies cannot be condoned or overlooked. Iraq is now just a few hundred thousand barrels short of the 2.6 million barrels of crude oil it produced before it attacked on Kuwait. Even with war reparation, which Baghdad pays, the recent rise in oil prices has filled its coffers. The only real concern left of the international community is seeing to it that whatever Iraq earns is not spent on re-building Saddam's military machine. This means maintaining UN control on the oil sales and export earnings of Iraq. But the sun should now be set on the inspection programmes, the no-fly zone and the bans on civilian economic movement between Iraq and the world.

In the post cold war period the US throws its weight around to a greater degree than even before. The figures on sanctions, provided by US business lobby groups, form the context for one of the more unexpected initiatives of the new Bush administration. When Colin Powell visited the senate for hearing on his nomination as Secretary of State, one of the issues he raised were sanctions. "There were too many of them," he said,[42] "they often did not work and what was more, they gave America a bad name. The repeated use of sanctions as a foreign policy weapon shows a degree of American hubris and arrogance that may not serve our interest all that well."

Does this presage a new dawn of enlightenment for governments of Havana, Delhi, Damascus, Tehran, Kabul, Beijing and elsewhere? Powell was explicit about two cases: Iraq and Libya. Here the sanctions would remain. There is another consideration that gives pause. Sanctions are not always bad and they do sometimes work: the example of South Africa during the apartheid era is often given. And it will be remembered that many big business, including some British banks, fervently opposed them. The recently imposed UN curbs on the West African war-stoking trade in "Blood Diamonds" are another example of sanctions that are morally desirable and will hopefully work.

France.[43] Call it a Napolianic pride or Guallist defiance, the French leaders have often pursued an independent line in foreign policy. By sending a passenger flight to Baghdad, defying the UN sanctions, Paris has given notice to the US that the sanctions have outlived their utility and that France will no longer care to abide by the existing embargoes.

Russia.[44] Russia has been contemplating regular commercial flights to Baghdad. It has already sent a humanitarian flight to Iraq. US and Britain have regarded Russian revival of its scheduled flight to Iraq as breaching the sanctions regime. A Russian spokesman claimed that commercial flights were not covered by UN resolutions against Iraq. Scheduled passenger flights between Moscow and Baghdad would drive a hole through the crumbling sanctions regime and encourage President Saddam Hussein to continue to defy the West. There have already been individual flights from Russia and France but scheduled flights would be a big change.

In London a foreign office source said: "The resumption of scheduled flights amounts to a resumption of trading relations and that would be a breach of sanctions." On the other hand, in order to shore up the sanction regime, the US and Britain send their war planes over Northern and Southern Iraq, denying air space to Iraqi fighters. The resumption of Russian commercial flights would complicate an already tense and dangerous situation. Both Russia and France—eager to do business with Iraq—have tried at the UN to persuade US and Britain to end to no-fly zones set up after Baghdad cracked down on Northern Iraq's Kurds and Southern Iraq's Shiites following the Gulf war. The new move by Russia should be taken, the London spokesman said, as a signal that the world community must act to overcome this impasse.

Arab World.[45] There has been the weakening of international support for sanctions, particularly, due to a sense that the Iraqi people are being unfairly punished. Turkey finds it increasingly difficult to justify the economic sacrifices it is making to maintain the trade embargo. A related issue is the future of Iraqi oil export. It is to the benefit of other oil producing countries that sanctions are maintained for when they are lifted the Iraqi oil that comes to the market may further depress prices.

The continuation of UN sanctions against Iraq is perceived by Arab in general as vindictive and inhumane leading to expression of sympathy for the Iraqi people even if less so for

Saddam. Saddam's argument about a hegemonic threat from United States is gaining credence and there has been resurgence of interest in Saddam's wartime themes of 'Pan Arabism' and the fall of monarchies.

Venezuelan President Hugo Charvez crossed into Iraq from Iran by car, thus, becoming the first head of state to visit Iraq since 1991 war. The Indian Minister of State for External Affairs, Ajit Panja also went to Baghdad and has called for immediate lifting of UN sanctions on the ground that these have become counter productive. Jordan has asked for UN permission to resume Air services to Iraq. More and more Arab countries have also called for easing of sanctions against Baghdad. Despite reservations about Saddam Hussein, even some of the Gulf States have begun to make a case of Iraq's return to the Arab fold to strengthen peace and stability in the region.

Iraq.[46] These emerging perceptions and their mutual reactions led to the realization of the fact that while the regime was slowly eroded, in the short run, Saddam was not likely to be overthrown. His grip over Iraqis and the mobilizing power of the ruling Baath party was demonstrated by a snap referendum in October 1995 in which Saddam was overwhelmingly re-elected President.

It is argued that despite defeat Saddam still harbours ambition with regard to Kuwait. He has stoked tension with Kuwait, accusing it of stealing its oil. As may be recalled it was the similar charge a decade ago which led to the Iraqi incursions into Kuwait. Kuwait is very afraid of a second invasion. Its desire for a defence treaty, which promises more protection than the United States is currently willing to give, is evidence of the Kuwaiti concern about the long term threat of revenge on the part of Iraq. Iraq is working overtime to weaken the UN sanctions by playing its oil card.

Sanctions have their limitations and these developments on the diplomatic front by France, Russia, Arab world and others are exposing them. The US and Britain have become increasingly isolated. While the international community feels repugnance towards President Saddam Hussein, there is also a growing sense that the sanctions and no-fly zone are hurting civilians rather than the regime. Sanctions have led to the starving of thousands of Iraqi and killed innocent children, something, which an increasing number of countries are finding unacceptable even if it is known that Saddam Hussein has been using the sanctions to create rifts in the Western alliance. It is clear enough that the earlier Western hope that the deprivation caused by these harsh measures will compel the Iraqis to rise against their cruel dictator has not come true. Now the cracks in the Western line up are more visible than ever, Saddam Hussein can be said to have regained some of his lost prestige.

Thus, the "cracks" as well as the "regaining," confirm the fact that sanctions on Iraq are increasingly proving "counter productive."

III. APPRAISAL

The assessment of sanctions on Iran and Iraq manifest two broad areas: the US-European differentiated position on sanctions and, as a result the contentious issue of sanctions itself. Both the aspects, in turn, are discussed as under:

The domestic pressures on foreign policy form a considerable barrier to reaching common ground on US-European policy[47] and the problem is perhaps more daunting in the United States where members of the administration regularly do battle with elements in Congress over US foreign policy. If Middle East peace process left unresolved it will continue to feed insecurities in the Gulf. Even here the United States is criticized for its Israeli bias, and Europe have their differences. Suggestions for bridging the gap like carrot-stick, wait and watch etc. have their own deficiencies.

The suggestion for creating the forum for dialogue is also not possible. Revolving European representation often leaves out major European players and can lead to misperception that differences in US and European positions are greater than they are. Structure and formality similar to trade talk is often a hurdle though require for effective discussion. US is more sensitive about the idea of forum, which is perceived as limiting its sovereignty in national decision. European countries already loaded with a vast array of European Union related committees, are unlikely to be amenable to yet another forum for discussion.

On these grounds the idea of forum is unworkable. However efforts of consensus are going on.

Beyond the conflicts inherent in the policy of sanctions and away from the problems and difficulties involved in an effort of structural contiguity, the United States and Europe differ in their choice of strategies to achieve on policy objectives. Such policy disparities between the USA and Europe manifest more prominently in respect to sanctions on Iran and Iraq. Broadly, while the United States relies, significantly, on economic sanctions, the European states resort to 'critical dialogue.' While Europe deems economic sanctions counter-productive, the United States views European policy weak-willed, uncritical, preferential to trade rather than the security consideration, and perceives absence of articulating the relationship between trade and dialogue in clear terms despite forming the basis of European Union's official policy towards Gulf region. This clash in policies is based on divergent assessment of the threat to Gulf stability. Bridging US-European differences both in policy prescription and threat perception is difficult.

Both US and Europe list the security threat in Gulf as follows: Weapons of mass destruction (WMD), terrorism, political instability, and political Islam. Despite such commonality, differences appear on the perceived level of threat. United States perceives that it is ultimately responsible for international security and that WMD proliferation is primarily an American problem, not a European one. Despite effective US-European cooperation, disparities in policy did arise over conflicting position on how broad or narrow non-proliferation effort should be. While Europe sees trade and diplomatic relations as a tool to help stem a country's desire for WMD, the United States sees non-military trade as a source of revenue that allows state to pursue WMD programme more easily.

The US leadership role in the region is manifested by its broad military presence, which includes[48] some twenty war-ships and support vessels in the Gulf since the end of 1990, 40-50,000 military personnel and over $ 1.2 billion of military equipments. Such a commitment points to the accountability of the United States if Gulf security is breached. US-Europe differences on policy prescription draw from this sense of US accountability.

Europe focuses more on internal development within state and less on outward assessment of state's military capabilities. The United States, on the other hand, bases its assessment of state's intention primarily on military capabilities and judges more on external action. Oil plays a more critical role in the formation of US policy towards Gulf whereas European concerns about access to oil were eased by a sense that Gulf States, regardless of political developments, will always need big markets for their oil.

The United States and Europe both reap advantages and suffer some disadvantages. Out of the existing system in the Gulf, the United States have to bear significant military cost even with the considerable subventions by regional rich oil states such as Saudi Arabia and Kuwait, but it also enjoys benefit to its domestic defence industry and gains a leading role in both oil and politics in the region.

Europe, on the other hand, sees much of its oil interest protected under the extended US security umbrella without having to pay the cost but is somewhat at a disadvantage when it comes to its role in the oil sector and influence in the politics of the region. Europe feels that the present security arrangement in the Gulf is unsustainable. It considers the US presence in the Gulf de-stabilizing and fear that this US position provides it the incentive to act unilaterally with or without consulting Europe.

Europe notes the continuing tendency of the United States towards unilateral sanctions: For instance Iran-Libya Sanctions Act (ILSA) extends sanctions to foreign companies; Freedom from Religious Persecution Act (FRPA) seeks to impose sanctions on countries engaged in campaign of religious persecution, targeting Cuba, Vietnam, Laos, North Korea and Islamic countries in general; ranges of sanctions under FRPA to be imposed include banning export there, ending US support for multilateral assistance, ending support for World Trade Organization membership and cancellation of visas. A third piece of legislation, supported by US businesses, requires that the Congress and White House prepare a cost-benefit analysis before sanctions are imposed. But the bill is facing a considerable obstacle to its enactment.

Europe also criticized the United States for its policy of 'moving the goal post' on UN resolutions concerning Iraq, mainly US insistence that UN resolutions remain in place until Saddam Hussein leaves or is removed from power. As a result Saddam Hussein has strengthened his grip on Iraqi people exploiting their frustration with the Western embargo. Such US policy is seen as damaging the integrity of the United Nations. It is pointed out that sanctions can be removed gradually while monitoring stations remain in place. Sanctions are not likely to last indefinitely as they are currently enforced as support for them is eroding from within the Security Council and the coalition as well as within the region.

The US policy is built around the threat posed by Iraq. But Europe often fails even to discuss it. No doubt, Europe, which has grown complacent, needs to be more vigilant. But the attempt of focusing Iraq policy around the figure of Saddam Hussein and attempt to remove him, as the United States does, is itself destabilizing. In fact Europe perceive Iraq, as one of the three (the other two being Iran and Saudi Arabia) big powers in the Gulf region, will always potentially be a threat. Even a change in regime would not change its geographical weakness—lack of sea outlet—or ameliorate ambitions to reverse that weakness. Thus, sanctions placed on Iraq, as Europe perceive, are the most extensive ever imposed.

Where the United States and Europe are largely in agreement on specific effort to cut off the weapon trade in the region of instability such as Gulf, the main problem is to bring states like Russia and China into weapon control regime as they are reportedly cooperating with Iran and Pakistan to build Missiles. Moreover weapon control regime, MTCR is not fool proof; it can delay the weapon programme or dissuade a less determined country from making a purchase. The Waasenar Agreement,[49] unlike other regimes, which focus on one weapon system or country, has a broad mandate: to consider regional stability in making arms transfers. As no set means exist to measure regional stability it is difficult to see how the principles of the Waasenar Agreement will be implemented.

The unilateral actions imposed by the United States, affect the investment, as most service companies are Americans. It is believed that as and when embargo will be lifted, Iran and Iraq will want to diversify their investment resources. So in the context of assessing the relative advantages and disadvantages, it would be a case of one getting a slice, only of different size.

In the light of the ramifications of different policy posture of the USA and Europe, the nearly eight-year-old sanction policy of "Dual Containment,"[50] initiated by Clinton administration to isolate and economically weaken both, Iran and Iraq, is in need of review. The Duel Containment policy has not been effective. Although sanctions have made resources scarcer in Iraq, the government has chosen to respond by further abandoning its responsibilities to the Iraqi people and by committing all available resources to the reconstruction of its military forces. Saddam Hussein's control is more absolute than it was eight years ago and Iraqi opposition groups are generally more divided. Saddam's regime continues to profit from the sale of oil, while the latest round of Israeli-Palestinian violence complicated the discussion of so-called smart sanctions in the UN Security Council.

Iran, in contrast, has been undergoing more positive change in the last eight years. But these changes have been limited almost entirely to domestic issues and there is no evidence to suggest that they have come as a result of US policy. The US concern—support of violent opposition to the Middle East peace process, backing international terrorism directed against US interests, and efforts to develop weapons of mass destruction and missile capabilities—is arguable. But it is highly unlikely that such changes as there may have been were driven by a lack of resources, as a consequence of sanctions. Those who oppose a change in US policy towards Iran often find themselves caught in a contradiction, arguing on the one hand that Iran's behaviour is more egregious than ever, and on the other, that current US policy is worth continuing because it has succeeded in restraining Iran's behaviour. Iran's international conduct has been, and continues to be determined not by US sanctions, but by internal politics. Those sanctions may have handicapped the ability of the United States to elicit greater cooperation from Tehran in the campaign against terrorism. With or without sanctions, Iran almost certainly has sufficient funds to pursue advanced nuclear weapon capabilities and to fund opposition to Israel for years to come.

In addition to being inconsistent and ineffective, Duel Containment has, since its inception, proven injurious to other US national interests. It has aroused the ire of European allies, created discord between the United States and its Arab partners, compromised the credibility of US diplomacy, prevented potentially lucrative US investment in Iranian oil industry and deprived the US government of influence over the scale and direction of Iranian weapon programmes.

Although Europe has generally supported sanctions against Iraq, there is growing disagreement on how to ensure that those sanctions achieve their stated goals, France and Britain are often divided in the UN Security Council, while those European countries supporting the French position on Iraq bemoan Anglo-American rigidity. Additionally the European Union has taken frequent umbrage at the secondary sanctions of ILSA intended to prevent foreign investment in Iran's petroleum sector, threatened to raise the issue at the World Trade Organization and took seriously that ILSA, renewed for an additional five years in August 2001, should have never been imposed. Encouraged by an ongoing dialogue with Iran, many European states argue that 'engagement' is a better tool than are sanctions. Finally most of Arab countries have increasingly demonstrated a preference for accommodation (rather than confrontation) with Iraq.

In light of these considerations, the Dual Containment policy seems not only ineffective, but out of touch with current international political reality. Meanwhile, the rigidity of Dual Containment has contributed to a general decline of US diplomatic credibility. Iranian opinion of US diplomacy is particularly sceptical. Iran's ambiguous response to US attempt to encourage it to play a more active role in the anti-terrorism coalition, is in part a reflection of domestic division and in part a reflection of concern that any assistance will be "rewarded" with a continuation of sanctions. Iranian leaders may justifiably reason that the uncompromising US position is unlikely to change and that, therefore, significant cooperation would only make Iran appear weak and pliant to US demands.

US policy, especially toward Iran, consistently appears aimed more at punishment than at achieving reform or ending problematic behaviour. However, the negative effects of Duel Containment are felt more by the US economy and US geopolitical interests than by either Iran or Iraq. US-imposed sanctions are a windfall for foreign companies that are not forced to compete with US firms. Moreover, US economic and long term-energy security interests are damaged by the continuing underdevelopment of petroleum reserves in both Iran and Iraq. And while both countries would certainly be richer but for sanctions, no sanctions regime would be likely so to constrain the economy of an oil producing state that it would be unable to finance problematic behaviour (such as development of WMD or support for international terrorism).

Duel Containment has led the United States to focus so intently on combating certain concerns—state-sponsored terrorism, violent opposition to the Middle East peace process and the development of WMD—that it has neglected other interests, which can be pursued simultaneously and without tremendous opposition from Iraq and Iran: energy security, regional stability, increased commercial activity and reduced drug trafficking. This last area of possible cooperation would also help stamp out some of the sources of funding of terrorism. Indeed, there is good reason to believe that greater engagement, at least with Iran, might aid in the realization of a host of old and newly understood common interests.

By its nature, Dual Containment is a reactive policy intended to minimize the damage done by Iraq and Iran to US interests. It assumes (and, indeed at times seems to prefer) a continued hostile relationship with both countries and is lacking in positive incentives. In the face of active-reactive syndrome, it is most likely that Iraq may refuse to change despite proposed smart sanctions regime (which, according to US perception, inherently contains the element of "rewarding" Iraq for its belligerence), the US may be justified to adopt more forceful policy. In the case of Iran, however, there are signs that improved relations are possible and that cooperation on problems affecting both countries would be fruitful. Furthermore, maintaining current policy towards Iran would demonstrate continued hostility despite three democratic elections in the last four years, each providing overwhelming mandate for reform. Thus on both fronts, the United States must demonstrate that its ire is directed at certain policies of the governments in question, and not at the people over whom they rule. Against this background, the following principles have been suggested to guide the reformulation of US policy toward Iran and Iraq.

USA must treat Iran and Iraq as separate entities, despite geography and their common opposition to US "hegemony." Iran is a stable country with a democratic form of governance and a highly educated population, consistently infusing enlightened spirit in the Islamic regime. Iraq is mired in a humanitarian crisis of unknown proportion and is ruled over by a dictator who has, in the last decade, invaded a neighbouring country and used poison gas against his own people. Instead of lumping of 'Iran, Iraq and North Korea, into an "Axis of Evil,"[51] or returning back to "Duel Balancing," there is the need for the differentiated treatment of each. The ways in which decisions are made in each country are very different; the US efforts to affect decision-making must reflect this fact.

The complexity of the task of promoting national interests requires the 'high politics' of engagement, rather than 'low politics' of Sanctions. Moreover the goals and interests cannot be protected alone; the efforts to rehabilitate the worsening relationship between United States and the Muslim world and to maintain strong relations with its allies in Europe and Asia require pursuing the most important interests far more effectively. Experience and analysis suggest that sanctions, barring few as effective instrument of foreign policy, are more effective when they are multilateral and when they target very specific sectors such as the importation of dual use technologies. To the extent sanctions remain in Iraq and Iran, this should be an important consideration.

Even during the Cold War, the United States maintained an embassy in Moscow. If the United States really wishes to achieve greater peace and stability, it needs to design a policy, which relies more on diplomatic engagement rather than political and economic isolation. To this end, the United States will need to communicate more effectively with the states of Iran and Iraq, particularly, and with the Muslim world in general.

Suggestions are often lost in the vagaries of politics; the only substance of issue, as its victim, remains for analysis. The uniqueness of Iran-Iraq episode lies in its short impact of sanctions on the target states and a long shadow of frictions between the US and its European allies. As such analysis escapes away from sanctions to float in its universe. Another difficulty is that both the target states are "allied-turn-adversaries." As such the Conflict Expectation Model, which is usually applicable in a neat division between ally and adversary, like North Korea and South Korea, cannot be a suitable framework for analyzing the implications of sanctions in respect to Iran and Iraq.

Even if it is presumed that analysis runs into difficulty because of the 'universe of sanctions,' gaining ascendancy over sanction, as well as because of the isomorphic effect of allied-adversary mixed situation, it can safely be stated that in respect to Iran and Iraq, the US appears in a dual role of an "initiator" and "protestor;" but the difficulty is that the 'initiator of the situation' cannot be accepted as the 'protestor of its consequence.' This norm of US foreign policy is creating difficulty elsewhere as well, for instance in Afghanistan. This, in essence, is the problem of the Western Coalition, which resulted in the complications, discussed, behind the sanctions imposed on Iran and Iraq. The moment this inherent dichotomy between "initiation" and "protestation" is resolved, the adverse implications of sanctions regime in respect to Iran and Iraq, can easily be resolved or at least the trend can be reversed back.

REFERENCES

1. David H. Saltiel & Jasonn S. Purcell, Moving Past Dual Containment: Iran, Iraq and future of US Policy in the Gulf, *Bulletin*. The Atlantic Council of the United States & The Stanley Foundation, Vol. XIII, No. 1, January 2002, p. 1.
2. *Ibid.*
3. Theodore A. Couloumbis and James H. Wolfe, *Introduction to International Relations: Power and Justice,* Prentice Hall of India, 1986, p. 244.
4. Frederic, S. Pearson & J. Martin Rochester, *International Relations,* Random House, New York, 1984, 406.
5. *Ibid.*, p. 124.

6. Couloumbis & Wolfe, *op. cit*, p. 245.
7. Rochester, *op. cit*, p. 292.
8. *Ibid.*, p. 293.
9. *Ibid.*, p. 237.
10. Couloumbis & Wolfe, *op. cit*, p. 188.
11. *Op. cit*, p. 189.
12. US-European Policies in the Persian Gulf: Beyond the Friction, *The Persian Gulf Project*. Sponsored by The Royal Institute of International Affairs & The Stanley Foundation, September 11-12, 1997, Chatham House, London, UK, 1997, p. 20.
13. *Ibid.*, p. 21.
14. *Ibid.*, pp. 21-22.
15. For detail on US-European Policy, see *Persian Gulf Project*, 1997, *op. cit*, as well as of 1998.
16. *Op. cit.*, 1997, p. 3.
17. *Ibid.*, p. 13.
18. *Ibid.*
19. *Ibid.*, 1998, p. 9.
20. *Ibid.*
21. *Ibid.*
22. *Hindustan Times*, October 17, 2001.
23. *Ibid.*
24. *Ibid.*
25. *Ibid.*
26. *Ibid.* (Refs. 22 to 26: The *New York Times*: Elain Scioline/Neil A. Lwis, Washington, October 16 as reported in *Hindustan Times*, Wednesday, October 17, 2001, p. 14).
27. The Persian Gulf: Challenges for the new Administration, 37th Strategy for Peace, US Foreign Policy Conference, The Stanley Foundation, 1996, p. 10. For detail on Iran see: Richard W. Cottam, *Khomeini, the Future, and US Options* (Policy Paper 38), The Stanley Foundation, Muscatin, Iowa, USA, 1987.
28. *Bulletin*: NGOs Coordinating Committee on Human Rights (NCCHR)/ 66; 67, September 15, 2000, p. 4.
29. 37th Strategy for Peace, 1996, *op. cit.*, p. 12.
30. *Ibid.*, pp. 12-13.
31. *Bulletin*, *op. cit.*, p. 4.
32. *Ibid.*
33. *Ibid.*
34. *Ibid.*, pp. 5, 10.
35. *Hindustan Times*, November 30, 2000.

36. *Bulletin, op. cit.*, p. 10.
37. *Hindustan Times,* May 18, 2001.
38. *Ibid.*
39. *Hindustan Times,* May 19, 2001.
40. *Hindustan Times,* June 29, 2001.
41. 36th Strategy for Peace (Stanley Foundation), 1995, pp. 8-10; 37th Strategy (Stanley Foundation), 1996, p. 13; *Hindustan Times,* October 4, 2000, November 30, 2000 and February 10, 2001.
42. *Hindustan Times,* February 10, 2001.
43. *Hindustan Times,* (editorial), September 26, 2000.
44. *Ibid.*, and *H.T.* October 4, 2000.
45. *Hindustan Times,* (editorial), September 26, 2000; *HT,* November 30, 2000; 36th Strategy, 1995, *op. cit.*, pp. 8-9.
46. *Ibid.*
47. On US-European Policy Differences see: *The Persian Gulf Project,* 1997 and 1998, *op. cit.*
48. *The Persian Gulf Project,* 1997, *op. cit.*, p. 7.
49. *Ibid.*, p. 12.
50. Moving Past Dual Containment, *op. cit.*, pp. 2-4.
51. *Hindustan Times,* July 26, 2002.

6

INDIA AND PAKISTAN

In the wake of nuclear tests, conducted by India and Pakistan in 1998, the USA imposed sanctions on both the countries. Two extreme viewpoints emerge in the US administration. Gilman Benjamin, Chairman of the House of International Committee, said: "The strongest possible deterrents, short of military action, are needed in South Asia to ensure against any move from weapon testing to weapon deployment." But Stuart E. Eizenstat, Under Secretary of State for Economic, Business and Agricultural Affairs, pointed out: "Sanctions are not a panacea and they are not cost free." He stated that frequency of imposing sanctions have increased: The US has applied sanctions for foreign policy purposes a total of 15 times since World War I, 104 times since World War II and 61 times since 1993. Thus, more than half the sanctions imposed in the past 80 years have been imposed in only the past four years.

The President's Export Council estimated in mid-1997 that about 75 countries were subject to or were under the threat of sanctions. Recent estimate of such countries is now 90 and the trend is towards broader unilateral sanctions even though the council concluded that the unilateral economic sanctions have a very poor record of success. The list of countries includes some against whom sanctions have been in force for more than 38 years such as Cuba. Others against whom strict economic sanctions are being maintained include: Cuba, Iran, Iraq, Libya, Myanmar, North Korea, Serbia, Sudan and UNITA (Angola). Sanction against Cuba was imposed in July 1963 and the one against Sudan was put into effect in November 1997.

Undeterred by such frequency and volume of sanctions, the USA applied costly unilateral economic sanctions to India and Pakistan in response to their nuclear tests. Eizenstat stated that "Economic sanctions should be a last resort with diplomatic action being the first line of action. Multilateral support is essential if sanctions are to be truly effective means of influencing the policies and behaviour of other countries. Except for Japan, Canada and few more European nations the US has not found such support for sanctions against India and Pakistan."

He also called for careful balancing of benefit against cost: "Do the likely benefits of sanctions outweigh the economic losses to our business and workers?" Sanctions that are ineffective, that impose substantially more cost on US interests than on the sanctioned country, that are unable to garner broader support, even of closed allies, do not send a message of US resolve of commitment rather than send a message of US irrelevance.

The official also pointed out two essential conditions for sanctions to take hold: The targeted country had to be small and vulnerable; and Economic Sanctions had to be supported by other nations. The first condition clearly did not apply in the case of India. And given the disagreement among "Members of G-7 and a half," the second condition also did not apply.[1]

Owing to mixed initial reaction and also because of the fact that the Glenn Amendments were imposed for the first time, the US administration was careful to reduce the rigours of the sanctions, particularly when it impinges adversely on the American private sector. American banks have been allowed to operate in India and permitted to keep government securities to maintain their liquidity. But despite precautions and apparently safeguards of US interests, a degree of self doubt was starting to manifest itself and rethinking was beginning to surface: Has our reaction been too hasty and too harsh? Will the sanctions lead to more instability on the sub-continent and lesser opportunities for American companies, already strapped by unilateral sanctions around the world?

The senator Connie Mack, Florida Republican said on the floor of senate on July 16, 1998:[2] "It is a strange logic behind rewarding inappropriate actions by the Chinese Communist party leaders while simultaneously sanctioning the democratic leaders in India. There is something inherently wrong with sanctioning a democracy legally acting in its perceived national interests while rewarding a single party communist state which threatens regional security in violation of international law." The senator pointed out[3] that "India did not sign NPT basically it was discriminatory, but also because the treaty meant that China, the internally oppressive and undemocratic, occupying force on India's border, would be permitted to have nuclear weapons whereas India, fearful and insecure, would be denied any recourse to such weapons." Senator Mack also pointed out[4] that India had never been a proliferator of nuclear weapons and missiles, but China, a nuclear power, had proliferated time and again. In fact some estimates indicated that 90 per cent of China's weapon sales went to states that border on India, with Chinese proliferation of weapons technologies to Pakistan being of particular concern. Despite the record, India has been denied the same nuclear and technical cooperation, which the US has accorded to China. India and China both have commercial electricity needs that are among the largest in the world. The US signed a nuclear cooperation agreement with China but it continues to maintain restrictions on nuclear power agreements with India.

These spontaneous reactions within the sender country about the targeted 'Indian Subcontinent,' which is amounted to mean South Asia as a whole, is very significant in the sense that sanctions, unlike applied elsewhere, has become controversial as policy instrument in this context. As such the details of the 'action-reaction syndrome' of the sender and targets may be helpful to judge the quantum of effectiveness and ineffectiveness of the imposed sanctions.

I. INDIA

(a) Evolution

India's nuclear programme is totally indigenous and does not involve any foreign assistance and is not under IAEA safeguards. As such none of the nuclear transfer provisions—concerning enrichment transfer; reprocessing transfer; and explosive transfer—apply to India. However. since India is not a nuclear weapon state according to the NPT definition, the US imposed the sanctions after the Pokharan tests.

The USA, justifies the imposition of sanctions on India as follows:[5] "The US government shall terminate assistance to that country under the Foreign Assistance Act of 1961, except for humanitarian assistance or food or other agricultural commodities" [Sec. 102(b)(2)(A)]. The United States has been extending economic assistance to India since 1951. But its contribution has declined substantially in recent period. Indeed, if debt-servicing payments are taken into account, there is a net flow of funds from India to US account of development loans. While US estimates the loss on account of termination of development assistance at $ 142.3 million, the government of India figures of utilization of aid from the US put it at lower figure. Under this Act, the USA has imposed seven different types of sanctions on India. The sanctions and their probable effects are discussed as under:[6]

First, "The US government shall terminate sales to that country any defence articles, defence services or design and construction services" [Sec. 102(b)(2)(B)(i)]. US sales of defence articles and defence services to India have never been of much significance to either country. Indian purchases have been low. Deliveries of such items under the Foreign Military Sales (FMS) programme amounted to $ 1.329 million during the ten years period 1987-96. During the past five years, however, they have averaged only about $ 23000. The US put the effects of sanctions at $ 775000! However it is a fact that outstanding deliveries under the FMS agreements already calculated come to $ 6.124 million on 30th September 1996.

The other two elements under this heading are defence services and the International Military Education and Training (IMET) programme. There have been no sales of defence services from the USA to India. As regards IMET, they are minimal averaging $ 263000 per year in the period 1987-96. The programme is primarily due to the US desire for closer service cooperation with India than any major Indian need for such education and training.

Second, "The US Government shall terminate licences for the export to that country of an item on the US Munitions List"

[Sec. 102(b)(2)(B)(ii)]. There have been only limited commercial purchases of US military articles by India. Items have included purchases made on account of defence research projects such as the LCA rather than for operational purposes. The value of commercial export licensed under the Arms Export Control Act for period 1987-1996, was $ 325 million. While bulk of items, required for the LCA project, has already been acquired, there are still few items that have not been delivered. While their value may not be high, their critical requirements need some study.

Third, "The US government shall terminate all foreign military financing for that country under this Act" [Sec. 102(b)(2)(C)]. There has been no US financing of military sales to India since 1962.

Fourth, "The US government shall deny to that country any credit guarantees or other financial assistance by any department, agency or instrumentality of the US government" [Sec. 102(b)(2)(D)]. The principle US agencies involved in this section is the Export-Import Bank of USA (EX-IM Bank), the Overseas Private Investment Corporation (OPIC) and Trade and Development Agency (TDA).

EX-IM Bank's operations consist primarily of support for export of capital goods through long-term loans and guarantees of commercial bank financing or medium term loans, guarantees and insurance. During financial years, October 1996-September 1997, EX-IM Bank's authorization in respect of India, amounted to $ 304.999 million, consisting of loans of $ 20.308 million and medium term insurance for $ 4.217 million. Over all EX-IM Bank exposure in India amounted to 1403.498 million at the end of September 1997. The effect of EX-IM Bank sanctions affect US export to India.

The OPIC is the key federal agency encouraging American investment in developing countries. Its operation consists primarily of: Protecting US investors against political risks overseas by providing insurance; Financing US business expansion overseas by providing long term, limited recourse project financing; and making equity capital available for investments in eligible emerging markets by guaranteeing long-term loans to private equity investment funds.

OPIC's exposure in India amounted to $ 320 million insurance coverage in financial year 1996, and in single project financing of $ 50 million in financial year 1997. OPIC is concerned with promotion of US exports. According to a OPIC press release, the sale of $ 200 million in political risk insurance to Enron Oil and Gas Company in 1996 will result in $ 310 million worth supplies of US goods and services to the project in its first five years of operations, creating and supporting some 1100 American jobs. The White House release has estimated the loss on account of OPIC at more than 10 billion. This estimate, too, seems to be more on the basis of expressed interests or probable applicants than on any historical basis. The total exposure of OPIC in any one year is far less than $ 5 billion.

TDA is a US government agency, providing funding for US companies to conduct feasibility studies related to major projects in developing countries. In this manner TDA helps US companies get involved in projects that offer significant export opportunities. Funding varies year to year, but average less than $ 1 million per year. It should be remembered, however, that the funding is for US companies to conduct the studies and is, therefore, a subsidy to US companies and not assistance to India.

Fifth, 'The US government shall oppose in accordance with 701 of the International Finance Institution Act, the extension of any loan or financial or technical assistance to that country by any international financial institution" [Sec. 102(b)(2)(E)]. This section would require the US Executive Director on the Board of such institutions as the World Bank, ADB, IMF and IFC to vote against all loans and assistance to India. This is serious and should not be underestimated. The efficacy of US action will be contingent upon a number of factors.

As a matter of historical record, this is not the first time that such an action has been taken. For a period of three years from late 1974 to 1977, the USA had opposed all IDA loans to India, 26 in all, as a requirement arising out of the "check" amendment. The US Congress, as punishment in 1974, passed this amendment. The US was alone in its opposition and had no success. All the 26 credits were approved. As a consequence the US Congress repealed the amendment in 1977.

As a matter of record, the US has never been able to block any loan to any country in multilateral financial institutions such as IBRD, IFC, ADB, AFDB etc. during all these years because it could not gather sufficient support to block any of these loans. And by itself it does not have voting strength in any such institutions. The US opposition to specific project proposal should have to be accompanied by the opposition of other members before a project could be formally denied. In the World Bank, for example, its share is 17 per cent. As resident representative of that bank explained, to block any loan, the opposition needs to muster 50.1 per cent of votes. To do so the US has to have the support of not only G-8 countries but also a number of other countries, many from the developing world. It is unlikely that it will be able to do so, especially when countries such as UK, France etc. have expressed their opposition to any kind of sanctions. Therefore, the approach used was to defer loan applications from India till such time as the matter is resolved, as has been done on two occasions since the imposition of the sanctions.

There is another important factor that needs to be taken into account. Even if the US were to mobilize such support, it can block only the fresh loans. It cannot stop disbursements under loan agreements already approved. Such disbursements are not subject to Board approval. They are dependent solely on the fulfilment of contractual obligation on the part of the country. Typically in any year, more than 80 per cent of India's withdrawals from these institutions are in respect of loans approved two or more years earlier. Therefore, any stoppage of fresh loan approvals will begin to take effect with a lag of more than two years. It is, of course, quite possible that the US might begin to raise objections to withdrawals by India on technical grounds. However, that is different matter and its effect would be dependent on government of India's ability to respond creatively to such technical objections. It should be noted that India's unutilized loans are substantial. At the end of March 1996, they were more than $ 16 billion. They should provide sufficient cushioning for a drop in fresh commitments. The US could not maintain the coalition for any length of period and the opposition to loans to China collapsed in the face of the strong stand by China.

Sixth, "The US government shall prohibit any US bank from making any loan or providing any credit to the government of that country, for the purpose of purchasing or other agricultural commodities" [Sec. 102(b)(2)(F)]. The Indian government has not taken any loan from commercial banks from US (or for that matter from any other country). Therefore this should not have any direct effect. However, the US government has some degree of freedom in making things difficult for India.

The enforcement of economic and trade sanctions against targeted countries is administered and enforced by the Office of Foreign Assets Control (OFAC) of the US department of Treasury. It does so by issuing Foreign Assets Control regulations for (a) the Financial Community; (b) the Securities Industry; (c) the Export and Import; (d) the Insurance Industry and (e) the Tourism Industry.

The current list of US government sanctions against India, do not in any manner impact directly on the operation of the last three groups of entities. It may impact on the first two. Even this requires some careful and detailed analysis because this is the first time the US government has imposed sanctions under the Glenn Amendment. Unlike other sanctions currently being maintained by the US government, there are no trade sanctions against India. Nor are these any against investment in India. Tourism is not prohibited and there are no insurance companies operating in the country.

Seventh, "The authorities of the Section 6 of the Export Administration Act of 1979 shall be used to prohibit to that country export of specific goods and technology" [Sec. 102(b)(2)(G)]. The Nuclear Proliferation Prevention Act (NPPA) defines "goods and technologies" as "nuclear materials and equipment and sensitive nuclear technology...and all technical assistance requiring authorization under Sec. 57b of the Atomic Energy Act of 1954."

India is already subject to details of such goods and technology as a result of its refusal to sign NPT. In fact as a result of such refusal, it is subject to even stricter denial regime, including the MTCR, the NSG, Zangger Committee etc. Therefore this item will not put any additional burden on India.

India and the US signed a MOU in 1984 on export of technology and goods. Nevertheless, the US government has contrived to place obstacles in the way of Indian access to US technology and goods. In recent years the value of Import Certificates issued by Government of India under the MOU has fallen to levels much below $ 100 million. Moreover many of these items have begun to be freely available from the non-US sources such as France. In addition, the advances in technology have made such control regimes quite ineffective. A recent study has pointed out, many Indian computer manufacturers offer machine of much stronger capabilities than those allowed under the export control regimes. The Indian parallel processing super-computer technology is quite advanced, offering machines of quite high speeds, far in excess of the 2000 MTOPs limit placed by Bureau of Export Administration (BXA) on computer export to India.

As per the latest BXA guidelines, no licences will be issued for duel-use items controlled for nuclear or missile non-proliferation reasons for all end users. All export licences will be denied to the published BXA list of entities involved in such activities. On the other hand, BXA will continue to give favourable consideration on case-by-case basis to other duel-use export to other Indian government and non-government entities. No Indian private sector entity is currently listed in the BXA Entity list.

The sanctions, under these seven categories, have minimal impact on India in a short run. Moreover the very nature of law, common to many of the US anti-non-proliferation legislation, is self-defeating. Once instituted it can only aggravate the situation without leaving any recourse to negotiation. Any remedy of the situation requires a fresh legislation by the US Congress. Once Symington Amendment was invoked to put sanctions against Pakistan, the only way the US could get around the sanctions, for whatever purposes, was to enact new acts and amendments. Still, as recent disclosures about China-Pakistan transfers have shown, the US has been unable to resolve the matter in a meaningful manner. This happens because US non-proliferation objectives are not clear and therefore the concerned laws contain ambiguity.

The role and the use of sanctions as instrument of US foreign policy are already under discussion. The commercial concerns have also played a role in the enactment of laws diluting the sanctions. The US Congress has amended the requirements of sanctions under the Arms Export Control Act to allow for use of US government funds to guarantee export of agricultural products. This was the direct consequence of the Pakistani decision to open tenders for white wheat. Since the tenders were to close on July 15, the US Congress rushed to pass the law before July 14.

There are other bills pending before the Congress that would limit all sanctions present and future, to a period of two years. Extension of such sanctions would require separate Congressional approval. Furthermore, the President is required to file elaborate declarations and analysis explaining the rationale for the sanctions as also the setting forth the costs and benefits of such sanctions. All these efforts, however, should not be construed as a prelude to the lifting of sanctions against India.

It is a long drawn process. There must be give and take from both sides. Any attempt by the US to dictate unconditional acceptance of its terms will only result in failure. While all efforts should be taken into account some of the US concerns such as proliferation of weapons of mass destruction (WMD) there is no way Indian security concerns can be compromised to please the US. The task of restoring good relations between India and the US will be difficult but not impossible if both sides are willing to address each other's concerns.

India's economy, as Brahma Chellaney stated[7] has performed better under economic sanctions imposed after 'Shakti Tests' than in the previous 18 months. Sanctions are however, a potential political instrument to mount pressure on weak-willed states as India's case exemplified. Rigid sanctions spur 'fudging,' a classic case being the inaction as Chinese nuclear and missile transfer to Pakistan. Clinton gained executive flexibility in relation to US Arms Export Control Act under which economic sanctions were imposed on India and Pakistan. This flexibility provided the choice to dangle carrots and reward 'good behaviour.' Despite being armed with blanket authority by Congress to waive punitive actions, Clinton has kept India under pressure by maintaining the most biting sanctions—World Bank lending curbs—but extending waivers on sanctions hurting US companies' interests.

The World Bank related curbs, as stated, are estimated to cost India few hundred million dollars annually in higher interest rates from increased commercial borrowing. By imposing this additional burden on the Indian economy, even though manageable and free from strings attached to World Bank loans, the Americans have strengthened their political leverage. A second set of sanctions relates to technology control and denial and predates the shakti tests. In this respect there is no hope of liberally interpreting the progressing export control laws. The Entities List is the third type of sanctions for applying pointed pressure on specific firms. In contrast to Export Controls targeting specific technologies, entity related sanctions blacklisted particular companies, not for breaking US or international law, but for contributing to their home country's strategic programmes. The United States blackballed 200 large Indian private and state-run enterprises, months after the Jaswant Singh-Strobe Talbott talks began. It also helped ease International Financial Institution (IFI) lending curbs against Pakistan but not against India. Both actions were motivated by a desire to strengthen negotiating leverage against India.

The Indian enterprises, as he informed, now removed from the Entities List should never have been blackballed, as they are involved in innocuous activities such as clothing, food-preservation, fire prevention and control, terrain survey, basic research, and manufacture of small arms. More significant is Clinton's continuing reluctance, despite new authority from Congress to remove from the Entities List major Indian private sector firms like Larsen and Toubro, Godrej and Walchand Nagar industries or even the Indian Institute of Technology. Although Congress gave Clinton 60 days to streamline the Entities List, namely October 25, 1999, he had timed his step with an eye on India's CTBT consensus building effort. None of the 51 of the 204 Indian private and state enterprises taken off the Entities List, which had previously sought a US export licence. Nor does their removal permit them to purchase any high-tech items. As long as India is under stringent technology sanctions, the Entities List will remain only a pressure tool against (and warning to) the Indian industry.

In real terms, R. Ramachandran pointed out[8] that the US administration cancelled $ 27 million in aid to India. The American companies dealing with India will loose $ 300 million from OPIC, and $ 500 million in EXIM financing. Though the law requires the US banks to close their operation in India, the administration has not requested them to do so. The US exported $ 3.6 billion in goods to India of which duel-use technology exports (banned to sanctioned state under law) were $ 300 million. Under the decision of case-by-case review policy only 20 per cent of such restrictions could be affected; it works out $ 60 million. Voting against Indian loans at IMF and World Bank is not clear; so far pipeline loans have not been affected. The Farmer's Export Relief Act amended an arms export control law to exempt government loans and credit guarantees programmes that support the sale of food and other agricultural products including fertilizers. In fact this Act was being rushed lest Pakistan buy its wheat from elsewhere. For India's economy these restrictions are peanuts; in due course they got further clipped.

Despite meager impact or easing of the stringent effect, sanctions, besides being the political instrument of pressure, did inflict some difficulties in real terms. For instance owing to the sanctions, the British manufacturer could not export the American components needed for Indian Navy's Sea-King helicopters as the transaction was deemed to be violative of US's Arms Export Control Act. Indian Navy's Sea-King 42-B anti-submarine warfare helicopters had been virtually grounded after US imposed sanctions on India following nuclear tests at Pokharan in May 1998. India had purchased these helicopters from UK based Westland Helicopters with US based Sirkorsky company. As number of critical components in the Sea-King helicopters was of US origin, its British manufacturers could not supply these parts or service them till the US sanctions were lifted. This has left a large number of 'servo-packs' and 'gear-boxes' of Sea-King helicopters lying un-serviced in Britain due to lack of US spares.

While the Navy was facing the similar problem of spare parts for its Sea Harrier jump jet-fighters, the matter was apparently resolved with Hindustan Aeronautic Limited (HAL) being able to manufacture these parts indigenously. The Sea-King fleet, on the other hand, had been hamstrung and was operating at around 25 per cent of its capability with severe flying restrictions for the past two years. The Navy was around three squadrons of Sea-King 42-B helicopters, which along with Sea Harrier fighters form the backbone of India's forces.

Thus the US sanctions have forced the Indian Navy to restrict the flying hour of its anti-submarine warfare and fighter aircraft by over 25 per cent. Unofficially, Naval sources concede that the curtailment is ever higher. Export describes the cutback in flying as a serious set back on the navy's operational readiness. Repair and servicing of the British assembled Sea-King anti-submarine warfare (ASW) helicopters and Sea Harrier fighter-cum-maritime reconnaissance jets have been put on hold because several crucial parts requiring replacement are American. The US manufacturers cannot supply the parts because of sanctions. The UK is also constrained by its commitment to the US-led NATO arrangement.

While declining to confirm the quantum of reduction in flying, Vice-Chief of the Naval Staff, Vice-Admiral Madhavendra Singh admitted that part of several aircrafts, which require servicing, were lying in the UK. "We have twin strategy to deal with the sanctions: reduce flying to increase the longevity of the machines and approach domestic industry for replacing the parts required. Our experience with the domestic industry has been encouraging. In fact the sanctions will make us stronger."

But experts are worried. They point out that some aircrafts have been cannibalized to keep others flying. "Restricting flying hours will have a bearing on the Navy's operational preparedness. The anti-marine warfare—all whether and all seas—is a tricky business. Skills have to be honed only by steady practice. Reduced availability of aircraft means less training." This has also caused a set back to the Navy's plan to ensure an integral air element (in the form of on board Sea-King 42 B and Kamov 25 ASW choppers) on all major warships. The Sea-Kings primarily have an anti-submarine warfare role, although the navy also has the commando (42-C) and Airborne Early warning versions. The two squadrons of the Sea Harriers, which compliment the aircraft carrier INS Viraat, have reportedly been operationally reduced from 27 to about 15. The reduction in force levels have circumcised the 'huge technological advantage in the air,' which the Harriers—with their all-whether day and night flying, short take-off and vertical landing capability—enable. The torpedo-equipped Sea-Kings, with their dropped sonar buoy capability to detect sub-marines, are meant to be deployed in large numbers in the Western Fleet in view of the security requirements. Depletion in squadrons at the INS Kujali (Mumbai) and the INS Garuda (Cochin) are emasculation. One consolation for the Indian Navy is that Pakistan too is reeling under similar sanctions. The Pakistan Navy is also stuck with its grounded Sea-Kings.[9]

Beside impact on defence, particularly Navy, more than three years after the echo of nuclear explosions died down in Pokharan, the 'developmental activities'[10] came to a grinding halt as a result of sanctions. The forest department is feeling the tremors because this has had an adverse impact on the employment. Nearly 4500 people are rendered unemployed once this development work stops. Two of the major projects that are being currently carried out with Japanese financial assistance are withdrawn since they are unlikely to get further extensions. These include the Afforestation and Pasture Development Project (APDP) targeted at the Indira Gandhi Canal area and the Forestry Development Project (FDP) aimed at the development of 14 non-desert districts of Rajasthan. These two projects together employ nearly 4500 people.

Further, Rajasthan is unlikely to get Rs. 1600 crore it requires as financial assistance for projects envisioned in the Tenth Five Year Plan. "In the early 1998 the Japanese Bank of International Cooperation (JBIC) had appraised and agreed to fund the nearly Rs. 730 crore phase II of the Aravalli Afforestation Project (AFP). However, in the aftermath of the Pokharan blasts, Japan refused to sanction further loans." The project is with the Centre, which is yet to find a donor since 1998. Another comprehensive project titled Forest Development Agency (FDA) has been included in the Five Year Plan. But no major donors are coming up to fund the nearly Rs. 500 crore project. The department needs finances also for its third project that is likely to cost Rs. 570 crore. Japanese used to be a willing donor for forestry projects in Rajasthan till the blasts. Now nobody wants to touch the projects. It is imperative that the state government implores the centre to attract funds for these projects.

Thus, sanctions on India may be ineffective in the short run. But they are adversely affecting the defence and economy in the long run as is exemplified by implied consequences on Navy and direct financial crunch on afforestation projects of Rajasthan. The full impact of sanctions on the Indian economy needs a separate detailed study. But the examples are sufficient to realize that sanctions have already started to show themselves, at least parochially though not comprehensively.

(b) Evaluation

The categories of sanctions and their differentiated impact on Indian economy, discussed in the previous section, naturally lead to evaluation of the nature of restrictions and the assessment of the waiving, relaxation and lifting of the sanctions, which is the main concern of this section.

The restrictions are against the spirit, if not the letter, of WTO. China is not the member of WTO, but the USA runs to it for trade. China is signatory of NPT but openly flouts it by transferring nuclear technology to Pakistan. The US expects other countries to sign CTBT while its own senate refuses to ratify it. Its own laws ignore WTO. Such mismatching convinces that international laws are designed to keep weaker countries in check. It is argued that capital flows promote investment and lead to productivity advancements through the introduction of new technologies. Such argument is fallacious because capital includes financial flows, which had been the major cause of economic disasters in Thailand, Malaysia, Korea and Mexico. Chile, the pioneer of free trade, could protect itself from the similar crisis by its restriction on investment. India's own experience confirms that in spite of her opening up for the past 15 years, she is still technologically behind except where it was forced to develop 'swadeshi' technology, *e.g.* the nuclear tests.[11]

Another fallacy is related to 'gain from trade' concept. The argument that trade is beneficial to both partners, pre-supposes the equality between trading partners. But trade between unequal partners like India and US amounts to exploitation of the weak by the stronger. It is no surprise that the US senate passed the law to have no restrictions on such trade. It is said that the economic growth requires market friendly policies. The acceptance of this policy resulted in promoting multinationals and subverting national interests in the garb of globalization.[12]

Against such fallacious argument and the minuscule size of the restrictions against Indian trade and investment, the question naturally arises: Why is so much noise about sanctions? The reason is that even if economically sanctions have little impact on India's national interests, these restrictions do affect a small but vocal section of Resident Non-Indian (RNI) elite that sells information, goods and skills to the US. The accustomed imperialist attitude manifested by our RNI and respected in US media, have created a myth of sanctions. For instance the *Wall Street Journal*, the spokes media for the US multinationals, that control the US government agenda, headlines: "US hits India and Pakistan with sanctions." Note the master-slave language of 'hits' and 'sanctions.' Again "the Senate voted unanimously (89-0 vote) to exempt agricultural products from US economic sanctions aimed at punishing Pakistan and India." What an oxymoron! Senate is seeking trade from those to be punished. In the same way see the 'patronizing' and 'offensive' coverage by CNN and BBC on Washington's decision to lift sanctions: "President Bush has 'rewarded' India for its contribution to the fight against terrorism." The phrase 'sanction', whether inflicted or lifted, conveys not only the imperialist attitude but also hopes to produce the myth of US 'Rights' and 'Means' to punish or reward others. It is a myth because the US neither has this right nor the means to punish or even to reward, which, given with political expediency, becomes, ultimately, a bribe. Its only hope is to propagate this myth with the help of Indians themselves.[13]

A partial lifting of sanctions[14] in the last week of October 1999 serve two-fold purposes: to create a positive atmosphere in Indo-US relations in preparation for the visit of President Clinton to India and Bangladesh. Secondly, it is a gesture to encourage to India to fall in line with the US agenda on non-proliferation, which remains intact despite US Senate's vote against the ratification of the CTBT. Such removal of sanctions signify the US desire to engage India constructively on important issues about which there are differences of opinion between the two countries whether they are related to non-proliferation or WTO. Secondly, the removal of sanctions implies an acknowledgment by the US that India is not likely to succumb to punitive attitude or economic pressure at the cost of its basic national interests. Thirdly, sanctions, which have been removed in their specificity, imply a willingness to expand bilateral economic and commercial relations and to slowly cooperate in the field of defence cooperation, wherever possible.

Clinton has removed sanctions of development aid, which may revive bilateral defence training and a private US bank's participation in Indian commercial and economic operation, which may encourage exchange programme. This may be a forward movement but it is yet to be seen what the US will do to remove sanctions of greater significance to Indian interests. Will the restrictions on the transfer of dual-use technologies be removed? Will the restriction on the Indo-US cooperation for peaceful uses of space and nuclear technology be removed? Will the US government's 1998 order banning interaction and cooperation with what they have called "Entities," which can enhance India's nuclear and space capabilities, be set aside? Will Clinton follow up the removal of sanctions on US private banks operating in India by authorizing the US representatives to tell the IMF and IBRD to restore financial flows to India back to normal level? Will the restriction on contacts between scientists and technical experts of India and US be removed?

These questions are relevant because the US Congress has authorized the President to remove these sanctions though with the discretion to revive any of these if he so considers necessary under the relevant US legislation. From Indian point of view, the removal of these sanctions will be a significant political move reflecting a paradigm shift. But this is not the case so far. From US point of view, the present move reflects a desire to expand bilateral relations based on mutual trust. As for as the most substantial sanctions go, the US is likely to relate them to the non-proliferation benchmarks because it is still a high priority matter on the global and regional strategic agenda of USA. At the moment the efforts are to transcend differences of opinion on some basic issues and to establish a practical and working relationship. But the real shape of Indo-US relationship shall ultimately depend on three factors: The stance that India will take on CTBT, the responsiveness of India's economic policies to global economic trends led by the US, and the manner in which India manages its relations with Pakistan.

President Clinton is on a weaker wicket to pressurize India on signing the CTBT, having been refused ratification by US Senate. As for as economic policies go, there is a gradual interaction between the two countries. If US endorse the flow of funds from IMF and IBRD to India, it may overcome the mounting fiscal deficits. In the sphere of Indo-Pak relations, the US, for the first time, de-linked its relations with India from its relations with Pakistan. So far military regime persists in Pakistan, there is no point for India in opposing this element in America's South Asian policies. Only the precaution of maintaining responsiveness and avoiding military confrontation with Pakistan is required on the part of India and that too as for as possible.

In short there is no paradigm shift in the United State's Indian policies, but there are notable undercurrents and impulses indicating Washington's desire to structure a stable and mutually beneficial relationship with India. India should be responsive to these trends without, of course, wishing away basic differences with the US on some vital issues.

Easing sanctions is merely of the extension of the waivers that expired[15] on October 21, 1999. In exercising the authority given to President Clinton by Congress, he waived the same set of sanctions he had lifted on December 1, 1998. Those sanctions had been hurting US commercial interests more than India's economy. President maintained the one punitive action that really affects India—the prohibition on credit lending by international financial institutions (IFIs). Equally important is the fact that the US still maintains rigorous technology sanctions. These include not only the technology controls pre-dating the May 1998 Indian nuclear-weapons tests but the additional dual-use export barriers that were imposed in the months following Operation Shakti.

The essential message that comes out from the partial easing of sanctions against India is that the US is seeking to protect its commercial interests while maintaining political leverage. For the first time US invoked section 102(b) of its Arms Control Act, which had no implementing regulations. But since then, the administration and Congress worked together to evolve regulations that seek to arm Washington with leverage but ensure that US business do not get hurt in the process.

It is a mistake to interpret Clinton's latest sanctions waivers as permanent. They are without a time prone but can be annulled at any point. It will be a bigger mistake to read his action as favouring India more than Pakistan. Clinton bailed out the military regime of Pakistan by resuming IMF assistance flow through especially waiving sanctions of commercial banks lending to Pakistan. While India has no need for IMF assistance, as it is not facing a balance of payment crisis. But it does want credit from the World Bank, which provide long-term development loans. While taking care of Pakistan in respect to IMF, India continued IFI lending curbs.

Sometimes relaxation from time to time serves either to protect the commercial interests (as happened when, within months, many post-Shakti economic sanctions were lifted) or to give the illusion of a softening in the attitude (illustrated by the removal of some Indian enterprises from the Entity List). Sanctions relaxations in one area, sometimes has been followed by new punitive measures in another. Five conclusions emerge out of the impact of US sanctions:[16]

First, post Shakti sanctions has had a minimal economic effect. The economy has performed better in the 20 month period after the imposition of sanctions than in the previous 20 months. The US International Trade Commission confirms this fact when it concluded: "Overall, the Glenn Amendment sanctions appear to have had a relatively minimal medium-to-long term impact on India's economy. They are also benefiting alternative supplies."

It is true that the International Financial Institution (IFI) sanctions have hurt India, but its loss due to extra non-concessional commercial borrowing is difficult to estimate. First, the loan denials by World Bank and ADB have not prompted India, in a majority of cases, to turn to higher interest commercial borrowing. Had it done so, the interest differential would be up to 800 million a year. Second, having got into the habit of securing loan commitments far in access of actual utilization, India still has access to old, un-utilized credit totalling billion of dollars. For the same reasons the impact of the halt to new Japanese ODA approvals has proved to be very little.

The calculated economic impact of the post Shakti sanctions thus has been under 0.2 per cent of India's G.D.P. No doubt the initial psychological effects of US sponsored sanctions were greater, resulting in down turning in the Indian financial markets, down grading of India's foreign currency debt-risk assessment and delaying in some company bond issues, but by 1999 India's credit worthiness upgraded and initial concern about investment inflows dissipated mainly because of the rising of $ 4.2 billion, internationally through the "Resurgent Indian Bonds," which actually restored some exchange-rate stability.

The very factors that protected India from the effects of the 1997-98 Asian financial crises have insulated it from the rigorous of the economic sanctions. Indian economy is not dependent on exports. Moreover, successive government have pursued cautious, step by step liberalization approach, maintaining capital controls that shield the country from abrupt short-turn capital movements and keeping the volatile short-turn foreign debt at a manageable level. The Indian economy relies neither on access to the American or any other single market on multilateral assistance. In the process of liberalizing its economy India took care of a balanced approach limiting external vulnerabilities.

Second, sanctions, nevertheless, remain a potent political weapon to mount pressure on a weak-willed state. The India-Pakistan Relief Act of 1998 and the Greater Sanctions Waiver Authority conferred on President by Congress reflect the flexibility to dangle carrots and reward 'good behaviour'—thus sharpening the political value. The US has employed the sanctions card to build leverage in negotiations with India. Months after the talk began, it blackballed 200 large Indian enterprises, 'a discretionary action' outside the purview of the Glenn Amendment. And it helped ease IFI lending curbs against

Pakistan but not against India. India, although publicly stating that it will not negotiate on sanctions, has allowed itself to come under pressure on that issue.

Third, the pre-existing sanctions actually motivated India to go overtly nuclear. The sanction bugbear was employed by outside powers for years to dissuade India from crossing the nuclear threshold. Shafts at Pokharan were drilled in the early eighties but the testing plans remained frozen, beginning to thaw from late 1995 when an internal government assessment showed that the cumulative international costs of nuclear restraint outweighed the potential cost of overt nuclearisation. Far from winning any rewards, India realized its unique nuclear restraint had increasingly made it a target of technology sanction. A point was finally reached when threat of further sanctions could no longer buy continued Indian restraint. Over-use and prolonged-use had blunted the sanctions tool. Pre-existing sanctions thus played an important role in nudging India to gate crash the nuclear club.

Fourth, a nation's international understanding needs not be affected by sanctions. Instead of getting isolated, a sanction-slapped but indigenously nuclear potential India is increasingly being seen across the world as emerging power with whom cooperation is desired. It was inconceivable two years ago that India would have the kind of strategic dialogues it was conducting with some major powers.

Fifth, sanctions cannot be fought with a clear strategy. As a target of sanctions for decades, India has to evolve a counter strategy that implies a limited leverage it has gained from its market opening initiatives. Sanctions should not remain a one-way street. The same elasticity of the Uruguay Round Agreements and WTO regulations said to permit sanctions and export controls on national security grounds also justifies reciprocal punitive steps. Obviously India cannot hit back in the same areas where it faces punitive actions but will have to select sectors where the sanctions-clamping nation has significant commercial interests. The US strategy of rewarding 'good behaviour' can be emulated by New Delhi to provide favoured market access, especially in the consumer and other lower technology sectors, to nations behaving well towards

India. By enacting a reciprocal Sanctions Act, India will put sanctions imposing countries on notice.

However, circumstances changed, which ended the phase of 'sanction relaxation' and started the era of the lifting of sanctions. The new administration in US gradually developed a perception that sanctions are no more beneficial; quite contrary they are creating hurdle in the required Indo-US relations. Christina Rocca, President Bush nominee to run South Asian affairs publicly stated[17] "the US post-Pokharan-II sanctions against both India and Pakistan must go as they have outlived their usefulness." As Assistant Secretary of State she said:[18] "Two separate sanction reviews were going on in Washington. The first dealt with the general sanctions that the US has accumulated over the past few decades. The second review was about sanction specific to India and Pakistan. The first step in the latter process was looking into sanctions resulting from the 1998 Glenn Amendment." Robert Blackwill, at his confirmation hearing before a Senate panel more or less echoed the views of new Assistant Secretary for South Asian Affairs, Rocca when he said:[19] "Sanctions do not constitute a viable strategy in pursuing America's non-proliferation goal." Senate Foreign Relations Committee Chairman, Joseph Biden urged:[20] "Bush to act speedily by exercising his authority to waive sanctions until the Congress takes action." Another influential Democrat, Tom Lantos announced[21] that "he plans to introduce a legislation in the House of Representatives for lifting the sanctions against India;" that "these restrictions have outlived their usefulness and are no longer in the interests of the United States;" that "economic sanctions apart, the non-proliferation issue should not be allowed to stand in the way of engaging India in greater scientific and defence cooperation either. The US is likely to get further commitments and compliance from India on non-proliferation and test ban agreements by lifting sanctions and engaging in greater scientific and defence cooperation."

Even excesses, inadvertently committed during sanctions were acknowledged and apologized. For instance the US ambassador to India, Richard Celeste said:[22] "Sanctions on science and technology institutions, not involved in research in nuclear warheads and delivery systems was wrong. It was a mistake on our part;" "Sanctions were more of an emotional reaction by the US administration when it felt aggrieved, deceived and spurned by the friend;" "As a result of blanket sanctions some 'crystallography' projects, most importantly the one carried out by Atomic Energy Commission's Chairman, R. Chidambram were also affected. Chidambaram was even refused a visa to the US, where he was to attend a conference relating to his research in the field. It was a mistake to discourage him to participate in the meeting related to his work in 'crystallography,' which had nothing to do with nuclear research. Since he was a nuclear scientist, he was affected by sanctions;" "We need to rise our scientific collaboration so that future misunderstanding do not spill in this area."

Under such growing support for the Bush administration's plan, the United States lifted the 1998 economic and military sanctions against both India and Pakistan. Bush proclaimed:[23] "I hereby determine and certify to the Congress that the application to India and Pakistan of the sanctions and prohibitions contained in the Arms Export Control Act would not be in the national security of the United States." Certifying the scope of Bush's order, US Secretary of State Colin Powell said:[24] "The lifting of sanctions against India and Pakistan was partial. While the post nuclear sanctions were being lifted, other sanctions would remain. In India's case, the Clinton administration had waived a substantive number of commercial restrictions, but key sanctions related to military sale transfer of duel-use technology and economic assistance through international financial institutions remained in place. Some of the restrictions on the export of duel-use technology predates the 1998 sanctions."

India shall be able to overcome the roadblocks in multilateral financial forums and expects to get a wide range of development assistance. After 1998, sanctions by developed countries like US, Japan and Canada, it has had to rest content with the humanitarian aid. As a result of lifting of sanctions, the benefits are:[25] "World Bank, IMF development loans; Blacklist diluted; doors open for full-fledged military ties with US. The existing impact are: Many sanctions on India were waived earlier by Bill Clinton, but waiver are temporary, not the same as repeals.

Pre-Pokharan-II nuclear and technical sanctions remain on both countries."

Technology Transfer. The United States has spurned its dreaded 'Entity List' that bars technology transfer and equipments to a host of Indian Institutions. However, organizations directly engaged in India's nuclear missiles and space programmes will continue to face the squeeze. The revised list liberates a large number of institutions under the Defence Research and Development Organization (DRDO) and several other engaged in diverse activities.

In the DRDO family 21 of 25 institutions have been removed from the list. Units such as Hindustan Aeronautics, Bharat Heavy Electronics Ltd., Bharat Earth Movers, Centre for Development of Advanced Computing and Electronic Corporation of India have all been freed. The bar of premier institutions like Indian Institute of Sciences, Bangalore, IIT Mumbai, IIT Chennai, National Aerospace Laboratory, Bangalore and a number of private sector units also go. In the case of nuclear missile and space related entities of both India and Pakistan, American exporters will require a licence. However it is pointed out that licensing in these cases will now revert to a case-by-case review. The implication of the lifting of sanctions and the pruning of the Entity List are likely to become clear after the close study by the user organizations.[26]

What still stays on the US 'Hit-List' are as follows:[27] (1) DRDO subordinates: Armament R&D Establishment, Pune; Defence R & D Laboratory, Hyderabad; Missile R&D Complex, Hyderabad; and Solid State Physics Laboratory, New Delhi. (2) Department of Atomic Energy Entities: Bhaba Atomic Research Centre, Mumbai; Indira Gandhi Atomic Research Centre, Kalpakkam; Indian Rare Earths Ltd.; Nuclear Reactors Fuel Processing and Enrichment facilities; Heavy Water Production facilities. (3) Indian Space Research Organization's (ISRO's) subordinates: ISRO Telemetry, Tracking and Command network; ISRO Inertial systems Unit, Thiruvananthapuram; Liquid Propulsion System Centre; Solid Propellant Space Booster plant; Space applications Centre, Ahmedabad; Sriharikota Space Centre and Vikram Sarabhai Space Centre, Thiruvananthapuram. (4) Bharat Dynamics Ltd.

Defence Sphere. In the first relaxation of American sanctions in the defence sphere, the Bush administration permitted the sale of spare parts for Indian Navy's Sea-King helicopters. Indian Navy's Sea-King helicopter fleet, thus, got a fresh lease of life. With the arms export market plummeting down by 30 per cent, it seems the US, perhaps, after weighing the commercial benefits and pleas of the British aircraft industry, had little option but to relax the ban. Another significant factor that may have contributed to the lifting of the ban is Rs. 6000 crore Hawk AJT deal, which is being negotiated by India with British aerospace, and the possible purchase of US passenger jets for India's civil aviation sector. However it was a relief for Indian Navy when Bush administration had relaxed the ban on the sale of helicopter spares by Britain to India even if they contained parts of US origin.[28]

Contrary to reports crediting President Bush with more to relax US sanctions on the sale of British Sea-King helicopter spare parts to India, it was former President, Bill Clinton who made this crucial decision on his last day in the office. Clinton signed it on December 19, 2000, but all these things were part under review. The new administration has signed off on it also. The US administration did not notify the Indians on this because it was not the Indians who requested that we do this waiver, it was the British because they were the ones who had the parts. This is a limited number of parts for the Sea-Kings, which India had sent to British and these were stuck there because of sanctions. The waiver allowed these to be sent back to India and that is all the waiver covers.[29]

The Indo-US Defence Policy Group (DPG) on December 3 and 4, 2001 discussed US sanctions on the transfer of dual-use technology. The US is expected to lift sanctions related to nuclear and missile related technology on a case-to-case basis. Sanctions on duel technology were slapped after Pokharan nuclear explosion in 1974. These have been in force since, and India had been forced to take the indigenous route in its defence and space projects. Earlier, the presumption for transfer of technology to India was denial. Now the presumption to any Indian application will be approval, unless there are specific objections, which can be substantiated. Of course, such transfers of technology have to be considered under the ambit of the relevant multilateral regimes.[30]

A US official said:[31] The question will not be what the US has to offer India. It will be what India wants to purchase. The US, in September, had lifted defence related sanctions clamped on India after the Pokharan II nuclear tests. These sanctions related to the joint development of the flight control system of India's Light Combat Aircraft (LCA), technologies with regard to the advanced Light Helicopter programme, servicing and spares for the Sea-King helicopters and the Sea Harrier jets, and the sale of weapon locating radars. India can now approach the US for acquiring these systems. It is also reportedly interested in transfer of technology for the LCA engine, and the acquisition of submarine rescue vessels and the Harpoon anti-ship missiles.

US cleared the sale of seven weapon-systems to India. A Joint Technical Group (JTG) has reached point of agreements in the process for lifting of nuclear and missile related technology sanctions against India. At the third meeting of DPG, held for the first time since Pokharan II, cleared the sale of seven weapon systems sought by India. Since the waiver of the 1998 sanctions, seven applications for export of licences have been approved by the US department of state and defence and are in the process of notification to the Congress. These include the licence for the weapon locating radars (required in Kargil and Siachin). The US has also agreed to expeditiously process the rest of the applications, which includes engines and systems for the Light Combat Aircraft, component for jet trainers and high performance jet engines. To assist the licensing and sale process requirements, a security cooperation group will be set up.[32]

Lifting of sanctions after Pokharan nuclear blasts in 1998 may not be of much consequence to India as punitive provisions were already nullified by the Clinton administration. Two major areas where there could be some relief to India are duel-use technologies and international lending by multilateral agencies like World Bank and Asia Development Bank (ADB). Bharat Heavy Electrical Ltd. (BHEL), Bharat Earth Movers Ltd. (BEML), Larsen & Turbo (L&T), Godrej Boyce, Electronic Corporation of India Ltd. (ECIL) and Kirlosker, which figured in the list of 39 Indian companies, identified by the US administration not to be dealt with, will breath a sigh of relief. Even for these companies, the impact was not either earthshaking or 'adverse' in terms of revenues. But, definitely, it would be a psychological booster for corporates. Export and import of 'duel-use-technologies,' which has hitherto been banned by US even for civilian use, would now be open to India. With regard to defence supplies, lifting the sanctions will help go shopping for 'mission critical high tech components' especially in missiles development projects and spares for the existing hardware.[33]

Psychologically, no doubt, India will have an advantage in export markets. In particular, it would make research in space, biotechnology and chemicals with duel-uses easier with free exchange of information and data worldwide. In the case of foreign lending, the US-exam and other American lending agencies had already diluted the impact of sanctions on exposure in Indian projects. But definitely it will be easier for these lending agencies to take exposure in Indian projects on principles of commercial jurisprudence. With regard to World Bank and ADB, loans were already sanctioned to India on 'humanitarian grounds.' But flow of funds of these agencies to the power sector, roads and highways were definitely affected. For instance, the USA $ 400 million loan of Power Grid Corporation of India Ltd. (PGCIL) was blocked at a Board meeting of World Bank as US representatives vetoed the same. Similarly, NTCP's funds flow under 'time license arrangement' was also delayed. ADB's second line of credit worth US $ 500 million was inordinately delayed. Though large chunks of 'golden Quadrangle' highway project connecting North-South-East-West regions of the country was posed to World Bank, alternative sources of funds were being lined up by NHDP due to sanctions. These proposals may see the light of the day in case India was still interested in sourcing its funds from these multilateral bodies.[34]

On the whole the impression about lifting of sanctions is that those, which the United States had imposed on India after Pokharan-I in 1974 still remained; they were far more stringent. Moreover it is still not clear whether the lifting of sanctions also meant that transfer of technology in nuclear-related and defence fields would be allowed to India.

II. PAKISTAN

Pakistan has been groaning under the weight of multi-layered American sanctions on issues ranging from nuclear proliferation to human rights, democracy and refugee issues. In fact, Pakistan's burden is greater than India's. It had sanctions which President Bush could not waive until his administration could "certify the return of Democracy."[35] The United States has categorically told Pakistan that the lifting of economic sanctions would be possible only if Islamabad reigns in militant groups active in Kashmir and Afghanistan, restores democracy, cooperates in nuclear non-proliferation and improves relations with India.[36]

Washington's sanctions linked to the 1999 coup in Islamabad are expected to remain. Pakistan was under sanctions under the Pressler Amendment even before Chagai Hills nuclear tests. In 1990, Republican senator Larry Pressler campaigned successfully to clamp military and humanitarian aid to Pakistan when proof of country's nuclear programme was available.[37]

The United States has decided to impose sanctions on a top Chinese arms manufacturer for continued sale of missiles technology and components to Pakistan in defiance of an agreement reached last November. Though Beijing and Islamabad have been denying the missile transfer but US intelligence officials have pointed to Pakistan receiving 12 shipments of missile parts from China this year. The parts are meant for production of Shaheen-I missiles and development of the more ambitious Shaheen-II with a range of 1240 miles.[38]

Apart from nuclear and democratic issues, Pakistan is confronted with a new problem. It is among 23 countries put on notice by the United States for failing to tackle human trafficking and could be denied aid unless the issue is addressed by 2003. The first omnibus state-department report on the subject estimates that at least 700,000 people, mostly women and children are victims of trafficking round the world every year: some 40,000 to 50,000 of them end up in the US. The report follows a mandate by the US Congress, which last year (2000) passed the "Victims of Trafficking and Violence Protection Act." To deal with the growing magnitude of this "modern-day form of slavery," the legislation stipulates withholding of aid to countries that do not effectively tackle the problem. "Our report should make it abundantly clear that trafficking is going on all over the world in both developed and developing countries, even within the United States," Secretary of State Colin Powell said while releasing the report. In the US the task force is to be set up to protect the vulnerable and punish the traffickers. Pakistan, according to report, is a "source, transit and a destination country for an increasing number of trafficked persons. Women and children are trafficked for purposes of sexual exploitation, bonded labour, and domestic servitude to the Middle East." It is also a source of country for young boys kidnapped or bought and sent to work as camel jockeys in the Gulf countries.[39]

Despite multi-layered sanctions, the US administration was never dismissive of Pakistan. It talks of US's "long standing friendship" with Pakistan and the need to "sustain and enhance it." Wendy J. Chamberlin, appearing before the Senate Foreign Relations Committee for her confirmation as US ambassador to Pakistan used "Tough Love" as an alternative to 'pressure' relating to sanction issues.[40]

The US administration's swift move, after months of vacillation, owes so much to 'a friend in need is a friend in deed' perception and is largely being viewed as a bid to reward Pakistan for its logistical support to the impending operation against Osama Bin Laden in the wake of development following the September 11 attacks. While the post nuclear sanctions were being lifted, the additional sanctions imposed on Pakistan after General Musharraf's coup in 1999 remain. There is little doubt that Pakistan, as opposed to India, stands to gain for more.[41]

The US senate Foreign Relations Committee, on October 4, 2001, approved a bill, authored by senator Sam Brownback, lifting the remaining sanctions against Islamabad for two years, clearing the way for US assistance to Pakistan. This waive was in addition to last month's waiving of sanctions on both India and Pakistan that had been imposed after both countries conducted their first nuclear tests in 1998. Sanctions related to the 1999 overthrow of the government in Pakistan, however, remain in place, and it is those sanctions that are the subject of the current bill because as senator Brownback said:[42] "Today the Senate took one step closer to helping solidify our national coalition against terrorism. This represents significant progress on an issue that is so important to freeing the administration's hand in working with Pakistan;" and as the Senate Foreign Relations Committee Chairman Joseph Biden said:[43] "Pakistan has chosen to stand with the United States. We need to assist this important front-line state." Thus, the bill, S. 1465, lifts the sanctions imposed on Pakistan following the 1999 coup that overthrew a democratically elected government and brought General Parvez Musharraf to power. The sanctions bar the United States from providing economic and military assistance to Pakistan.

The bill waives the restriction against the countries where a democratic government has been overthrown by a military coup, for fiscal year 2002. Once the bill is to be approved by full senate, and passed by the House of Representatives, President Bush may waive the restriction in fiscal year 2003 if he determines that doing so will facilitate the transition to democratic rule in Pakistan, and if it is important in the fight against terrorism. In addition, the Brownback bill permits an expeditious waiver of sanctions imposed last fall against Pakistan's Ministry of Defence for violation of the Missile Technology Control regime. Under current law, the President may waive these sanctions in the interest of national security, provided he notifies Congress 45 working days before doing so. This bill allows the President to exercise the waiver without delay. Finally, the bill waives provisions of law, which restrict assistance to nations in areas on their payments of official debt to the United States. The United States just rescheduled some of the Pakistan's debt, but that rescheduling does not take effect for 30 days, so this provision allows assistance to flow to Pakistan in the meantime.[44]

In the light of this Bill, besides reviewing the US economic and military cooperation, Islamabad is counting on Washington's support for a massive IMF assistance. It also looks forward to the rescheduling of $ 600 million in debt through the Paris club of creditors. Benefits: World Bank, IMF Development loans; US guarantees and loans; Eligible for military spare parts and officer exchanges. Existing Impact: Pakistan still remains under section 508 sanctions imposed after coup (which is much diluted by Brownback bill, if Bush so desires); Pre-Pokharan nuclear and technical sanctions remain on both countries.[45]

III. APPRAISAL

Regarding sanctions on India and Pakistan a question has usually been raised: Will the United States lift the nuclear related sanctions against Pakistan when it improves these punitive measures in the case of India? The state department is vague on the subject. On the linkage of sanctions *vis-à-vis* both countries, the state department said: "The US was conducting a separate but similar review of policy while looking at sanctions against India and Pakistan." Department spokesman commented in the same breath that any lifting of the nuclear-related sanctions would have less impact on Pakistan since it faced additional restrictions because of 1999 military coup. These curbs would be firmly in place until the country returns to popular rule. The comments on the sanctions came on a day when President Bush announced a waiver, permitting the export of spare parts and ammunition for certain Pakistan Helicopters and armoured personnel carriers. But this waiver is purely to enable Pakistan operations in Sierra Leone as the member of the UN Peace-Keeping force. On nuclear related sanctions *per-se*, Islamabad's contention is that its tests were in response to the Indian Tests in May 1998, so any lifting of the US's sanctions ought to cover both countries.[46]

Another crucial significance is the time and circumstances under which the sanctions has been lifted. Bush administration's lifting of sanctions are widely seen as a "reward" for Pakistan for supporting the US expected military campaign against the Taliban for harbouring Osama Bin Laden. India has been included to avoid resentment and accusation of US one-sidedness.

On May 13, 1998, the then US President Bill Clinton reported to Congress that he had imposed sanctions against India under section 102 of the Arms Export Control Act (Glenn Amendment). It led to termination of assistance under the Foreign Assistant Act of 1961, except for humanitarian assistance for food or other agricultural commodities. Add to that, sale of defence hardware and services was banned; military financial credit and guarantees by US government agencies was denied; bank loans to purchase food was prohibited, besides a ban on export of specific goods and technology which may have civil and military (duel) use unless licensed by the US commerce department. A spokesperson of the MEA said that New Delhi had always maintained that punitive measures clamped in the wake of Pokharan tests were counter productive. The decision to lift them would lead to a 'mutually beneficial relationship'. Sources said that unless the decision included removing the ban on the duel purpose technology, which was there even before Pokharan II, there would be no significant change. If this is removed, there could be possibilities for industrial joint ventures and scientific collaboration.[47]

Food exports were removed from the sanctions umbrella on July 9, 1998 by a senate vote. But later that year, a two year ban was imposed on all US licensed exports to the Indian Space Research Organization as its deal with the Russian Space Agency, Glavkosmos, was found inconsistent with clauses in the Missile Technology Control Regime (MTCR).[48]

With Pakistan set as a launching pad for America's second Afghanistan war, Indian foreign policy is entering one of its more challenging phases. Once again Washington is rewarding a military regime in Islamabad for yielding itself to be used—this time against the Taliban created by Pakistan's state-run terrorist complex. The new rewards approach was underscored by the rapidity with which Bush lifted the remaining 1998 sanctions against Pakistan and India. For almost eight months, the Bush team had been dangling the carrots of the sanctions waiver and the strategic partnership to make Indian foreign policy amenable to its vision. But even after India reversed its policy of isolating the Musharraf regime and held the disastrous Agra summit, the sanctions were not waived because, as the Drezner's 'Conflict Expectation' analysis resounds, the carrot had become a source of vulnerable leverage.

Now within days of Musharraf being forced to sell out the Taliban, Bush lifted sanctions, more to come to the immediate aid of Pakistan's battered economy than to befriend India as part of a strategic plan. Bush's action was designed to be symmetrical in appearance. But not only is its timing self-explanatory, its impact later proved to be asymmetrical. The benefit of the action largely reached Pakistan whose economy had been smothered by the sanctions. The effect on India was marginal and largely symbolic. This is because Bush had withdrawn only the 1998 sanctions, whose effect was minimal on India but severe on Pakistan. The US has not withdrawn the real sanctions that hurt India—the technology controls that began after New Delhi stayed out of the NPT and expanded when it conducted its first nuclear tests in 1974.

In any case, most of the 1998 sanctions against India were waived by late 1999 and those still in place (such as World Bank lending) had been gradually relaxed. With their formal withdrawal, there will be a smoother flow of World Bank Loans to India and greater room for military to military ties. For Pakistan, the Bush action means much needed relief. Washington had already persuaded its close allies such as Japan and Australia to resume aid to Islamabad. This relief will not significantly alter Pakistan's grim economic situation, with the impending war likely to drive away even risk-taking investors.[49]

The American decision to lift the sanctions imposed in 1998 on India and Pakistan was a beginning of a history. The measures were meant to punish the two countries for their attempt to gate crash into the exclusive nuclear club. The step was in keeping with the earlier US efforts to persuade India and Pakistan to sign CTBT and where India was concerned, to cap, roll back and eliminate whatever nuclear weapons it may have. These decisions were taken by Washington with a view to enforce the nuclear non-proliferation Treaty.

All that is now history. Since the sanctions have been deemed by the US to be no longer in keeping with the national interests, they have been withdrawn. As an immediate effect, what it earns is that the status of India and Pakistan as nascent nuclear powers have been recognized, if not approved. The removal of sanctions signaled that the US has little choice but to accept that India (and Pakistan) have moved into the nuclear club. The US, of course, had been moving in this direction for quite sometime, especially under the Republican regime, which has always been more pragmatic in this matter. At the moment, however, it is not the new status of two countries, which is of any relevance. Far more important is the American objective for taking the step. The US is no longer interested in hairsplitting about the nuclear order but about combating the menace of terrorism. Since it has identified Pakistan as a front-line state in this endeavour, it had no option but to be nice to it and lift sanctions. Given its compulsions, the US might have lifted the sanctions imposed after the coup in Pakistan as well. But that is strictly not necessary at present when military and economic cooperation will be enough to keep Islamabad happy.

Having dispensed with the sanctions on Pakistan, these also had to go where India was concerned. The Bush administration had been more amenable toward India in any case. But what it will hope for at the moment is that these steps will ensure a measure of stability in Pakistan while the operation against Taliban is conducted. Since it is going to be a long drawn affair, with the US unlikely to leave the job unfinished as when it lost interest in Afghanistan after the Soviet withdrawal, the impact of lifting of sanctions will be closely watched. Clearly the US will use this show of generosity as a stick to keep Pakistan in line.[50]

The Deputy Secretary of State, Richard Armitage, is reported to have told a Pakistani official that[51] "history began on September 11 when the latter had mumbled something about 'much history' being involved in his country's relations with Taliban." But history also began with the lifting of sanctions to serve as a stick to keep Pakistan in line. Only the reaction of Pakistan in view of its conflict expectation shall be the subject of analysis under the 'Conflict Expectation Model.' As for as India is concerned, it, being neither ally nor adversary, is already outside the purview of this model. Moreover, the lifting of sanctions, which was 'intentional' in respect to Pakistan under the compelling circumstances, was just an 'incidental blessing' or 'spill-over effect' for India. No doubt the September 11 blast had actually blasted the intact cap of sanctions on India and Pakistan. But this blast of the 'capped sanctions,' in respect to Pakistan, was deliberate while in respect to India, was a 'consequential inevitability' of just protecting it from 'unintentional injury' in the process. That is why the condition of 'return of Democracy' in respect to Pakistan has been, conveniently, ignored under the extraordinary situation of national interest while the incidental opening up of the cap of sanction is, consciously, kept intact in areas like duel-use technology in respect to India, which hurts it most.

Such "accidental" change of circumstances, which resulted into "incidental" blessing for India in the form of lifting of sanctions cannot be properly assessed within the framework of the Conflict Expectation Model—as model, consciously developed on the sequence of occurrences, cannot cover 'accidents' and 'incidents' and their consequences. Circumstances change; status of countries differs; priorities clash. As such the application of sanctions, even if identical in nature, is bound to produce different "tone" and "tune" as the cases of India and Pakistan manifest.

NOTE

Except Matto's edited book, referred below, in which the initial impact of India's sanctions, in the context of Glenn Amendment, has been thoroughly investigated and analyzed, the rush of events and rapid changes in waiving, relaxing and lifting of sanctions in the most affected defence and development areas, owe largely to Newspaper reports, write-up and editorial comments.

REFERENCES

1. *Hindustan Times*, June 22,1998.
2. Quoted by N.C. Menon, "Re-thinking on Sanctions," *Hidustan Times, Ibid.*
3. *Ibid.*
4. *Ibid.*
5. G. Balachandaran, "Sanctions and Economic Consequences," in Amitabh Matto (edited), *India's Nuclear Deterrent: Pokharan-II and Beyond*, Har Anand Publications, New Delhi, 1999, p. 228.
6. See for detail concerning US laws, their amendments, various waiver clauses and their impact on India's sanctions, *Ibid.*, pp. 225-36.
7. Brahma Chellaney, "US Action underscores Politics of Sanctions", Hindustan Times, December 19, 1999.
8. Romesh Diwan, "Reality versus Myth," *Hindustan Times*, June 16, 1998; Also see for the 'pruning by the United States of the List of Entities identified for post-Pokharan II sanctions,' R. Ramachandaran, "Sanctions and Contradictions," *Frontline*, Vol. 17, No. 19, September 16-29, 2000, pp. 82-84.
9. Concerning Impact on Defence, see Vishal Thapar, "US Sanctions Crippled Vaval Aviation," *Hindustan Times*, February 4, 2001; *Hindustan Times*, February 3, 2001; and *Hindutan Times*, August 31, 2001.

10. Concerning Developmental activity see Sandipan Sharma, "Pokharan After-shock: 4,500 May Loose in Rajasthan," *Hindustan Times*, August 16, 2001.
11. Romesh Diwan, *op. cit.*
12. *Ibid.*
13. *Ibid.*
14. On partial lifting of sanctions see J.N. Dixit, "A Paradigm Shift?," *Hindustan Times*, November 10, 1999.
15. On easing of sanctions merely the extension of waiver see editorial, "No Cause for Cheers," *Hindustan Times*, October 30, 1999.
16. Brahma Chellaney, "Carrots and Sticks, *Hindustan Times*, March 9, 2000.
17. *Hindustan Times*, May 19, 2001.
18. *Ibid.*, July 25, 2001.
19. *Ibid.*, June 28, 2001.
20. *Ibid.*, August 30, 2001.
21. *Ibid.*
22. *Ibid.*, January 1, 2001.
23. *Ibid.*, September 24, 2001.
24. *Ibid.*
25. *Ibid.*
26. *Ibid.*, September 30, 2001.
27. *Ibid.*
28. *Ibid.*, February 3, 2001.
29. *Ibid.*, February 4, 2001.
30. *Ibid.*, December 1, 2001.
31. *Ibid.*
32. *Ibid.*, December 5, 2001.
33. *Ibid.*, September 24, 2001.
34. *Ibid.*
35. *Ibid.*, July 7, 2001.
36. *Ibid.*, August 2, 2001.
37. *Ibid.*, September 24, 2001.
38. *Ibid.*, September 1, 2001.
39. *Ibid.*, July 14, 2001.
40. *Ibid.*, June 28, 2001.
41. *Ibid.*, September 24, 2001.
42. US Department of State, International Information Programmes, links to internet, Susan Domowitz, Washington File Staff Writer, U.S. Senate Committee Recommends Lifting Pakistan Sanctions, Brownback bill passes senate Foreign Relations Committee,

October 5, 2001, (IIP home/ Index to this site/ Webmaster/ Search this site/ Archives/ U.S. Department of State).

43. *Ibid.*

44. *Ibid.*

45. *Hindustan Times*, September 24, 2001.

46. *Ibid.*, August 15, 2001.

47. *Ibid.*, September 24, 2001.

48. *Ibid.*

49. *Ibid.*

50. *Ibid.*, September 25, 2001.

51. *Ibid.*

7

U.N. Sanctions

I. JUDICIALIZATION OF SANCTIONS

Any form of law, as Jones and Rosen explain,[1] has, as its incentives, a variety of normative, utilitarian and coercive sanctions. For instance, an individual may drive his automobile lawfully because he fears the consequences of wrongdoing (fear of coercive sanction); he may do so as a matter of personal safety (utilitarian sanction); or as a contribution to orderly social co-existence (normative sanction). Likewise among states, compliance with rule of law is rather consistent, and is grounded in normative and utilitarian motives. Governments do generally regard reciprocal behaviour as mutually beneficial, and are often sensitive to international pressures. They wish to avoid reprisal and embarrassing declarations and resolutions brought on by untoward behaviour except when perceived needs exceed the risk of external criticism. Furthermore, states rarely enter into formal international agreements unless they intend to benefit, and unless they intend to comply with them. Nor do they acquiesce in custom over the long run without anticipating benefits. Accordingly, it is not at all extraordinary that state should normally comply with their voluntary obligations. When a state is not a party to formal normative or utilitarian sanctions generally applicable, its behaviour with respect to others may be controllable only through the threat of coercion. Thus coercive sanction takes over where all else fail.

Traditionally, responses to illegal behaviour have been left to aggrieved states. Indeed, international law includes a doctrine of 'self-help,' which permits each state to launch punitive responses to illegal or other noxious acts. But while the doctrine of self-help (a by-product of absolute sovereignty) tries to provide international politics with formal and legal means for sanctions, it is apparent that abuses or excesses actually contribute international anarchy. Primarily for this reasons, twentieth century international organizations have striven to replace unilateral sanctions by collective sanctions.

This process was begun by the League of Nations Covenant (Article 11), which inscribed the principle that "Any war or threat of war...is hereby declared a matter of concern to the whole of League." This concern was activated through Article 16: "Should any Member of the League resort to war...it shall be, *ipso facto*, deemed to have committed an act of war against all other Members of the League, which hereby undertake immediately to subject it to the severance of all trade or financial relations, the prohibition of all intercourse between the nationals of the Covenant-breaking state and the state and the prevention of all financial, commercial or personal intercourse between the nationals of the Covenant-breaking and the nationals of any other state, whether a Member of League or not." The Covenant further authorized the Council to recommend to states what military forces they should contribute for implementation of Article 16.

The principles of League of Nations were greatly expanded in Charter of the United Nations. The Chapter VII of the Charter, entitled "Actions with Respect to Threat to the Peace, Breach of the Peace, and acts of Aggression," authorizes the Security Council to determine the existence of a threat to international stability and to recommend either peaceful measures for its solution or coercive acts short of force. Ultimately, however, in Article 42, the Security Council is authorized to call upon states to use armed force in behalf of the Organization.

This principle of 'all against one'—the entire world against the aggressor—is termed 'Collective Security.' This differs both from self-help, which is the doctrine of unilateral action, and from collective self-defence, which is an alliance arrangement by which a few states agree that attack upon one shall be considered an attack upon all.

Despite the limitlessness of Security Council authority on enforcement action the Council has never undertaken an act of enforcement within the full meaning of the expression and of the Charter provisions due to following reasons: (1) The United Nations is not a government and as such depends upon separate nation state for military forces; (2) Since the Military Staff Committee failed to create a stand-by force in the wake of cold war rival blocs, the ability of the Security Council to act still rests upon state's willingness to be the Council's agent; (3) To this end Article 48 provides that action required to carry out the decision of the Security Council for the maintenance of international peace and security shall be taken by all the Members of the United Nations or by some of them, as the Security Council may decide; (4) Demands for action have been highly politicized and have failed to achieve the concurrence of a majority of the Security Council members—including the permanent members; (5) In creating the United Nations, the great powers sought to prevent action against their own interests by including in the Charter the principle of great power unanimity. Article 27 requires that the matter of substance be decided by a majority of nine of the 15 members, including the concurring votes of the permanent members.

These impediments of the Security Council's actions were responsible that United Nations could vote enforcement in only two or three cases. And even in these cases it cannot be said that collective security was involved within the full meaning of the Charter because, in Korean situation in 1950, the Soviet Union was absent as a result of boycott after UN refusal to seat the Peking representative and in Iraqi case, the concurring vote of Russia was taken for granted in the wake of the collapse of Soviet Union.

Enforcement measures are not the sole means of the United Nations sanctions. Other methods involve diplomatic interventions. Those who consider the economic sanctions as alternative than substitute to enforcement and peace-keeping, regard the later as separate category of UN action though at the initial stages, when such sophisticated classification was not possible (even between enforcement and peace-keeping) the entire Security Council action were counted as varied types of sanctions.

Today the sanction has acquired a definite meaning of its own and is regarded as alternative to force and as non-coercive entity. Today the use of force is considered to be the defeat of the purpose of sanction, *e.g.*, to avoid war. As such economic sanctions acquired special status despite the fact that this category like coercive one, existed since League days. In its economic sanctions, the United Nations has followed in the path of the League of Nations, which undertook economic sanctions against Italy in 1935-36 for its attack upon Ethiopia. In the UN period, the most celebrated economic sanctions have been those voted against China by the General Assembly in 1951 as a result of China's intervention in the Korean war and 1967 decision of the Security Council to isolate Southern Rhodesia for its policy of racial separation following its unilateral declaration of independence from Britain.

As in other cases of economic sanctions, effectiveness in the Rhodesian situation was limited by the twin problems of (i) achieving universal participation and (ii) facing the resistance of national elites to external coercion, especially when the issue was one of prominent international concern. With respect to universal participation, even states usually sympathetic to Britain's policy demonstrated weak compliance. The United States, for example, by executive order imposed restraints upon imports originating in Rhodesia, "provided, however, that the prohibition against dealing in commodities or products exported from Southern Rhodesia shall not apply to any such commodities or products which prior to the date of this order, had been lawfully imported in the United States."

As a matter of international interests, the United States sought formally to implement the Security Council sanctions. But as a matter of self-interest, the US government demurred from full implementation by interpreting the sanctions to affect only commodities in which trade had not customarily occurred between the two nations. The reason was that Southern Rhodesia was a prime supplier of Chromium to the United States, and the continued flow of this resource is necessary for production of steel alloy needed in, among other things, military hardware.

This decentralization of sanctions remains one of the major weaknesses of international law. While international bodies sometimes make decisions in the implementation of sanctions, member states must implement them. The states are the importers and exporters in the international system. They command industrial economies and the passage of goods across national boundaries. Just as Stalin once remarked that pope has no military decisions, so too does the United Nations have no troops of its own, no industries to produce the coveted commodities which, if withheld, might alter the external or internal policies of the states. The UN has no Chromium deposits to withhold from the United States! Furthermore the United Nations is wholly dependent upon its members for operating funds, and whatever decisional authority its members give it, its ability to take action depends not only upon decision, but also upon means. Without the support, the wealth and material assistance of national governments, the United Nations is incapable of effective sanctions. The resistance of governments to a financially dependent UN arises principally from their insistence upon maintaining control over sanctioning process in international politics.

In the absence of reliable system of collective sanctions, individual and group sanctions must be accepted as legitimate within current international law. Until states can achieve their demands through collective actions, governments and their close allies will invoke coercive self-help. As a result, the imposition of individual sanctions is common. Some cases in which sanctions are threatened see no actual implementation. The United States, for example, did not impose measures upon those Latin American states, which nationalized privately owned American property, despite legislation that authorizes to President to discontinue aid in the absence of adequate compensation. In the same way, the Jackson-Brock Amendment imposed restraints upon American trade with the Soviet Union until the latter recognizes and permits its Jews citizens to emigrate. Because Moscow regarded these restraints as interventionary and politically exorbitant, it declined to enter into a commercial agreement offering it most-favoured-nation-status (tariffs no higher than those required of other major trading partners of the United States). Other acts of unilateral sanctions may also be noted. In the fall of 1975, after the United States suffered several embarrassing defeats at the

United Nations, including the majority declaration equating Zionism with racism, it became American policy to threaten with economic sanctions those of its friends who contributed to the continuing embarrassment. In another instance, as a potential recipient of sanctions, the United States was informed by Britain and France early in 1976 that if it refused limited landing rights in American air-ports to the supersonic plane Concorde, they would initiate economic sanctions against the US.

The frequent resort to individual sanctions leads some to conclude that international law is incapable of restraining states, yet the fact remains that much of the conduct of states is regulated by legal means. For instance the law of the high seas is highly developed, though laden with modern complication; except the peculiar situation in Iran (1979-80), diplomatic and consular personnel may rely upon foreign governments for specified treatment, that there exists developed principles for international exchange of fugitive through extradition; and that the host of relatively non-political functions are regulated by international conventions. At the same time it is equally true that power-relations of governments are but sparely regulated and even then imperfectly. The Kellog-Briand Pact of 1928 was considered inapplicable in cases of self-defence, and each state retained the right to determine the conditions and needs of its defence. Article 51 of the UN Charter continues to permit 'individual or collective self-defence' prior to the Security Council's assumption of responsibility. By the same token, neither France nor China entered into NPT until after having achieved its desired level of deterrent capability. And while US, Soviet Union and Britain foresworn nuclear testing at sea and in the atmosphere, they reserved the right to continue nuclear competition by underground testing.

Thus, the 'judicialization of sanctions,' as the 'law of the political context,' is an on-going process, which tries to give to the normative distinction between law, ideology and politics, to the practical distinction between war, coercion and peace, to the sanctity of co-existence and mutually binding obligation, and to the entire spectrum of relationship between international jurisdiction and national jurisdiction, a 'Universal Validity.'

This entire process has been identified with the term 'judicialization,' the sole purpose of which is to erase the "illicity" of sanctions and to minimize the adverse effects on unintended targets. Some of such efforts within the UN system have been undertaken in the subsequent sections.

II. REVITALISATION OF THE UNITED NATIONS

Since the end of cold war, policy makers, political analysts, and the media have heralded a new life for the United Nations in a new world order, citing possibilities for cooperation through a revitalized Security Council and the new role for the United Nations. In addition this new optimism has been echoed in the adoption of sanctions following the military overthrow of the democratically elected Haiti government as well as in response to ethnic conflict in the former Yugoslavia.

Renewed global interest in multilateral sanctions questions the conventional wisdom which rates sanctions as ineffective and disregards them as an alternative to the use of force. Specially, the increased use of sanctions in recent years raises questions about the role of international and regional institutions for the successful implementation of multilateral sanctions, the relationship between sanctions and the use of force and the possibilities for and limitations of, developing the underlying consensus or 'political will' that may be requisite to developing sanctions into a more effective and specific policy instrument. In addition, as sanctions are applied in a broader range of international disputes, questions arises over the different types of target states and the appropriateness of a variety of these specific sanction measures.

In order to assess the usefulness and limitations of sanctions the following areas have been identified:[2] First is the area of goals and targets. The cases of sanctions against Iraq, Haiti and Yugoslavia clearly demonstrate the substantial variation in the goals of multilateral sanctions. Doubts are expressed that the same policy instruments could be equally appropriate for coercion (such as demands for withdrawal of troops, as in the case of Iraq), the enhancement of democratization and human rights (as in the cases of Haiti and South Africa), and peace keeping and promotion of negotiation (as in the case of former Yugoslavia). However following four goals have been identified: (1) Avoiding the use of military force; (2) Appearing to take action; (3) Promoting Human Rights and (4) Creating incentives for collective action on global and environmental problems.

It is realized that the goal of 'appearing to take action' may weaken the 'substance of taking action' and thus contributing to the conventional wisdom that sanctions are ineffective. They may be effective where timing is not crucial and immediate action not required and where target can be isolated. The issue of unintended injury to third parties, including domestic populations of target states has been raised as additional and compelling reason to develop better methods of targeting and to identify more clearly the goals of international actions. The targets of sanctions in addition to national governments are specified as follows: Private firms, corporations or banks; individuals, including national leaders as well as civilians; social groups which have direct or indirect influence on government policies or decisions. Identifying such targets and choosing of sanctions in accordance will actually determine the extent of the vulnerability of target states and the nature of the ambiguity associated with the 'success' of sanctions.

Second is the area of international institutions, enforcing policy choices. The relationship between instruments, goals and targets necessarily involved a broad range of questions about effective implementation of various sanctions measures as well as calls for improved mechanisms for compensating unintended victims of sanctions. As such numerous potential changes in international organizations have been suggested which include: Strengthening the UN Secretariat; Altering the membership and procedures in the UN Security Council; Building bridges between the General Assembly and the Security Council; Developing compensation mechanisms such as under the aegis of Article 50 of the UN Charter; Strengthening the role of the International Court of Justice. Suggestions for changes outside the United Nations include: Promoting a more effective role for regional organizations, such as the European Community and the Organization of American States, in order to decentralize incentives for compliance with the multilateral sanctions; Involving financial institutions such as International Monetary Fund and World Bank in implementing sanctions; Taking advantage of non-governmental organizations in monitoring the implementation of multilateral measures; Considering procedures, which would enable pre-emptive implementation of sanctions. Secondary sanctions measures to be implemented against third parties (collateral participants) in order to enforce compliance with primary sanctions have also been recognized.

Third is the area of developing political will and international consensus. Issues of implementation raised fundamental questions of costs and the political will required for international cooperation. The possibility and improbability of expanding the legitimate powers of the international institutions in relation to sovereign nation state led to consider whether or not states would support such fundamental changes in the international system. While hypothetical change in international organization was recognized as one potential means for increasing international cooperation, the difficulties of developing international consensus on how the Security Council might be restructured, had been emphasized and also doubts expressed if the United States, as leader of Gulf war coalition, would be willing even to consider such a restructuring. To some it seems unrealistic expectation for generating consensus among states that have different goals, interests and domestic constraints; the UN consensus on sanctions against Iraq should not create undue expectations for repeating this kind of broad-based consensus for adopting sanctions in the future. Others point out that perhaps it is unimportant that member states had different reasons for adopting sanctions as long as they are willing to adopt sanctions to attain their diverse goals.

The roles of domestic politics, bureaucratic factors, international media and legal considerations are important in exploring the sources of state's goals and willingness to adopt sanctions. Furthermore, in assessing the influence of domestic politics, not only the importance for leaders of packaging sanctions, acceptable to their domestic audience, but also the importance of domestically generated pressures to adopt sanctions—such as in the cases of South Africa and China in the United States—must also be taken into consideration.

Fourth is the area of expectation and direction for the future. The future use of sanctions depend upon the understanding of the current changes in the international economic and political systems, which have implications of state's perceptions of the utility of sanctions as well as the efficacy of those measures. While the direction of such global changes is uncertain, the changing international role of the United States and an increasing global economy could be potential enough to both enhance and detract from the general utility of sanctions. For instance it is pointed out that if increased international interdependence increase opportunities for using economic instruments for non-economic goals, the costs to sender state of implementing sanctions also rise in such circumstances. In addition, the opportunities for loopholes and difficulties in monitoring substantially increase. Furthermore, recent trends towards economic liberalization in many countries may facilitate the effectiveness of sanctions in influencing target governments because of changes in their domestic constituencies.

The evolving concepts of sovereignty are also adding new issues to the international agenda, such as human rights and bio-diversity. These emerging issues are particularly noteworthy, both because they do not justify the use of force—indeed they make threats of the use of force non-credible—and because they make influence by non-military measures such as economic and diplomatic sanctions more likely. The growing global perception of the need of multilateral, rather than unilateral, action on global environmental problems will promote more effective use of sanctions for enforcing compliance with cooperative measures. Finally, it is also necessary to develop understanding of costs and benefits of using sanctions not only to increase their effectiveness for multilateral policies but also to minimize the adverse effects on unintended targets.

III. APPLICATION

After the end of cold war, the situation in the Security Council substantially changed. Unsolved ethnic, territorial and border problems, particularly, after the dissolution of socialist federations, and the change of regimes in other socialist states, as well as the problems related to the democratization and protection of human rights in all parts of the world, have been internationalized. The maintenance of peace and security calls for a new look.

At the same time, in the Security Council, the readiness of

permanent members to start close cooperation became more and more visible. Consequently, the Security Council allegedly became an active factor in searching solutions for the existing international and other conflicts. And their unanimity in reality appeared to be a new qualitative element in the activity of Security Council. The authority of the decisions of the Council increased. Those concerning the implementation of collective measures under Chapter VII and in the field of peacekeeping forces were adopted without specific difficulties. On the other hand, the political influence of the General Assembly became more and more marginal and not only with respect to the preservation of peace. Moreover the political authority of Secretary General was growing as the head of peacekeeping operations, but also marginalized in practice, by the great powers, the permanent members of the Security Council. The concentration of political activity in the hands of the Security Council may be considered now a confirmed fact.

One of the main results of this development is the new experience emerging from the implementation of the Chapter VII[3] to which Security Council resorted more than before. Trying to contribute to the solution of existing international disputes and conflicts, the Council adopted decisions, which sometimes could be of controversial character. In this respect, undoubtedly, the action against Iraq, because of its occupation of Kuwait (the Gulf War), armed conflicts in the territory of the former Yugoslavia, particularly, Bosnia and Herzegovina and the operation in Somalia—all that put the Security Council in a very awkward position. In all of these three cases, the action was undertaken under Chapter VII and the decisions concerning the implementation of collective measures adopted on the basis of different legal considerations.

In the case of Gulf War, as declared, it was a "violation of the international peace and security" because of the 'invasion' by Iraq and its 'occupation' of Kuwait. However the armed intervention of the organization was not organized on the basis of Article 42 but under Article 51 of the Charter, allegedly involving the "inherent right of individual collective self-defence." The Security Council applied the solution adopted in the past concerning China in the Korean War. The armed action was organized under US command. Whether and to what extent the

UN had the possibility to control the action of the coalition is a question raised by some people. The Security Council, quoting Chapter VII, decided to give to member states the permission to apply the necessary measures to restore peace in the region. In the case of former Yugoslavia, the decisions were adopted under the heading of 'threat to peace' in relation to very different aspects manifested during the long evolution of conflicts on its territory. Starting with the embargo of armed trade, then in many resolutions on humanitarian assistance and security in the protection zones up to the decision establishing International Tribunal for the prosecution of persons responsible for the grave violations of international humanitarian law, the Security Council relied on Chapter VII of the Charter.

Looking at the subjects of these resolution the questions may be, perhaps, asked what are the reasons of this approach? It is not, however, difficult to answer this question. The necessity for ensuring the implementation of adopted measures (insisting on their binding force on the basis of Chapter VII) forced the Council to act in that way. The same may be said for the UN action in Somalia to provide humanitarian assistance to a country devastated by civil war. Undertaken by the US, under the authority of Security Council that action was continued through the engagement of the UN forces that at one point applied reprisals. The action, in fact, was unsuccessful.

The implementation of economic collective measures in the cases of Iraq and Yugoslavia, by their rigidity and scope, qualitatively expanded the previous practice. They were adopted as instruments of political and economic pressure and the condemnation of the behaviour of these two countries. However, looking at the methods of their realization in practice, from the political and economic point of view, it is possible to raise the question of the nature of the effects reached by the adoption of these measures. It seems that the economic collective measures were understood more as a panel punishment rather than an instrument of political pressure. The conclusion may easily be deduced from the argumentation explaining the partial suspension of economic sanctions in the case of Yugoslavia.

Two more recent practices of the Security Council relating to Chapter VII deserve special attention. The first was initiated at the end of the operation in the Gulf War and represents the intervention in Iraq concerning the protection of Kurds by the air force of the US and UK before the adoption of the resolution by the Security Council. Later the Council took the decision to relate the reasons to the protection of human rights and the maintenance of peace and security. Nobody reacted to the Iraqi complaint that the sovereignty and territorial integrity of Iraq was violated. At the same time, the UN observers were sent to the region where Kurdish camps were located. The importance of the second action is of a general nature. It is the question of the consequences of decisions of the Security Council involving NATO in the protection of UNPROFOR and of humanitarian assistance in the armed conflict in Bosnia and Herzegovina. The problem of joint intervention of Chapters VII and VIII of the Charter involved in this action should be carefully considered. Also, the preservation of neutral position of the UN in cases of cooperation with military agreements should not be underestimated.

There has been considerable interest in the application of sanctions both as a response to a flagrant breach of peace and as a preventive measure that might keep a festering problem from becoming a full-scale crisis.

The Security Council has applied sanctions only seven times in its history but five times since 1990.[4] Six countries—South Africa, Iraq, Yugoslavia, Somalia, Liberia, and Libya—remain targets of sanctions. The sharp increase in the application of sanctions coincides with a period in which the Council has also launched numerous peacekeeping operations. Public has began to see the United Nations as a system of law, order and justice. But governments have not equipped it for the size and number of operations now being demanded. This reflects their deep ambivalence about the role they really want for the organization.

The importance of sanctions in the system of collective security has been controversial. On one end of the spectrum is the view that Article 51 of the UN Charter—which provides for self-defence and alliance—is the centerpiece of the security system. On the other end is the idea that sanctions should be the central security enforcement element in a world in which war is increasingly unacceptable. Sanctions, however, while perhaps not the first policy choice for governments, will continue to be used more frequently.

The legal authority for the Council to levy sanctions lies in Chapter VII of the UN Charter. As such, sanctions are enforcement tools meant to address a breach of peace, or a threat to peace and security. The Charter never uses the word "sanctions." Rather Article 41 says the Council "may decide what measures not involving the use of armed force are to be employed to give effect to its decisions." The measures which have been employed include: arms embargo, financial embargo, trade embargo, embargoes of selected goods or commodities, reduction in the status or expulsion from international bodies, cultural and sport boycotts, suspension of technical assistance, air embargo, severance of postal and communication services, and war crime proceedings, among others.

Historically, when the Council has taken action under Article 41, it has most often applied comprehensive sanctions. This is appropriate in cases where there is an egregious breach of the peace such as Iraq's invasion of Kuwait or Yugoslavia's support of Serbian insurgency against the government of Bosnia and Herzegovina. However sanctions need not always be comprehensive. Their most effective use might lie in more limited application at an earlier stage of a conflict.

Usually when the Security Council passes a sanction resolution, its explicit goals are to punish a state for its behaviour and to bring it into compliance with the will of international community as expressed by the Security Council. The legally stated goals—punishment and coercion—are quite clear. However many factors complicate the situation: First, the political goals of some Council members may be more extensive, complex, and even fluid than the Council's various resolutions. For instance, over time, the United States and United Kingdom have publicly stated that they seek Saddam Hussein's removal from power. But that is not the goal of the Council or of many other member states. Given that circumstances, it is extremely difficult to reach agreement on what conditions must be met in order to lift the sanctions.

Second, ambivalence arises as citizens of a target country feel the pain of the sanctions. Most target countries are led by authoritarian regimes, which have insulated themselves from economic privation and democratic pressures. Over time, humanitarian coercion arises. The international community must struggle with the question of how long to impose punishment on the citizens of a country whose leaders are beyond their control.

Third, the interests of neighbouring states and major trading partners must be taken into account. The Council relies on member states to enforce the sanctions. If some of those states are severely damaged by curtailing activity with the target country, their enthusiasm for enforcing the sanctions may wane, even if they generally support the Council's stated goals. The UN Charter provides for international relief to those countries; but, in reality, the resources available for such relief are scarce.

All these concerns are taken into account by the Sanction Committee, which the Council sets up separately for each of the sanction resolution. However these committees are terribly over-burdened. They are engaged in routine administrative matters that became highly politicized in a Committee. For example the Iraq Sanctions Committee had debated whether the delivery of forty cases of Scotch Whiskey should be humanitarian exception to the sanctions. This diverts the Committee's attention from more serious concerns.

Four general categories of sanctions are identified. First, they can be intended to change the behaviour of the target nation. Second, they can be used to limit worsening of a conflict situation. Third, they can be seen as a prelude or alternate to military intervention. Fourth, they can be applied with the intent of changing a nation's regime. However, this final purpose is not a legitimate one for UN sanctions. It would be a clear interference in the internal affairs of a nation and would never be approved by the Security Council.

Further complications arise from the changing role of the Security Council. The Council's more frequent use of sanctions reflects its determination, in recent years, to assert its authority more often. The Council has broadened the definition of a threat to peace and security to include among others, massive violations of human rights and humanitarian disasters. There is a perception among some members of the United Nations that the Council has gone too far and that it is too responsive to the interests of the major powers. The result is that the Council's goals in applying sanctions may not really be embraced by some of these states.

Another evolution is that the council is increasingly interested in representative actions when historically it has been reactive. If sanctions are to be used more frequently and effectively as well as in more preventive applications, visceral actions should be replaced by more systematic planning and targeting. Goal-keeping for more limited sanctions, applied before a dispute erupted, could be more precise. If so measuring their effectiveness would be somewhat easier.

Recent experience with sanctions operations yields two clear lessons: first, the UN Secretariat has insufficient staff and resources to plan and manage this level of activity. Second, there is a lack of clarity regarding the role the United Nations should play in the implementation of sanctions. In order to bolster the sanction capacity of the United Nations, the specific recommendations are made in the areas[5] of option assessment, intelligence, monitoring and enforcement, and mitigating third party spillover effects.

Option Assessment. Sanctions can be effective policy tool if they were designed to fit the specific goals and circumstances of each individual case and if they were applied earlier. Recently Security Council practice on sanctions resolutions has been to simply refer back to the most recent sanctions resolution adopted and approved, almost unchanged, whatever language was used before. For example, the sanctions resolution against Iraq was largely copied from 1960's sanctions resolution against Rhodesia. The resolution against Yugoslavia was modelled on the resolution against Iraq.

This approach is fundamentally flawed. Sanctions that were appropriate for one case may not be best in the next. The goals of sanctions are not identical in all cases. Simply modelling one resolution from the last one does not allow for policies to be crafted to fit the specific circumstances. Further, it risks omission of important provisions. For example humanitarian provisions were initially not included in the Iraq resolution simply because they were not included in the Rhodesian resolution. Humanitarian provisions had to be added later in a separate resolution.

United Nations must develop new options assessment capabilities. The overall goal must be to put the Security Council in a better position to weigh different options and to tailor sanctions to the goals and circumstances of the specific case. Knowledge of the possible options may also give the Council the opportunity to initiate sanctions earlier in a crisis would be more effective than comprehensive sanctions imposed, only after egregious acts have become widespread.

The report to the Council should have several elements. First, it would identify vulnerabilities of the target country. This would include an analysis of the structure of the target country's economy and information on which imports or exports are most important. There should be an analysis of which sanctions would have the quickest impact and which sanctions would have the greatest impact on the leadership of the target country. This information could be used by the Security Council to design sanctions that are targeted specifically for the policy goals in mind. It would also reveal potentially effective options short of comprehensive sanctions. Arms embargo on Yugoslavia was particularly ineffective because the country was already heavily armed and a net arm exporter.

Second, the report should analyze not only which options would place the greatest pressure on the leadership of the target country but also the impact on its innocent people. This could help the Security Council in crafting sanctions so that they have the greatest chance of success. The inevitable estimation and information about humanitarian costs could be used to identify possible options which would minimize harm to innocent members of society while focusing the burden of the sanctions on the vulnerabilities of the governing elites within the target state. Unintended consequences of the sanctions could be reduced if decision-makers had more information about what the effect of their decisions would be.

Third, the report of the Council should anticipate the possible enforcement problem for each policy option. For example, if certain imports or exports are to be embargoed, an assessment should be made of how those goods currently enter or exit the country and how easily those flows could be halted. An assessment of how easily the sanctions could be circumvented should also be made. This information could help the Security Council to craft sanctions that could realistically be implemented. Possible difficulties could be identified in advance, and measures could be taken to address them. Additionally, the Council could have a better sense of how effective various sanctions might be.

Fourth, the report should assess the impact that various sanctions option would have on neighbouring countries and important trading partners of the target-state. Not only could unintended consequences of sanctions be reduced but also possible humanitarian concerns in third countries could be taken into account. The report could explore ways to cushion the native impacts sanctions would impose on third countries. This type of advance planning could reduce unintended consequences and increase the likelihood that sanctions would be supported and enforced by other countries.

If this sanctions impact report was to be useful for decision-making, the research and analysis must begin early. Also by having this information in front of the Security Council early, the Council may be better able to act at the early stages of a crisis with a less than comprehensive targeted sanctions programme, which may be able to prevent the escalation of international conflicts. Developing such option assessment capability report, though essential, would be a significant departure. The United Nations has never had the capability to carry out this type of international, dispassionate analysis in the past. To move in this direction would require the support of member states. At the same time, if sanctions are going to be employed effectively by the United Nations, developing an internal options assessment capacity is essential.

Intelligence. Currently the Security Council relies on the intelligence-gathering and analysis capabilities of a small number of states that have large national intelligence operation, necessary to use sanctions policies more effectively. The problem with this approach is that in many cases the national intelligence analysis of one country is not credible to other member states. Without an independent source of intelligence analysis, concerns can be raised that a state may distort its intelligence assessment to support the policy outcome that state prefers. Conflict over the reliability of intelligence assessment may cause difficulty in reaching a decision to implement a sanction programme.

The United Nations does not need direct intelligence gathering function, but it should develop an intelligence analysis capability. Rather raw intelligence information is readily available from member states, the media, non-governmental organizations, and the public domain. What is needed at the United Nations is the capability to then independently analyze and assess that information.

Intelligence information from a wide variety of sources is gathered and then analyzed by, for instance, the type of Special Commission set up by the Security Council to enforce Iraqi compliance with the destructive weapons provision of the Council resolution. Confidentiality of information has been rigorously maintained. Even members of the Security Council receive only general overviews of the intelligence reports. Information trading between the Special Commission and intelligence sources has improved the quality of the intelligence being gathered. Such analysis capability may be beneficial in activities such as preventing diplomacy and peacekeeping operation.

Monitoring and Enforcement. In addition to developing option assessment and intelligence capabilities, the United Nations should strengthen its capacity in sanction monitoring and enforcement. Currently, the enforcement of the mandatory sanctions is left entirely to individual nations-state. If the Security Council receives a report that sanctions have been violated, the government of the country involved is asked to investigate the incident. The difficulty with this approach is that the countries asked to investigate sanctions violation occurring within their borders have little incentive to report violations, which have occurred. A national government is unlikely to admit to an official policy, which permits or encourages violations of its international obligations. Even in the case of violations by private parties, the government may not want to report violations, which, if stopped, could injure national economic or political interests. Indeed, in practice, countries routinely reply to the Security Council that they have fully investigated the incident and there is no foundation to the allegation of a violation of the sanctions.

To make the sanctions more effective, it was argued that the United Nations should take a more active role in the monitoring and enforcement operations. Several proposals were made along these lines. First, Security Council name a sanctions Coordinator at the same time a sanctions resolution is passed. This person should be experienced senior diplomat who would be charged with the responsibility of coordinating efforts to implement and enforce the sanctions.

Second, the United Nations should draft a model law that nations could follow to translate their sanctions responsibilities into their own legal systems. This would make it easier for states to fulfil their sanctions enforcement obligations. United Nations already provides model laws in such areas as direct foreign investment and humanitarian matters.

Third, the United Nations develop direct monitoring capabilities by posting UN monitors at critical points along the borders of target countries to assure that the sanctions are complied with. The UN terms would be composed of trained custom officers who would monitor the work of national custom officers. These UN representatives would not actively engage in the enforcement activities, such as using force to halt illegal imports or exports. The actual interdiction and enforcement operations would remain the responsibility of local authorities. Rather the UN monitors would report sanction violations to the United Nations. It would be up to Security Council to decide if action would be taken against nations, which do not carry out their enforcement responsibilities. It should be noted that the United Nations is given authority to engage in such activities by the UN Charter. Article 2.7 states that the prohibition as interference in the internal affairs of states, "shall not prejudice the application of the enforcement measures under Chapter VII."

It is suggested that the Sanction Assistance Missions (SAM) programme of the Conference on Security and Cooperation in Europe (CSCE) could provide a useful model for the United Nations. The SAM programme has been used in Europe in the effort to enforce sanctions against Yugoslavia (Serbia and

Montenegro). In this programme, trained European Custom officials have been dispatched to neighbouring countries and key transportation points to monitor compliance and act as a consulting resource for the local enforcement efforts.

Such programme can result in significant improvement in the level of compliance for a very modest investment of resources. At the same time, it was recognized that the UN monitors would not be effective in all situations. For example, if a country had a long coast line or vast expanse of desert along its border, monitors would probably be less effective. However, there are many circumstances under which monitors could add significantly to the success of the sanctions monitoring and enforcement.

Fourth, the United Nations should be more deliberate in seeking to work with regional organizations, such as CSCE, to assist with monitoring and enforcement activities. Regional organizations would be especially valuable for conducting investigation of sanctions violations. Finally, a UN Black list or the imposition of secondary sanctions against companies or countries that violated sanctions has been advocated.

Spillover Effects on Innocent Parties. Sanctions impose significant spillover costs on neighbouring countries, significant trading partners, and private business. These costs are serious impediment to the effectiveness of sanctions. Neighbouring countries may not enforce sanctions because of devastating consequences on their own economies. There are many examples in which the general population of key trading partners has suffered because of sanctions against a neighbouring state.

These third parties should be compensated in some way for their losses. Such compensation would increase support and compliance of sanctions and reduce suffering and injustice burdens placed on the population of neighbouring states. At the same time, while Article 50 of the UN Charter gives injured countries the right to "consult" with the Security Council, the United Nations is not required to provide compensation to injured parties.

Historically the United Nations has not significantly compensated parties making Article 50 claims. It is contended that the funds needed to fully compensate all legitimate claims would be enormous and that it would be extremely difficult for the United Nations to raise the amount of money required. Additionally, it is difficult to evaluate the claims of damage brought before the United Nations. If the nation claimed damages in excess of what seemed reasonable, how would the UN decide what portion of the claim to compensate?

While these concerns are formidable, some ideas were advanced for compensating third parties. Certain states may be exempted from enforcing sanctions against neighbours and important trading partners. In practice 'turning a blind eye' to violations has been the most common response of the United Nations in these cases. A fund of pay compensation claims could be created, by raising money from member states. Alternatively, injured countries could be granted special assistance to mitigate damage or reduce dependence on the target state from international financial institutions such as the World Bank or the International Monitory Fund, but this would also require raising money so that the institutional capacity is not impaired. Finally, the Security Council could suggest to other agencies in the UN system that an injured country receive special attention. Another possible method for compensation would be to require the target state to pay compensation to injured state. However, it was pointed out that this might jeopardize target state reform and recovery and that it would be very difficult to enforce this transfer. It is acknowledged: even these solutions failed to address the issue of private organizations and businesses that were injured because of sanctions. For some sanctions to be effective the United Nations must have increased operational capability. Governments must decide how much of that capability they are prepared to give to the world body.

There are five Security Council Committees on sanctions,[6] namely, the committee established by resolution 661 (1990) concerning the situation between Iraq and Kuwait; the committee established pursuant to resolution 724 (1991) concerning Yugoslavia; the committee established pursuant to resolution 748 (1992) concerning Libyan Arab Jamahiriya; the committee established pursuant to resolution 751 (1992) concerning Somalia; and the committee established pursuant to resolution 841 (1993) concerning Haiti.

Some of these committees have to handle large volumes of work. For example, the Committee on Yugoslavia had to deal with more than 34000 communications in 1993 and more than 45000 communications so far in 1994. The Secretariat does not have adequate resources to process such huge volumes communications expeditiously, with the result that there is a serious backlog in many cases. There have been complaints from requesting governments and international organizations for the delays in responding to those requests. The committees have decided to devolve a great deal of work to their respective secretariats under the 'no-objection' procedure. This has, however, resulted in a further burden on secretariat.

Seven sanctions regimes[7] remain in effect and generate much work for the Council. In order to ensure the adequate servicing of various sanction Committees and the expeditious proceeding by the secretariat of applications for humanitarian supplies, the Secretary General has re-enforced the unit responsible in the department of Political Affairs. For their past, the sanction committees, drawing on their own experience, have initiated measures to streamline their working procedures and to ensure greater transparency in the conduct of their work in conformity with a set of measures[8] decided by the Security Council.

Cooperation on sanctions with regional organizations[9] has been important, with special reference to the contributions of the Organization of American States (OAS) in Haiti and EU and the Organization for Security and Cooperation in Europe (OSCE) in the former Yugoslavia. The temporary assignment of Liaison Officers from the EU/OSCE Sanctions Assistance Mission Communication Centre has provided the secretariat and the relevant committees with customs expertise and with advice on the practical implementation and monitoring of sanctions. Member state could further assist the efforts of the Committees and the secretariat by screening more effectively nation's applications to the Committees and by cooperating in further streamlining of the Committees' procedures.

In order to ensure that the sanctions remain a credible instrument for promoting international peace and security, Member state will need address a range of problems encountered in the implementation of sanctions. Recommendations in this regard were put forward in the supplement to "An Agenda For Peace,"[10] which, in respect to issues and their suggestions, already mentioned, explains the real difficulties, which the United Nations is itself facing. These recommendations are as follows:

Sanctions and recommendations are coercive measures[11] and, thus, by definition do not require the consent of the party concerned. Under Article 41 of the Charter, the Security Council may call upon Member states to apply measures not involving the use of armed force in order to maintain or restore international peace and security. Such measures are commonly referred to as sanctions. This legal basis is recalled in order to underline that the purpose of sanctions is to modify the behaviour of a party that is threatening international peace and security and not to punish or otherwise exact retribution. The Security Council's greatly increased use of this instrument has brought to light a number of difficulties relating specially to the objectives of sanctions, the monitoring of their application and impact and their unintended effects.

The objectives for which Specific sanctions regimes were imposed have not always been clearly defined. Indeed they sometimes seem to change over times. This combination of imprecision and mutability makes it difficult for the Security Council to agree on when the objectives can be considered to have been achieved and sanctions can be lifted. While recognizing that the Council is a political body rather than a judicial organ, it is of a great importance that when it decides to impose sanctions it should at the same time define objective criteria for determining that their purpose has been achieved. If general support for the use of sanctions as an effective instrument is to be maintained, care should be taken to avoid giving the impression that the purpose of imposing sanction is punishment rather than modification of political behaviour or that criteria are being changed in order to serve purposes other than those which motivated the original decision to impose sanctions.

Experience has been gained by the UN of how to monitor the application of sanctions and of the part regional organizations can in some cases play in this respect. However, the task is complicated by the reluctance of governments for reasons of sovereignty or economic self-interest, to accept the deployment of international monitors or the international investigation of alleged violation by themselves or their nationals. Measuring the impact of sanctions is even more difficult because of inherent complexity of such measurement and because of restrictions on access to the target country.

Sanctions, as is generally recognized, are a blunt instrument. They raise the ethical question of whether suffering inflicted on vulnerable groups in the target country is a legitimate means of exerting pressure on political leaders whose behaviour is unlikely to be effected by the plight of their subjects. Sanctions also always have unintended or unwanted effects. They can complicate the work of humanitarian agencies by denying them certain categories of supplies and by obliging them to go through arduous procedures to obtain the necessary exemptions. They can conflict with the development objectives of the Organization and do long term damage to the productive capacity of the target country. They can have the severe effect on other countries that are neighbours or major economic partners of the target country. They can also defeat their own purpose by promoting a patriotic response against the international community, symbolized by the UN, and by rallying the population behind the leaders whose behaviour the sanctions are intended to modify.

To state these ethical and practical considerations is not to call in question the need for sanction in certain cases, but it illustrates the need to consider ways of alleviating the effects described. Two possibilities are proposed for Member states' consideration. The first is to ensure that whenever sanctions are imposed, provision is made to facilitate the work of humanitarian agencies, work that will be all the more needed as a result of the impact of sanctions on vulnerable groups. It is necessary, for instance, to avoid banning imports that are required by local health industries and to devise a fast track for the processing of applications for humanitarian activities. Secondly, there is an urgent need for action to respond to the expectations raised by Article 50 of the Charter. Sanctions are the measures taken collectively by the United Nations to maintain or restore international peace and security. The cost involved in their applications, like other such costs (*e.g.*, for peace-making and peace-keeping activities), should be borne equitably by all Member states and not exclusively by the few who have the misfortune to be neighbours or major economic partners of the target country.

In order to address all the above problems the Secretary General should like to go beyond the recommendation made in 1992—An Agenda For Peace; and suggest the establishment of a mechanism to carry out the following five functions: First, to assess, at the request of the Security Council and before sanctions are imposed, their potential impact on the target country and third countries; Second, to monitor application of the sanctions; Third, to measure their effects in order to enable the Security Council to fine-tune them with a view to maximizing their political impact and minimizing collateral damages; Fourth, to ensure the delivery of humanitarian assistance to vulnerable groups; and Fifth, to explore ways of assisting Member states that are suffering collateral damage and to evaluate claims submitted by such states under Article 50.

Since the purpose of the mechanism would be to assist the Security Council, it would have to be located in the UN Secretariat. However, the expertise of the UN system and in particular, of the Breton Wood institutions should be available to it. Member state will have to give the proposal their political support both at the UN and in the inter-government bodies of the agencies concerned if it is to be implemented effectively.

In the "Agenda For Peace," the question of collective measures was not specially elaborated. However, in the "Supplement"[12] to the Agenda the possibilities of the Chapter VII were thoroughly analyzed. The use of armed collective measures (sanctions) and the collective action in general were considered on a large scale. It is easy, reading the supplement, to conclude that the experience of the Gulf War, of the armed conflicts in the former Yugoslavia, Somalia and the world in general have been very well understood. The lacunae of the Charter as well as the policies of the Security Council, decisions and actions were considered in depth with the aim to improve the UN activity in that field. So the Supplement insists that the concrete purpose of implementation of collective measures (sanctions) should be in all cases defined, clearly stating that in practice the Council was not ready to do it. Also the view is expressed that the collective measures do not represent penal sanctions and they should be interpreted as an instrument of political pressure. Moreover, it is understood that they should be of limited character and that the position of the population and the influence of the long-standing development of economic life should not be endangered. Humanitarian help should be secured as well as the other facilities important for the preservation of standards of normal life. Speaking about collective armed interventions, the Supplement is in favour of their realization by the members and not the passive attitude of the organization confronted with action of individual states. The control of the UN is much more preferable, but it supposes the presentation of regular reports to the Security Council in order to give it the opportunity to influence directly the action in the field.

All the recommendations of the Supplement, though deserve general approval, does not mention the need to proceed to the concrete legal regulations of the main aspect of implementation of collective measures and armed coercive actions it had examined. It remains confined in conforming behaviour with law, contributing to the efficiency of actions of the UN and assisting the work of the Security Council and classifying the rights and duties of the member states. Though the importance of such efforts cannot be neglected or underestimated, but the complex problems concerning the nature and contents of collective measures quoted in Articles 41 and 42 of the Charter, and the possibility to proceed to the use of other steps not foreseen by these provisions, as well as the conditions of their implementation, suspension and lifting are yet to be regulated in some acts and instruments. It is linked perhaps with the overall reformation of the United Nations and particularly with the imperative to enlarge the composition of the Security Council.

IV. SMART SANCTIONS

Sanctions issues and resolutions, covering mandatory measures and mechanism, discussed in the preceding sections, address also, though in a passing reference or up to the extent of realization and concern, the humanitarian exemptions and third state issues. No doubt, the sanction regimes, established by the Security Council, in recognition of such concern, normally do include humanitarian exemption, but some human rights treaty-monitoring bodies have stressed the need for such regimes to include specific measures protecting the human rights of vulnerable groups. The Committee on Economic, Social and Cultural Rights[13] has argued that such considerations must be fully taken into account when the sanctions regime being designed; that effective monitoring must be undertaken throughout the period when sanctions are in force, and that the party or parties responsible for imposition, maintenance and the implementation of sanctions should take steps to prevent any disproportionate suffering being experienced by vulnerable groups within the targeted country. The Committee on the Rights of the Child took a similar approach, pointing out that, in certain conditions, sanctions can act as an obstacle to the implementation of the convention on the Right of Child.

The Inter-Agency Standing Committee[14] composed of all humanitarian agencies emphasized that these humanitarian and human rights policy goals cannot easily be reconciled with those of sanction regime. It established policy guidelines on issues such as the link between human rights and humanitarian action and the humanitarian consequences of economic sanctions. In a statement transmitted to the Security Council in February 1998, the Inter-Agency Standing Committee expressed concern about the adverse humanitarian consequences of sanctions on civilian populations and urged that measures be taken to minimize them.

The embargoes on Sierra Leone, and particularly, the regional embargo imposed on Burundi by its neighbours, have curtailed the supply of foodstuffs and other material needed to alleviate the humanitarian consequences of those sanctions. Field evaluation of this potential and actual humanitarian impact of sanctions on Sierra Leone and the Sudan were undertaken in response to request from the Security Council.[15]

The United Nations experience in Angola, the Democratic Republic of Congo, Sierra Leone and elsewhere[16] have revealed what damage struggles for control over diamonds, timber, drugs, gum and other resources can do to a peace-process. The importance of this issue was highlighted during the year 2000 by debates in the Security Council and by the report of the panel of experts on sanctions against UNITA in Angola. The report revealed the extent to which violations of sanctions, in the form of illicitly mined diamonds, were sustaining the war in Angola. In respect to Iraq,[17] the distinction between having weapons and using them has been debated. While the 'non-use' is the legitimate objective to enforce, it is hard to justify the complete obliteration of Iraq's security system. If the latter is the objective of sanctions, it is uncertain that they will ever be lifted. It is also noted that the 'duel-use' principle adopted by the Sanctions Committee to judge requests for humanitarian exemptions is faulty—almost all goods necessary for human survival have military use, from truck tires to medical supplies. Furthermore, because military and economic measures were imposed as a 'package deal,' it is now politically difficult for the Security Council to lift economic sanctions while maintaining military sanctions. The result of all this is that Iraq's humanitarian damage has been severe; its economy has been destroyed, very few civilians receive full-required daily allowance of food, and disease runs rampant without proper medical supplies. The amount of oil that Iraq can sell under the Oil For Food Programme has increased but this is an empty action since Iraq is unable to pump oil per day with its dilapidated equipment. As is seen in the cases of Iraq and the former Yugoslavia, sanction can take a very long time to work. They can cause enormous collateral damage to civilians and other states before they achieve their objectives. Those who are capable to demonize the UN and those who support the sanctions strengthen rather than erode the support for the regime, thus neither achieving the objective of their own volition nor preventing the damage to civilians and other states.

While articulating principles behind sanctions, two types[18] of them must be taken into account—those, which target internal governance and those, which target international behaviour—with different expected outcomes. If sanctions are imposed with the intention of changing the internal behaviour, there must be domestic support for sanctions within the sanctioned states if they are to be effective. Sanctions imposed to change the international behaviour must be carefully targeted. Otherwise they can cause hardship and run the risk of creating domestic backlash. The Security Council lacks a way to deal with this counter-productive situation should it arise. It should seek alternative mechanisms for enforcing international norms of behaviour on states rather than indiscriminately punishing their civilians.

In this respect, 'financial' and 'diplomatic' sanctions are advocated[19] as the two easiest types to target towards offenders and away from civilians. However, it is argued that more research is needed on the effect of different types of selective and comprehensive sanctions and the experience of the past attempts to target them against transgressors of international norms. Financial sanctions, relatively new by promising innovation, especially merit research. To facilitate the targeting of sanctions, increased consultation among Sanctions Committees, affected states and experts are advocated. Sanctions Committees should improve their success to information and analysis of the facts of a particular case in order to target the initial sanctions and also to revise sanctions and to remain informed of collateral damage.

The Sanction Committees,[20] beside increasing the transparency and their working procedures and making information regarding sanctions and their effects widely available and instead of concentrating on petty punishment of unrelated offences, should allow the sanctioned state to appeal to them to increase humanitarian exceptions and to question the grounds of the sanctions. They should concentrate more to the humanitarian damage caused by sanctions. Humanitarian exceptions are not well designed or implemented; they are subject to abuse as has happened with the duel-use principle in Iraq. The issue of economic collateral damage done to the states that enforce sanctions against a targeted state is especially thorny in case of Iraq as the Oil For Food Programme affects the price of oil with serious ramifications for oil producing and consuming states.

Sanctions have had an uneven track record[21] in encouraging compliance with Security Council resolutions and in recent years their efficacy has been increasingly questioned. In some cases, little if any effort has gone into monitoring and enforcing them. In many cases, neighbouring countries whose trading relations are harmed by sanctions but which receive no compensation for the harm, suffered much of the loss from ensuring compliance; they have not been helped by the rest of the international community and as a result have allowed sanctions to become porous.

When robust and comprehensive sanctions are directed against authoritarian regimes,[22] a different problem is encountered. Then it is usually the people who suffer not the political elites whose behaviour triggered the sanctions in the first place. Indeed those in power, often benefit from such sanctions by their ability to control and profit from black market activity and by exploiting them as a pretext for eliminating domestic sources of political opposition. Thus the costs of sanctions have too often been borne by ordinary people, not by the authoritarian government against which they were directed. Paradoxically, the political elites that compose the regime themselves have often benefited economically from the black markets that have sprung up to circumvent the sanctions intended to exert pressure upon them.

Future sanctions regimes should be designed so as to maximize the chance of inducing the target to comply with Security Council resolutions while minimizing the negative effects of the sanctions on the civilian population and neighbouring and other affected states. A number of governments and numerous civil society organizations and think tanks[23] around the world have explored ways to make sanctions "Smarter" by better targeting them. Switzerland has an effort to design instrument of targeted financial sanctions, including drafting model national legislation required to implement them, and Germany is supporting work on how to make embargoes and other forms of targeted boycotts more effective. The UK and Northern Ireland and Canada have also contributed to the debate on how to target sanctions more effectively. These efforts are now sufficiently more advanced to merit serious consideration by Member states. The Security Council, in particular, must bear them in mind when designing and applying sanctions regime.

The debate on sanctions held in the Security Council in April and the subsequent establishment of an informal working group of the Council,[24] with a mandate to draw up general recommendation on how to improve the effectiveness of sanctions, demonstrated the Council's readiness to consider practical steps to improve sanction regimes. This is a welcome development that should help the Council to oversee the evolution of sanctions into a more potent instrument of deterrence and conflict prevention.

All such efforts resulted into the Interlaken, the Bonn-Berlin and the Stockholm processes, which require some illustration:

Interlaken Process. The Interlaken Process, hosted by Switzerland, is a forum for dialogue among representatives from national governments and regional bodies, central bank authorities, the UN Secretariat, the private banking sector and academia. It focuses on the practical and technical aspects involved in designing effective financial sanctions and ensuring their successful implementation. Mr. Staehelin (Permanent Observer of Switzerland) summarized the key results as follows:[25]

First, a better understanding of the specific technical requirements of targeted financial sanctions and the pre-conditions are necessary for them to be effective. Second, standardized language would enhance a more uniform drafting and implementation of resolutions in this area, as well as unambiguous interpretations. Third, the basic legal and administrative requirements for national implementation of financial sanctions should be identified. This included the development of elements for a national legal framework. Finally, there is the need for the United Nations to develop greater capabilities for the administering and monitoring financial sanctions, including the provision of guidance and technical assistance to help states implement sanctions on a consistent basis.

One of the essential pre-conditions to making targeted financial sanctions more effective is to be able to define the target clearly. And that also implies the effective identification of the actual economic beneficiary of assets. This is key element also for the fight against money laundering and for tracking and blocking more effectively financial flows used for terrorist acts, as demanded by Security Council resolution 1373 (2001).

The Interlaken Process has shown that the conceptual, technical and practical elements required to make targeted financial sanctions effective are available. It is now primarily the matter of mustering the necessary political will at the international and national levels to translate this into reality.

Bonn-Berlin Process. If the Interlaken Process is designed to achieve the goal of minimizing the unintended effects of sanctions on the civilian population of the targeted country and on third countries in the realm of 'financial sanctions,' the Bonn-Berlin Process (1999-2000), initiated by Germany to achieve the same goal with respect to arms embargoes and travel bans. Mr. Kastrup (Germany) explained:[26] These two types of sanctions are identified because they help to focus the unavoidable coercive element of any sanction regime on those most responsible for a threat to peace and security. Dealing with both issues at the same time seemed sufficiently concrete and politically desirable.

Stockholm Process. After the Interlaken Process of Switzerland and Bonn-Berlin Process of Germany, the Sweden government announced to continue the work and invited a broad range of government representatives, non-governmental organizations, regional organizations, academics and UN actors to participate in what is known as 'Stockholm Process.' This project is in continuing stage and final conclusions are yet to reach at the time of writing.

However Mr. Dahlgren (Sweden) explained:[27] The particular focus of Stockholm Process is on the implementation and monitoring of targeted sanctions and on suggesting improvements, building on what has already been done in the process so for. That includes the issue of how to achieve the more coherent and effective enactment of Security Council resolutions into national legislation. It includes how the United Nations and its Member states can better ensure truly effective monitoring of compliance and enforcement; there is much lacking there still. It is also looked at how Member States can best be assisted in implementing sanctions regimes and on what technical and financial support might be called for.

He also suggested a conceptual corrective:[28] If it were possible to find a clearer understanding within the international community of both the scope and limitations, then it might also be easier in practice to pursue a more effective sanctions policy. It is now under discussion how that can be done.

Thus these three processes have been the source of inspiration to the working of the United Nations in the realm of sanctions. An attempt is currently being made to put some Interlaken recommendations into practice concerning sanctions against UNITA. The knowledge gained at Interlaken has been successfully taped and put to use within the concept of the recently established Security Council Committee on Counter Terrorism. In the same way, many of the suggestions of Bonn-Berlin Process have been incorporated. For instance, in December 2000, by resolution 1333 (2000), the Council extended the flight ban and added an arms embargo to targeted financial sanctions previously imposed against the Taliban regime in Afghanistan. In march 2001, by resolution 1343 (2001), the Council imposed a travel ban and an embargo on diamonds from Liberia. In the same way the Stockholm recommendations are contributing to the improvement of the monitoring and implementation of Security Council resolutions. Since many of the Member states lack the capacity to monitor their implementation and require assistance in carrying out this primary responsibility, many of them advocate the establishment of a permanent monitoring mechanism to ensure better targeting and implementation of Smart Sanctions and to bring information on non-cooperation and non-compliance to Security Council's attention.[29]

In order to derive maximum benefit from the recommendations, the Working Group, established by the Security Council under the chairmanship of Ambassador Anwarul Chowdhury of Bangladesh to develop general recommendations on how to improve the effectiveness of United Nations sanctions, was specifically asked to examine a number of issues,[30] including the working methods of sanctions committees and inter-committee coordination; the capacity of the United Nations Secretariat to effectively monitor the implementation of sanctions; coordination within the United Nations system and coordination with regional and other international organizations; the design of sanctions resolutions, including the conditions for the maintaining or lifting of sanctions; assessment reports and the ongoing evaluation of sanctions; monitoring and enforcement; the unintended impact of sanctions; humanitarian exemptions; targeted sanctions; and assisting Member states in implementing sanctions.

All such efforts resulted into the concept of "Smart Sanctions" which seek to pressure regimes rather than peoples and thus reduce humanitarian cost. The challenge is: Maximizing the effectiveness of sanctions while minimizing the harm to civilians. The targeted sanctions are combined with targeted incentives. This is to be achieved by more selective targeting of sanctions or by incorporating appropriate and carefully thought through humanitarian exceptions directly in Security Council resolutions.

These three processes and the recommendations of the Working Group on General Issues on Sanctions prove a valuable contribution to the sanctions debate. These have made the international community conscious of the fact that the risk of adverse effect of sanctions on innocent populations or third parties highlights the tension inherent in the Organization's dual mandate to preserve international peace and to protect human needs. Now the international community realizes that sanctions should be forceful enough to persuade targeted leaders to move towards political compliance, but not so severe as to precipitate humanitarian distress that undermine the viability of the policy and of the instrument itself.

V. APPRAISAL

It is generally realized that 'comprehensive sanctions regimes' are less effective besides having negative humanitarian impact on civilian populations as well as the adverse economic effects on third states. The concept of Targeted Sanctions or Smart Sanctions addresses this concern. Both terms though inter-related but represents differentiated emphasis: The 'targeted sanctions' focus on individuals and groups, responsible for policies across the border or at home, regarded to be threat to international peace and security and as such condemned by the international community while ideally leaving other parts of population and international trade relations unaffected. Targeted means concentration on crucial issues such as finance and arms and focuses on specific groups; it also means regular reconsideration of the sanctions regime and its consequence. In designing sanctions attention is given to ruling elites, rebel movements and terrorists and the means of financing their actions. The objective is to change or restrict their behaviour. The only way to achieve that goal is to consider the imposition of targeted sanctions regimes wherever appropriate, in the form of financial or arms embargoes or of travel or aviation related sanctions.

The 'smart sanctions' assert that sanction regime should neither hit the innocent civilian population nor affect non-targeted nations. This assertion is based on the history of sanctions regimes, which has been guilty of paying a very little heed to the effects of sanctions on the innocent civilians of targeted state and on neighbouring states. Over the past ten years the Security Council has resorted to sanctions more frequently, which has caused international community increasing concern over the tremendous damage done to civilians by comprehensive sanctions. Making sanctions more clearly targeted, avoiding or reducing their humanitarian consequences and effectively resolving the economic problems caused by sanctions to third countries are the main points of emphasis for the advocates of 'smart sanctions'. To them it is not sufficient to select the targets to improve the effectiveness of sanctions but it is imperative that sanction regime must be crafted in ways that shield civilians from unnecessary harm.

Thus, the targeted sanctions concern with the "effectiveness" of sanctions while the smart sanctions concern with the "effect" of sanctions. Though both are mutually complementary, still the question is whether one can make these sanctions more 'effective' and at the same time more 'humane.' This question has, in fact, triggered the search for smart sanctions, which has been taken up through Interlaken, Bonn-Berlin and Stockholm processes. Under the impact of such processes, a broad consensus has emerged in support of sanctions that are designed to affect only those individuals whose behaviour are intended to be changed.

There has been a shift by the Security Council in its approach to the design of sanctions to targeting measures at the individual or individuals responsible for the behaviour or policies condemned by international community and at those elites or groups who directly benefit from such behaviour or policies. The Council now recognizes the need to consider fully the possible negative impact of sanctions on the humanitarian condition of civilian populations and on the economies of third countries. It is to be ensured now that sanctions regimes have no such unintended effects. Recent sanctions on Ethiopia and Eriteria, Sierra Leone, Liberia and the Taliban regime of Afghanistan have all been targeted. In designing these sanctions the Council borrowed extensively from the preliminary work of Bonn-Berlin and Interlaken Processes, as well as from the work of its own Working Group on General Issues on Sanctions. Implementation and monitoring of those sanctions have also followed, to a large extent, the recommendations contained in those two reports. It is a testament to the value of recommendations contained therein that even before they were finalized, the Council has already begun to pay heed to them.

The general discussions round the Interlaken, Bonn-Berlin and Stockholm Processes and accomplishment of Working Group highlights the ineffectiveness of and suggestions for improvement in the sanctions regimes. The views of delegates, expressed at the 4394th meeting of Security Council on 22 and 25 October 2001 are summarised as follows:[31]

Ineffectiveness. The main reasons for ineffectiveness have been enumerated as follows: First, the continuing defiance of and failure to observe sanctions gradually erodes their effectiveness. Second, there is an absence of clear objectives and targets in the sanctions regimes. Third, those who desire to give wider meaning to sanctions resort to extraneous interpretations of sanctions regimes. Fourth, the economic and humanitarian costs outweigh the benefits of the sanctions regimes. As a result some sanctions have not led to compliance with the United Nations Charter; others have led disproportionately negative side effects on civilian population and/or on third states and, in the worst cases, a combination of both. Even the most equilibrated and fine-tuned sanctions still depend on a prognosis of the aggressor's behaviour. The only measure for success is a halt to unacceptable behaviour. But quite contrary, even those with a substantial economic impact on the target, have led to little or no change in behaviour. Too many sanctions are being violated or circumvented. Numerous side effects emerged whereby vulnerable groups have been the hardest hit.

This total situation foils the working. For instance, the Chairman of the Sanctions Committee on Sierra Leone felt the frustration:[32] "Standing there on the border between the country and Guinea and seeing how easily it was to break the oil embargo just by taking another road through the jungle." Likewise, the Chairman of the Sanction Committee on Liberia experienced similar frustration:[33] He had to facilitate the implementation of travel ban list. Since this list was promulgated in June he experienced many difficulties, particularly for removal of targets from such list. But despite suggestions from Bonn-Berlin process, the Sanction Committees are not empowered to keep such list up-to-date. The fact is that these Committees do not have the resources to do this, nor is there any institutional follow up within the United Nations system to monitor the implementation of sanctions.

The representatives of Mali, Columbia, Jamaica, Mauritius and others assert that as a result of such weaknesses sanctions cause the economic woes of the targeted country which, in turn, damage the image of UN sanctions. But Ms Lee (Singapore) pointed out:[34] "This may be due in part to the unintended side effect of sanctions. However, in our view, much of the problem can be attributed to the less than effective implementation of United Nations sanctions to date. Thus, the credibility of the United Nations in relation to the implementation of sanctions has eroded badly in the last ten years. We must arrest this slide."

French representative Mr. Levitte raises another significant issue, relating to weakness, resulting in ineffectiveness of sanctions:[35] Two years of experience with the various *ad hoc* panels of expert created by the Council to monitor sanctions against UNITA, Sierra Leone, Liberia and Afghanistan, or to inquire into the illegal exploitation of the natural resources of the Democratic Republic of Congo, have demonstrated that the problems and the kinds of traffic are the same from one regional crisis to the next. The network and those responsible for violating sanctions and illicit trafficking are frequently the same and in each case the same causes produce the same effects.

He said: For example, the trafficker Victor Bout appears in every report. The panels of experts have worked in the same countries, with the same institutions, and have asked the same sort of questions. Some experts have even had to modify their itineraries in order to avoid arriving at the same time, or just after, their colleagues from another panel. The membership of the various panels has been remarkably similar for a very simple reason: the Council and its sanction committees always need the same kind of expertise, which is lacking in the secretariat. It is also the same expertise that is needed to monitor sanctions and to control and investigate the role in armed conflicts of illicit trafficking in raw materials. This is why an expert on diamonds, an expert on arms trafficking and yet another on financial network is, systematically, found in one committee after another.

The mechanism, which the French representative proposed, would be available to both the Council and the Sanctions Committees under its authority. It would be entrusted with specific task and called on by the Council to draft separate reports on various questions being examined. It would be a matter not mixing everything up, but on the contrary, of gaining full benefit of synergies that exist between the different subjects and crisis, which although not the same, are linked and interconnected.

Various panels have compiled a considerable amount of frequently overlapping data. It is time to use them and deal with them in a more cohesive way. In short, it is time for the Council to be more systematic and to set up an instrument that would avoid any duplication of panels with similar competence, which would waste less energy, time and money.. Another reason for the new instrument is the need to ensure permanence and continuity of the monitoring instrument so long as sanctions are in place. Otherwise, a disastrous political signal would be sent, as is the experience in the case of UNITA and request made by the government of Angola.

Suggestions for Improvement. The discussion on the weaknesses and the resulting ineffectiveness led the representatives turn to suggestions, beyond what is already said as a corollary, for the improvement of sanctions regime. If sanctions can be improved and be made effective, it will also strengthen the authority of the Council. Improving the effectiveness of sanctions requires the enhancement of internal institutional mechanism within the United Nations system, including the development of a more effective monitoring capacity within the secretariat, adequate staffing, streamlining of procedures and the homogenization of the guidelines and working methods of the Sanctions Committees, visits by the representatives of the sanctions committees, technical experts and support, and improved cooperation with regional organizations, non-governmental organizations and international financial institutions.

In order for a sanction regime to be effective and enforceable, Koonjul (Mauritius) suggested some achievable benchmark:[36] First, sanctions should be established and applied only in accordance with the provisions of the United Nations Charter. Hence, there is a need for more explicit, unambiguous and result oriented resolutions. Second, sanctions cannot be imposed on a state in perpetuity, and must be clearly targeted. There must be a 'sun-set' clause, based on either results or time frame. Third, sanctions should be imposed incrementally, with a gradual ratcheting up of the pressure. Fourth, sanctions should be reviewed and assessed regularly by the Council. Fifth, sanction regime should, at all costs, avoid collateral damage, especially to innocent civilians. Durrant (Jamaica), while echoing the same suggestions, added[37] that Interlaken and Bonn-Berlin processes should serve as guideline for streamlining the Council's design, implementation and monitoring of sanction regime. Levitte (France) suggested:[38] the adoption of the conclusions of the Working Group on General Issues on Sanctions as quickly as possible; the setting up of a unified, permanent instrument to monitor sanctions and the traffic in raw material in armed conflict; and making such permanent instrument possible to establish long term working relations with regional and technical organizations, such as the Organization of African Unity, the Economic Community of West African States, the Southern African Development Community, Interpol, the World Custom Organization and the International Civil Aviation Organization, whose cooperation is indispensable in order to ensure respect for sanctions. Fall (Assistant Secretary-General for Political Affairs) pointed out:[39] Beside serving as point of contact between Security Council and international and regional organizations, this 'Framework' might allow more systematic follow-up for those who violate the sanctions or who do not cooperate with sanctions committees. He emphasized that the technical expertise is urgently needed in the secretariat in such areas as military technology, illegal arms trafficking, illicit diamonds, customs regulations and investigations, and international finance and asset management. He recognized that the task of monitoring sanctions is no doubt the primary responsibility of Member states, but at the same time accepted the fact that many of them lack the capacity to monitor their implementation and require assistance in carrying out this responsibility. He suggested that the Security Council can encourage state compliance by continuing to devote greater attention to mitigating the negative effects of sanctions measures on civilian populations and third states. Providing support and inducements for neighbouring states could also greatly enhance the potential effectiveness of sanctions. He also pointed out that many Member states do not have the legal authority and administrative capacity for implementing these measures. To assist them, the United Nations could develop examples of model legislation that could enable interested Member states to make the necessary adjustments in their domestic laws and regulations to permit compliance with the United Nations sanctions. In short, he concluded, making sanctions smarter will not be enough; the necessary means and will are required for them to succeed.

Franco (Columbia) has streamlined the whole discussion round five aspects of improvement:[40] First is the effectiveness of sanctions in three areas as Bonn-Berlin process specified: The first area is the image of Security Council and the way in which it is perceived. If sanctions are not fair, if they do not have the proper basis and support, the Council's work will be perceived as inappropriate and improper and its relevance will be questioned. Secondly, if sanctions are not effective, the image and the legitimacy of the Council will be compromised. Sanctions must work; in other words, they must produce the anticipated results. Thirdly, the Bonn-Berlin and Interlaken Processes have prompted to think about the need for the Security Council to communicate with other actors—not only with non-members of the Council but, in particular, with protagonists that are relevant to the implementation of such sanctions, especially banks and other financial organizations, private sector enterprises, academic institutions and civil society organizations that have a relevant role to play in the implementation and monitoring of sanctions.

The first point, comprising three areas, is concerned with the effectiveness of sanctions. The second point is related to the 'effect' of sanctions. The challenge is to produce changes in the conduct of actors whose activities represent a threat to international peace and security. The difficulty for the Security Council, however, is how to produce that change in behaviour without affecting those who are not a threat to international peace and security—the civilians.

The third point is related to the concept of smart sanctions. This is not the static concept; it is a dynamic concept. New technologies, new ideas, new political circumstances and new international challenges should infuse dynamism in this aspect. Therefore the proposal to create a standing monitory mechanism deserves study to see if it is or is not compatible with the need to adjust to specific circumstances. In this context, the Stockholm Process, which provides an informal opportunity to discuss in depth the benefits and difficulties of this mechanism, should be recognized before doing it in the Security Council.

The fourth point is related to the implementation of Security Council resolution 1373 (2001). With the implementation of the A.41 of the Charter, a new path with great challenges has opened. Resolution 1373 has not created sanctions, but its implementation and monitoring could lead to the Council to undertake measures. In other words, a normative structure is created that will allow this organ to adopt decisions by means of smart sanctions. This could constitute an additional view of reflection for the Stockholm Process, as it involves substantively domestic legislative process and steps and actions taken at that level to implement them. Finally, the conclusions of the Working Group on sanctions must be adopted as other members have emphasized.

The entire discussion round ineffectiveness and suggestions for improvement manifest an irony: How to minimize the humanitarian impact of sanctions without weakening the impact of targeted sanctions as its possible inevitable consequence. Cunningham (USA), while accepting the sanction-approach—'greater than persuasion but less than the use of force'—to employ the collective will of the community, points out:[41] "There is some irony underlying the council's effort to develop and impose effective sanctions. Despite our best efforts, what can we do when a dictatorial regime itself holds its own people hostage? What are we to think when a state or government denies its own people food, medicine and shelter-items the international community is willing to provide to those most challenged? While the United States recognizes the importance of minimizing the humanitarian impact of sanctions, members of international community must also reflect on the humanitarian impact of not imposing sanctions. Such a decision has also consequences. This is a heavy responsibility for the Security Council members and one that we all should take most seriously."

Guofong (China) arrests:[42] that if harm to civilian population is checked, humanitarian consequences are avoided or reduced, economic problems caused by sanctions are taken care of, such targeted sanctions can be more effective, meaning thereby that the 'mentioned' irony can automatically be resolved. He further points out that sanctions are only a means and not an end in themselves. Recently there has been much talk about the so-called 'exit strategy' of peace keeping operations. We also need an exit strategy for sanctions—that is when deciding to impose sanction regime, the Council should consider and decide how to end the sanctions once the goal has been reached. There should be no more sanctions with no clear objective, no time limit and no well-defined conditions for lifting them.

Thus one emphasizes the danger of humanitarian consequences of not imposing sanctions, the other asserts the damage already done as a result of imposing sanctions in perpetuity without any clear goal and time framework. One conceive that too much emphasis on humanitarian aspect would inevitably weak the sanction regime itself, the other perceive that taking care of unintended effects would strengthen the sanction regime. This tussle, as well as the tilt to either side is reflected in every statement of the representatives. However, some delicate balancing has also been emerged: If sanctions are a useful tool that the Council can employ in specific circumstances, under the Charter, it is also true that because of their negative and undesirable effects, they have become the source of legitimate concern for the international community. That is why the Council must develop sanctions regimes that are functional and cause the minimum undesired secondary effect.

This tussle and the feasibility of balancing has ultimately made the international community extremely cautious of the fact that the introduction of sanctions is an extreme measure to be applied only where all other methods of bringing political impact to bear have been exhausted, and when the Security Council determines that there is a real threat to the international community. It is realized that sanctions must be introduced strictly in accordance with the provisions of the United Nations Charter and the norms of international law. They must seek clearly stated objectives; they must be carefully targeted; they must be subject to regular review; and they must set forth clearly the conditions for lifting them.

REFERENCES

1. Section: 'Judicialization of sanctions' draws on Walter S. Jones and Steven J. Rosen, *The Logic of International Relations*, fourth edition, Little Brown and Company, Boston, under the sub-heading: 'The Sanctions of International Law,' pp. 447-55. The material serves as the foundation of understanding the ongoing efforts discussed in the subsequent sections.

   Notes: The term "Judicialization," essentially, involves turning something into a form of judicial process. It is seen from two perspectives: Judicialization induced by the courts and Judicialization induced by politicians and administrators. In respect to sanctions, the politically inspired Judicialization is used to improve the defendability of decisions. It puts emphasis upon the role of reasons and of principle in the "Judicial," as distinguished from the "Legislative" or "Executive," appraisal of conflicting values. The Jurisdiction of the politics of Judicialization may roughly be said to signify upgrading the first principle at the expense of the second. Since 'ongoing process' is, recently, being, increasingly, reposed in the judicial process to shelter the conflicting issues of sanctions, hence, the term "Judicialization" seems preferable.

2. See the United Nations and Multilateral Sanctions: New Options for US Policy? Report of the Thirty-third Strategy for Peace, US Foreign Policy Conference, The Stanley Foundation, October 22-24, 1992, pp. 4-10.
3. The relevant sanction-related portion of the analysis of the Chapter VII of the UN Charter has been taken from: Milan Sahovic, "The Chapter VII of the UN Charter after the end of the Cold War," in

M.S. Rajan (editor), *United Nations at 50 and Beyond*, Lancer Books, 1996, pp. 161-63.

4. *See*: Political Symbol or Policy Tool? Making Sanctions Work, 24th United Nations Issue Conference, Stanley Foundation February 19-21, 1993, pp. 11-15.
5. *Ibid.*, pp. 15-24.
6. Boutros Boutros Ghali, S.G. of the UN: "Building Peace and Development," Annual Report on the Work of the Organization. UN, NY, 1994, p. 15, para. 32.
7. Boutros Boutros Ghali, S.G. of the UN, "Confronting New Challenges," Annual Report on the Work of the Organization, UN. NY, 1995, p. 20, para. 45.
8. See the Document: S/1995/234, March 29, 1995.
9. Annual Report, 1995, "Confronting New Challenges," *op. cit.*, p. 21, para 46.
10. *Ibid.*, p. 21, para 47 (Supplement to An Agenda For Peace, Doc. No. A/50/60-S/1995/1).
11. See for detail, Boutros Boutros Ghali, An Agenda For Peace, second edition with new Supplement and Related Documents. UN, 1995, pp. 25-28, paras 66-76.
12. For comments on the Supplement to Agenda For Peace see Milam Sahovic, *op. cit.*, pp. 163-66.
13. Kofi A. Annan, S.G. of the UN, "Partnership with Global Community," Annual Report on the Work of the Organization, UN. NY, 1998, p. 21, para 63.
14. *Ibid.*, p. 21, para 64 and p. 44, para 127.
15. *Ibid.*, p. 45, para 130.
16. Kofi A. Annan, S.G. of the UN, "Common Destiny: New Resolve", Annual Report on the Work of the Organization, UN. NY, 2000, p. 24, para 73.
17. United Nations of the Next Decade Conference, Stanley Foundation, June 7-12, 1998, p. 12.
18. *Ibid.*, pp. 21-22.
19. *Ibid.*, p. 22.
20. *Ibid.*
21. Kofi A. Annan, S.G. of the UN, "We The Peoples of the United Nations In the 21st Century," Annual Report on the Work of the Organization, UN, NY, 2000, pp. 49-50.
22. *Ibid.*, p. 50, Annual Report, "Common Destiny," *op. cit.*, p. 34, para 99.
23. *Ibid.*
24. Annual Report, "Common Destiny," *op. cit.*, pp. 34-35, para 101.

25. UN Security Council, Fifty-Sixth Year, 4394th meeting, 22 October 2001, p. 3.
26. *Ibid.*, p. 4.
27. *Ibid.*, p. 5.
28. *Ibid.*, p. 6.
29. *Ibid.*, pp. 6-7.
30. *Ibid.*, Resumed Meeting, 25 October 2001, p. 3.
31. See Security Council 4394th meetings, 22 and 25 October 2001; Watson Institute for International Studies at Brown University, Swiss, which has taken further additional research; Handbook which reflects the result of Interlaken Process; Handbook containing the practical results of the Bonn-Berlin Process; Kofi A. Annan, Secretary General, "Preventing War and Disaster," Annual Report, 1999, pp. 40-41, paras 124-26; Kofi A. Annan, Annual Report, 2001, pp. 34-35, paras 85-87.
32. Security Council Meeting 4394, 22 October 2001, p. 5.
33. Security Council Meeting, 25 October 2001, p. 9.
34. *Ibid.*
35. *Ibid.*, 22 October 2001, pp. 8-9.
36. *Ibid.*, 25 October 2001, p. 5.
37. *Ibid.*, p. 3.
38. *Ibid.*, 22 October 2001, p. 9.
39. *Ibid.*, pp. 7-8.
40. *Ibid.*, 25 October 2001, pp. 6-7.
41. *Ibid.*, p. 7.
42. *Ibid.*, pp. 10-11.

8
Conclusion

Sanctions, whether military or economic, in unilateral or multilateral initiatives, have long been used in international politics as instrument to secure political or economic advantage and maintain indirect control. Military sanctions may involve destruction, occupation, subjugation or domination; economic sanction may involve limitation on export, import, trade and services. But the important considerations are the purposes, the goals and consequences involved with measures of military or economic coercion. This consideration is particularly pressing in respect to economic sanctions because, comparing to quick, sporadic and immediate impact of military sanctions, the economic sanctions have complex and far-reaching consequences. If purposes, goals and repercussions are not clear, economic sanctions prove to be ineffective; even sanction itself may fall somewhere between diplomacy and violence.

Gradually a perception developed that reliance upon threat and coercion rather than rewards and incentives, provide an unbalanced spiral of negative responses; better outcome may be realized if policy is based on the notion of 'relationship management' rather than 'coercive reaction.' But it is argued that balanced policy cannot be sought so long the concerned nation modifies its behaviour. For instance, the US perceives that Iran must change its behaviour first, only then a balanced policy can be applied or adopted to resolve the current conflict.

This argument seems to be unconvincing, firstly, because it is based on "unilateral" rather than "mutual" interest; and secondly, because it manifests "differentiated" rather than "uniform" policy in its application. If despite unchanged behaviour, reflecting either in the violation of human rights or

MTCR regime, the USA is pursuing 'relationship management' rather than coercive relations with China, why should it postpone the 'relationship management' till Iran changes its behaviour? A reaction to uprooting from Iran and an aspiration to gain root in China may be the possible reason behind differentiated policy. But any such motive, if at all true, erodes the very basis of sanctions, which can only be effective in a state of neutrality and condition of impartiality. The restrained behaviour in respect to China while reactive behaviour in respect to Iran wears away the sanctity from sanction even before evolving the mechanism for its implementation. Such sanction becomes merely a strategy to secure political and economic advantage or settle a score and for this purpose to maintain an indirect control rather than an international regime to monitor and effectively control the untoward behaviour of any state.

If the strategic situation in relation to other states and the capacity to fight external aggression are crucial and recognized sources of strength of a country, then sanction regime definitely attacks the very concept of national sovereignty and freedom. This realization changed the attitude of Russia and China towards the use of arbitrary sanctions, which has already reflected lack of consensus on the issue within the UN. The strategies of imposing sanctions on the so-called 'rogue' nations in the past few years have helped the target nations to gain worldwide sympathy. Particularly, in order to force change, the USA imposed unilateral sanctions against Iran. Those sanctions have become problematic, as economic incentives for doing business with Iran have grown, tempting both European and American firms to pursue opportunities in that economy.

Thus, the unilateral sanctions, in particular, have had very limited success; they usually succeed when the USA holds disproportionate economic power or when the economies of the target state are particularly dependent on the US economy. Occasional and circumstantial success in sanctions cannot set precedent to be developed into a 'regime' in future.

Besides being ineffective for target states, the unilateral sanctions are not even in the interests of United States. They destroy the value of local investment that improves the situation of those employed by American firms; they force US firms to pass on an attractive business opportunities; they place US businesses at a significant disadvantage in comparison to competitive firms, not subject to US firms; they confuse private actors when, for instance, the US oil company responded to European competition in Iranian business while mixed signals were being sent by the US government; they impose limitation upon US corporations and thus force them to become unreliable partners. When the targeted state manages to acquire substitute goods and services from non-US firms, unilateral sanctions cause significant harm to US companies without creating substantial problem for the targeted state's economy.

It is pointed point out that sometimes it becomes necessary to respond to political demands made by important constituencies in the sending state, which want the government to align itself with their views; in such circumstances political loyalty rather than the effectiveness of sanctions becomes more important. Sometimes demonstration of disapproval of massive violence of human rights becomes necessary even if such demonstration involves ineffective unilateral economic sanctions.

Though such political pressure is unavoidable, still the fact remains that such public demands flow from the unfortunate necessity to develop policy by reaction to events rather than by anticipation and planning that would avoid wasteful responses. Sanctions, where moral response is necessary, are approved provided more effective means are adopted, which involve pro-active engagement in situations before they become crisis.

Due to such constraints the imposition of unilateral sanctions have become less preferable. But military sanctions have also their own constraints: Global economic interdependence, aberration of democratic constituencies to the loss of military and civil casualties resulting from the application of military force, the aversion of the voters to reliance upon military intervention as a political tool are the factors which diminish the support for increased reliance on military coercion. Quite contrary the possibility of cost sharing among the states of common interests have made the multilateral alternative to either military or unilateral sanctions more important.

Thus, multilateral sanctions are preferable not only because they have equal impact on all suppliers of the target state but also because, comparing unilateral sanctions, the multilateral sanctions have less possibility of becoming arbitrary. However, the multilateral sanctions programme that does not provide humanitarian assistance could cause civilian casualties at an unacceptable level making military force less heinous alternative. Moreover, military force cannot totally be removed from economic sanctions; naval task forces may well be the part of economic sanctions since they can be required to enforce measures at sea.

It is acknowledged that limitation on multilateral sanctions flow from political complexity of arranging the necessary cooperative effort. The political work that is required prevents the rapid implementation. However, collective action reflects consensus on the applicable norm. Although defectors from the sanction regime stand to make significant profit from illicit trade, the collective decision places that defector in an awkward position. Well-designed multilateral sanctions programme can be effective.

The imposition of pressure on the weakest and more vulnerable citizens of the target state provides limitation on any sanction programme and international news coverage of hungry children can cause resistance to multilateral sanction programme. In order to overcome this side effect such sanctions can narrowly directed towards responsible elites in the target country. These 'smart sanctions' can involve freezing foreign assets, limiting travel or interfering with financial transaction. The globalized economy, coupled with new technology, facilitated the option, not available earlier, to resort to narrowly focused financial targeting.

However, the multilateral sanction, though effective, but is still in its infancy—there is few effective mechanism for its implementation; there is a relatively passive approach in their use; there is little clarity on what sanctions mean; and there is a need for professionalism, planning and exit-entry strategies. In order to avoid such pitfalls, often the use of incentive rather than punishment is suggested as an alternative means to sanctions. These incentives may be political contacts with the target state or they may be economic, using success to foreign assistance of various sorts to encourage compliance with the relevant international norm by the target states. But reward for merely compliance with norms, obligatory for all states, is not sufficient to alter the behaviour of target state. It contains the element of appeasement. Moreover, it is doubtful that deeper international involvement and constructive engagement may provide significant incentives to bring about the desired change in the target state's behaviour. It did not lead to an alteration of South Africa's apartheid policy. Similarly it is doubtful whether engagement of China will lead to significant alteration in that nation's human rights policy. Greater engagement in the international community may offer good opportunities for long-term change, but near term compliance issues might not be resolved by this approach.

The entire discussion revolves round the "Unilaterality" and "Mutuality" of sanctions; the former generates 'arbitrary' behaviour while the later develops 'multilateral' behaviour. In respect to arbitrary behaviour, the question is: What are the safeguards, and how far, are they effective? Concerning the multilateral behaviour, the question is: how should one to overcome the involved dilemmas? Two safeguards have been provided against arbitrary actions of disputing states: They, instead of sitting in judgment on their own cause, may either resort to arbitration or to an impartial judgment of a third party. Though neither an arbitral tribunal nor the International Court of Justice has right or power to apply sanctions, but it is presumed that once states accept third party judgment, they would normally accept the results; enforcement action is rarely needed. Second the arbitrary action of state has been modified by various treaties such as League of Nations Covenant, Kellog Briand Pact and the United Nations Charter, restricting the freedom of states to resort to war or measures of reprisal.

But despite such safeguards and the attempt of modification of state's behaviour, the crux of the problem, as explained by Carr, is as follows:[1] "The element of power is inherent in every political treaty. The content of such a treaty reflect in some degree the relative strength of the contracting parties. Stronger states will insist on the sanctity of the treaties concluded by them with weaker states. Weaker states will renounce treaties concluded by them with stronger states as soon as the power position alters and the weaker state feels itself stronger enough to reject or modify the obligations."

Even after treaties have been quite voluntarily accepted, states sometimes conclude that they will gain more by violating them rather than observing them. This is especially true of treaties of Alliance; a state which finds that time has seriously reduced the benefit of alliance or increased its risk may not likely be prepared to abide by its obligation. Frederick illustrates:[2] "Since the possible effect of an alliance is to draw a third party into a war which is not of his doing, the strain on the treaty is very great unless both allies feel at the same time that they are equally threatened. It seems too much to expect that a nation, which has no interest in the outcome of war, will risk its very life merely to fulfil a promise contained in a treaty alliance." This is the dilemma of all the disarmament treaties:[3] "The further nations go by international agreement in the direction of eliminating bombs and installations the stronger becomes the temptation to evade the agreement." Such paradox is associated with sanctions as well.

The multilateral dilemma is reflected in the query once Dulles raised:[4] "If police force serves as deterrent to individual act of violence within states, why should we not in the international field adopt a similar procedure?" The reason is that domestic order is possible, not because the state is always prepared to suppress violence among the substantial part of the population, but because the state provides peaceful means for resolving conflict between individuals. As long as the peaceful procedures are available to them, most people will accept these alternatives to force. A police force can deal effectively only with marginal and usually abnormal elements, which do not accept the social forms agreeable to most of the people.

In the international field, sanctions play such a comparable role; they cannot themselves be a primary method of avoiding violence. This task can be achieved by the creation of a balanced form of world society. Until this is achieved, it is premature to consider sanctions. When it is achieved, the role of sanctions will have shrunk to small dimensions and the problem of their form will be one of management proportions. As it is, the premature development of sanctions has led to their discrediting in many quarters.

Sanctions manifest limitations in other two ways:[5] First, they may operate as a challenge to states. The dynamic nations, feeling themselves to be the likely subject of sanctions by *status quo* nations, are tempted to build up their armament and attain economic self-sufficiency. When state reacts in this manner, the result is accentuation of nationalism and the encouragement of the very policies, which the sanction concept is supposed to prevent. Second, sanctions encourage the tendency towards undeclared war. The invocation of sanctions is contingent upon the announcement of the existence of the state of war. But in an effort to avoid commitment the authority can pretend to see no war when none has been declared. The failure to declare war can thus disrupt the whole system of sanctions.

This phenomenon of sanctions is uncertain. As such it is suggested:[6] Sanctions work when they are swift, forceful and pursued in cooperation with front-line states. Comprehensive and rigorously enforced sanctions, which rarely sustain, may more likely to succeed than limited unilateral actions, which usually show the sign of failure even before their implementation. The dilemma is that the "swift" and "comprehensive" sanctions, which ensures success, is extremely a rare combination, while the "swift" and "unilateral" action, which is easily available at one's will, leads to failure. The resolution of this dilemma and the recommendations for a more workable sanctions regime are consistently under consideration within and without the United Nations. However, since sanctions, up till now, fail to achieve, fully, the purpose for which they are originally imposed, the down graded objective as narrow goal is usually accepted as a saving device. And even when sanctions do not achieve even narrow goal of inducing 'some' changes, they are useful symbolic tool for isolating violators of internationally accepted norms of behaviour.

This descending order of the justification of sanctions indicates that its success and failure, instead of inherently, should be extraneously determined. As such, more than the analysis of the 'apparent' failure and 'implied' success of sanctions, the assessment of the attitude and behaviour of the inflictors of sanctions must be treated as crucial and significant. Nelson Mandela, while giving interview to the Guardian, has drawn the attention to this very fact. He said:[7] I am resentful about the type of thing that America and Britain are doing together. They want to be policemen of the world; Britain has joined the USA in this regard. It is totally wrong attitude. They must persuade those countries like China and Russia, who threaten to veto their decisions at the UN. They must sit down and talk to them. They just cannot ignore them and start their own action.

Mandela was apparently upset at the bombing of Iraq and Kosovo by Britain and the US without taking a prior sanctions from the UN. He pointed out:[8] "The message they are sending is that any country which fear a veto can take a unilateral action. That means they are introducing chaos into international affairs—that any country can take a decision which it wants." Moreover, it[9] "undermined the role of the UN as a forum for the peaceful resolution of conflict around the globe. They send a message that the powerful will police the world. From there it is only a step to chaos in the world affairs, as power is substituted for the security of collective and democratic decision." He said that US and British planes petrol no-fly-zones over Iraq and frequently clash with air defences. The zones were declared by the West after the 1991 Gulf war and are designed to protect groups opposed to Iraq's President Saddam Hussein. NATO conducted a 78-day bombing campaign against Serbia to protect ethnic Albanians in the province of Kosovo. Against the description of this background Mandela asserted that[10] "powerful nations should not bully other members of the UN into following their line. The principle that all differences can be resolved through talk and negotiations applies also within organization like the Security Council of the UN and there can be no justification for unilateral action that imposes one's view over others in that body."

Mandela went on to imply that there was a racist motive behind the neglect of the UN. He illustrated that[11] "The US did not do this—unilateral decision—when the Secretary General of the UN was white. They are doing it now, ignoring the UN under Kofi Annan. And there are many people who are whispering that it is because the Secretary General is black. That perception is disturbing." Mandela warned that powerful Western countries, such as United States and Britain, risked sparking global conflict if they tried to police the world alone. He emphasised:[12] "When two nations take it upon themselves to police the world...without getting the authorization of the United Nations, we must condemn that because it can lead to another war."

All the suggestions for the improvement of the sanctions regime must serve, not as 'protective' of but as 'corrective' for the above cited attitude and behaviour. Such plane speaking is beyond any justification, interpretation or need for developing model to justify the initiator's behaviour or to prove, even if by other means, the niceties of success or failure. Such plane truth and bare facts confirm the essence of the cause behind all the difficulties, dilemmas and paradoxes mentioned in the preceding chapters.

The behaviour-corrective and effective policy tool feed on each other. Sanctions as a tool can be used to influence policy decisions. Like any tool, sanctions must be used selectively for the proper purpose to be effective. A wood chisel will not work on metal. A hammer serves a different purpose than a saw. Similarly tools can be altered and improved. A saw in meter-box will cut more precisely than a saw alone. The message here is that sanctions should be used only when they are the best available tools for the work at hand and when there is reasonable likelihood that they will do the job. Further they should be continually improved and sharpened to increase effectiveness.[13]

The record of sanctions has been mixed. Sanctions imposed on South Africa certainly influenced the government's decision to end apartheid. However, sanctions imposed on Serbia have not altered its policies towards its neighbours. Sanctions imposed on Rhodesia (now Zimbabwe) helped establish government representing all of the people while against Haiti, it failed to topple the military dictatorship. The Iraq sanctions raise, at least, three issues: Were the sanctions given time to be effective? Were they an appropriate response to an invasion of a sovereign nation? Is there real international agreement on the goals of continuing sanctions in Iraq? While circumstances in each of these and other cases are different, eight lessons are drawn from the past use of sanctions:[14]

First, sanctions are too often imposed without adequate thought to their objectives or a plan of action. Second, sanctions should be imposed with clear and defined goals, which are understood by all concerned. When this is the case, imposing and removing sanctions become easier. Third, sanctions are generally slow to affect the targeted country's leadership. Their impact must "trickle up" from the populace, as the poor and the innocent are generally the first to feel the pain. Fourth, sanctions take time. If sanctions are to be used as more than merely a symbol of censure or a precursor to military force, then they must be given time to work. Fifth, sanctions can be counter-productive. The targets of sanctions may succeed in portraying themselves to their people and others as victims. Overtime, sanctions may appear bullying and unfair. They can seriously distort the target country's economy, shifting wealth to unprincipled profiteers. Sixth, sanctions work best where there is continuing and substantial support from a segment within the targeted country and from business, media and other nations—particularly adjacent ones. Seventh, the external side effects of sanctions must be considered and remedied or compensated. Article 50 of the UN Charter acknowledges this, yet it has not been used in any meaningful manner. Eighth, the modalities and scope of sanctions should reflect their goals. The kinds of sanctions used to promote human rights or protect the environment should be different from those used to induce a country to withdraw its troops from another nation.

In short, if sanctions are to be effective in altering national behaviour, the United Nations must, before imposing them, carefully, plan, set goals, determine modalities, assess long term support, consider side effects and circumstances, and be prepared to give them ample time to work.

This leads to some critical questions about sanctions:[15] What are reasonable goals and expectations for sanctions? Under what circumstances are they likely to be effective in altering behaviour? Can some of these circumstances be defined generally or must they all be defined case by case? How can sanctions be honed to impact a specific target's group? Can they be designed to maximize pain on a nation state's leadership and minimize the harm to innocent citizens? What sanction-modalities—restrictions on the flow of particular goods, financial restrictions and blockades to name a few—will work best when sanctions are imposed? Despite the answer being country-specific, can guideline be developed? Can new forms of sanctions, such as inducements, prove effective in some circumstances? How can the international community build support for and maintain participation in the application of sanctions? How can the United Nations be strengthened to implement sanctions more effectively? What role can or should regional organizations such as the Organization for African Unity and the Organization of American States play in the application of sanctions within or outside of their regions? What steps are needed to activate use of Article 50 of the Charter to deal with 'spill-over' effects? Can inter-governmental and non-governmental organizations be used creatively to make sanctions work better? Can the International Monetary Fund be involved in designing and monitoring new financial sanctions? Can organizations such as Human Rights Watch or Green Peace participate constructively in the monitoring of sanctions in areas where they have expertise? What role do the media play? How can humanitarian relief be used to relieve the suffering of the poor and innocent? What should be the relationship between diplomatic sanctions and military force? Is a linkage between sanctions and military enforcement necessary?

These critical questions, spread over the entire canvas of the sanction issues and under consistent discussions at various forums, are put together to show that in an effort to find out the solution they manifest kaleidoscopic effects: If wide spectrum of these questions are taken into account, their interconnectedness leaves the impression of 'ramification' of sanctions; if adverse consequences are produced, they result simply to show the 'paradox' or 'dilemma' of sanctions; if the suffering of people rather than regime is emphasized, it hits and hurts the initiator; if the issue of the third party damage is taken into consideration, the problem of compensation' emerge. In short the attempt of resolving issues have generated further chain of issues but no clear picture of finally resolving the sanction issues has emerged so far. In order to overcome this vicious circle some suggested guidelines are proposed, which may be summarized as follows:[16]

There are limits to the ability of even the sole super-power with all its nuclear weapons to impose its will on other or to control conflicts and bring them to an end. The United States should utilize sanctions but as a part of consistent larger package of foreign policy tools.

Proper assessment of the overall situation is crucial. Policy-makers should understand the risk of humanitarian emergencies flowing from effective sanctions. Where multilateral sanctions are considered, the UN should rely on independent research analysis to obtain reliable statistics and information on the potential impact of future sanctions to consider the possible reactions to them and to critique the viability of implementation. With unilateral sanctions, an independent Commission should be established to perform similar function.

Promising technologies should be explored. Financial sanctions show promise. Freezing assets and prohibiting financial transactions can be effective, and new technologies can improve the prospects for sub-measures. Banks now have automatic name recognition programme that are being revised to eliminate false positive responses; other countries have been willing to cooperate in the use of these programmes.

The sanctioning multilateral body or government should expressly consider whether sanctions are more appropriate than other measures. The sending state or organization should decide on the ultimate goals in order to determine whether sanctions are more appropriate. For example, if the change of government is desired then the existence of a viable alternative governing group becomes critical. Without the existence of a viable political alternative, sanctions can generate defensive nationalism.

If broader sanctions, rather than targeted ones are chosen, then the sanctioning state or organization must ensure that humanitarian relief will be available to the victims of the policy. When the UN is the sending organization, there must be an effective aid-distribution mechanism managed outside of the United Nations to ensure neutrality and credibility. Money for humanitarian aid should come from voluntary contribution.

When sanctions are imposed, there must be constant monitoring of effects on the target state. Monitoring would allow progress to be observed; it will also allow flexibility in the implementation to allow adjustment.

Finally lifting of sanctions should be planned in order to maintain credibility. Every sanctions regime should have a 'sun-set' clause. The sending organization or country must ensure accountability by establishing a maximum time for application. Especially the United States should be wary of creating permanent sanctions by frustrating legitimate efforts towards compliance by the target state.

These suggestions are not new; they are the part of issue-analysis and outcome-evaluations. The purpose of their 'assemblage' at this point is to emphasize that sanction policy, instead of leaving it to political vagaries or whims of the initiator must be anticipatory and effective. Sanctions are not the plaything of 'throwing weight around' otherwise, for instance, "Bush would 'loose weight' of support on Iraq war;"[17] and now he is loosing at its consequences as well. This is the fate of every sanction if the 'corrective of selective nature' remains the real intention. This may conserve the arbitrary conduct but at the cost of developing any norm, leaving behind a long chain of paradox and dilemmas. Such repeated consequence suggests that diplomats must do their homework before using the tool. Government should not resort to sanctions for domestic political reasons or for expediency due to lack of consensus on more effective alternatives. Enforcement, compliance and consistency are all necessary ingredients to a successful sanction policy. Sanctions can be viable and credible policy if used rarely, cautiously, wisely and in concert with other foreign policy tools. Sanctions are acceptable under specific circumstances, provided they are free from 'political gain and civilian pain.'

REFERENCES

1. E.H. Carr, *The Twenty Years' Crisis 1919-1939*, Harper and Row, N.Y., 1946, p. 190.
2. Frederick Sherwood Dunn, "The Common Problem" in Bernard Brodei, (ed.), *The Absolute Weapon*, Brace and World, N.Y., 1946, p. 9, Quoted by Vernon Van Dyke, *International Politics*, (second edition), Vakils, Feffers and Simons Pvt., Bombay, 1966, pp. 284-85.

3. Frederick, *Ibid.*, p. 15.
4. Quoted. Norman D. Palmer and Howard C. Perkins, *International Relations*, Scientific Book Agency, Calcutta, 1969, pp. 198-99.
5. *Ibid.*, p. 199.
6. David Cortright and George Lopez (eds.), *The Sanctions Decade: Assessing UN Strategies in 1990s*, Lynne Reinner, 2000, review appeared in *Foreign Affairs*, Sept./Oct. 2000, p. 131.
7. Vijay Dutt from London April 5, *Hindustan Times*, April 6, 2000.
8. *Ibid.*
9. *Hindustan Times*, April 14, 2000.
10. *Ibid.*
11. *Ibid.*, April 6, 2000.
12. *Ibid.*, April 14, 2000.
13. Political Symbol or Policy Tool? Making Sanctions Work, 24th United Nations Issue Conference, The Stanley Foundation, February 19-21, 1993, p. 7.
14. *Ibid.*, pp. 7-9; Also see The United Nations and Multilateral Sanctions: New Options for US Policy? 33rd Strategy for Peace, US Foreign Policy Conference, The Stanley Foundation, 1992.
15. 24th United Nations Issue Conference, *Ibid.*, 9-10.
16. US Sanction's Policy: Balancing Principles and Interests, 38th Strategy for Peace, US Foreign Policy Conference, The Stanley Foundation, 1997, pp. 15-16; Also see 33rd Strategy for Peace, 1992, *op. cit.*
17. A Heading from *Hindustan Times*, August 17, 2002.

Bibliography

BOOKS

Adjer-Karssom, *Western Economic Warfare,* Alamqvist and Wiksell, Stockholm, 1968.

Amitabh Matto (ed.), *India's Nuclear Deterrent: Pokharan II and Beyond,* Har Anand Publication, New Delhi, 1999.

Andrew Mack (ed.), *Asia Flash Point: Security and Korean Peninsula,* Allen & Unwin, Canberra, 1990.

Anthony, H. Cordesman and Ahmad, S. Hashim, *Iraq: Sanctions and Beyond,* West View Press, Boulder, 1997.

Bela Bhatia, Mary Kawar and Marian Shahin, *Unherd Voices: Iraq Women on War and Sanctions,* International Study Team, London, 1992.

Bernard Brodei (ed.), *The Absolute Weapon,* Brace and World, N.Y., 1946.

Bruce Russett & Harvey Starr, *World Politics: The Menu for Choice,* W.H. Freeman and Company, Boston, London, 1989.

Carr, E.H., *The Twenty Years Crisis 1919-1939,* Harper & Row, N.Y., 1946.

Daneil Drezner, *The Sanctions Paradox: Economic Statecraft and International Relations,* Cambridge University Press, U.K., 1999.

David, A. Baldwin, *Economic Statecraft,* Princeton University Press, Princeton, N.J., 1989.

David Cortright and George Lopez (eds.), *The Sanctions Decade: Assessing U.N. Strategies in 1990s,* Lynne Peinner, 2000.

Donald, L. Losman, *International Economic Sanctions: The Case of Cuba, Israel and Rhodesia,* University of New Mexico Press, Albuquerque, 1979.

Eric Hoskin, *The Truth Behind Economic Sanctions: A Report on the Embargo of Food and Medicines to Iraq* in Ramsey Clark *et al. War Crimes: A Report on War Crimes Against Iraq,* Maissonneuve Press, Washington, 1992.

Fernando Teson, *Humanitarian Intervention: An Enquiry Into Law and Morality,* Transnational Publishers, N.Y., 1988.

Frederic, S. Pearson and Martin, J. Rochester, *International Relations,* Random House, N.Y., 1984.

Gary Clyde Hufbauer, Jeffrey, J. Schott and Kimberly Ann Elliot, *Economic Sanctions Reconsidered: History and Current Policy,* second edition, Institute for International Economics, 1990.

Geoff Simons, *The Scourging of Iraq,* second edition, Macmillan, London, 1998.

Hayes Peter, *Pacific Power-keg: American Nuclear Dilemma in Korea,* Lexington Books, Toronto, 1990.

Iraq Situation Report For SCF (UK). *Save the Children Fund,* London, 1991.

John Baylis & Steve Smith (eds.), *The Globalisation of World Politics,* Oxford University Press, 1997.

Lisa Martin, *Coercive Cooperation: Explaining Multilateral Economic Sanctions,* Princeton University Press, 1992.

Lori Fisher (ed.), *Enforcing Restraint: Collective Intervention in International Conflict,* Council on Foreign Relations, N.Y., 1993.

Loyed Brown John, *Multilateral Sanctions in International Law: A Comprehensive Analysis,* Praeger, N.Y., 1975.

Minoslav Nincic and Peter Wallensteen (eds.), *Dilemma of Economic Coercion: Sanctions in World Politics,* Praeger, 1983.

Mitchell Reiss, *Without The Bomb: The Politics of Nuclear Proliferation,* Columbia University Press, N.Y., 1988.

Oberdorfer, Don, *The Two Koreas: A Contemporary History,* Reading M.A. Addison-Weseley, 1977.

Palmer & Perkins, *International Politics,* CBS Publishers, Delhi, 1985.

Pramila Srivastava (ed.), NAM: Expanding Frontiers, Noida Publishing House, Noida (U.P.), 2000.

Rajan, M.S. (ed.), *United Nations at 50 and Beyond,* Lancer Book, Delhi, 1996.

Robert O. Keohane & Joseph S. Naye, *Power and Inter-Dependence,* Scott & Foresman and Company, Boston, 1989.

Sana-at-Khayyat, *Honour and Shame: Women in Modern Iraq,* London, 1990.

Soul Bloom, Miller, J.M., James Warner and Philippa Winkler (eds.), *Hidden Casualties,* Earthscan Publications, London, 1994.

Theodore, A. Couloumbis & James, H. Wolfe, *Introduction to International Relations: Power and Justice,* Prentice Hall of India, 1986.

Thomas, G. Weiss *et al.* (eds.), *Political Gain and Civilian Pain: The Humanitarian Impact of Economic Sanctions,* Rowman & Littlefield, Lanham, MD, 1997.

Vernon Van Dyke, *International Politics,* Vakil, Feffer & Simons, Pvt., Bombay, 1969.

Venter, D.J., *South Africa Sanctions and the Multinationals,* Cardin Publications, Sussex, 1989.

Willem, C. Smit & Jean Pierre Revel, *Report of the Assessment Mission to Iraq, January 11, 1994—February 11, 1994,* International Federation of Red Cross and Red Crescent Societies, Amman, February, 1994.

ARTICLES

Balachandaran, G. "Sanctions and Economic Consequences," in Amitabh Matto (ed.), *India's Nuclear Deterrent: Pokharan-II and Beyond,* Har Anand Publication, New Delhi, 1999.

Braken Paul, "The North Korean Nuclear Programme as a Problem of State Survival," in Andrew Mack (ed.), *Asia Flash Point: Security and Korean Peninsula,* Allen & Unwin, Canberra, 1990.

Bulletin: NGO's Coordinating Committee on Human Rights (NCCHR)/66; 67, September 15, 2000.

Christopher, C. Joyner, "Sanctions, Compliance and International Law: Reflections on The United States' Experience Against Iraq," *Virginal Journal of International Law.* Fall, 1991.

Denis, J. Halliday, "UN and Iraq's Weapons of Mass Destruction," *Current History,* February, 1999.

Diana Weathers, "Life Under Sanctions," (World Food Programme), *WFP Journal*, June, 1991.

Eric Roulean, "America's Unyielding Policy Towards Iraq," *Foreign Affairs*, Jan./Feb., 1995.

Franklin, L. Levin, "Asphyxiation or Oxygen? The Sanctions Dilemma," *Foreign Policy*, Fall, Carnegei Endowment for International, 1996.

Fredrick Sherwood Dunn, 'The Common Problem" in Bernard Brodei (ed.), *The Absolute Weapon*, Brace and World, N.Y., 1989.

Gale Cardoze, "A Slow But Steady Decline," *The Middle East*, August 1998.

George, A. Lopez and David Cortright, "Pain and Promise," *The Bulletin of Atomic Scientists*, May/June, 1998.

Hass Richard, "Sanctioning Madness," *Foreign Affairs*, 76 (6), 1997.

James Barber, "Economic Sanctions as a Policy Instrument," *International Affairs*, Vol. 55, No. 3, July, 1979.

James Blessing, "The Supervision of Foreign Aid: A Macro Analysis," *Polity*, 13, 1981.

James, C. Ngobi, "The United Nations Experience With Sanctions" in David Cortright and George Lopez (eds.), *The Sanctions Decade*: *Assessing UN Strategies in 1990s*, Lynne Pienner, 2000.

John Galtung, "On Effect of International Economic Sanctions" in Minoslav Nincic & Fetter Wallensteen (eds.), *Dilemma of Economic Coercion*: *Sanctions in World Politics*, Praeger, 1983.

John D. Green, "Strategies for Evading Economic Sanctions" in Minoslav Nincic & Peter Wallensteen (eds.), *Dilemma of Economic Coercion*: *Sanctions in World Politics*, Praeger, 1983.

Louise Coinker, "The Gulf War, Sanctions and Lives of Iraqi Women," *Arab Studies Quarterly*, Spring, 1993.

Man Dowty, "Sanctioning Iraq: The Limits of the New World Order," *The Washington Quarterly*, Vol. 77, No. 3, 1994.

Maggie Grey, "UN Sanctions Against Iraq: The Human Impact," *Current Affairs Bulletin*, May 1994.

Margaret, P. Doxey, "International Sanctions: A Framework for Analysis with special reference to the UN and Southern Africa," *International Organisation*. Summer, 1972.

Milan Sahovic, "The Chapter VII of the UN Charter after the End of Cold War," in M.S. Rajan (ed.), *United Nations at 50 and Beyond*, Lancer Book, Delhi, 1996.

Nicholas, J. Wheeler, "Humanitarian Intervention and World Politics" in John Baylis & Stev Smith (eds.), *The Globalisation of World Politics*, The Oxford University Press, 1997.

Nye Joseph, "Soft Power," *Foreign Policy*, 80, 1996.

Paul Taylor, "The United Nations and International Organization" in John Baylis & Stev Smith (eds.), *The Globalisation of World Politics*, The Oxford University Press, 1997.

Peter Wallensteen, "Economic Sanctions: Ten Modern Cases and Three Important Lessons" in Minoslav & Peter Wallensteen (eds.), *Dilemma of Economic Coercion: Sanctions in World Politics*, Praeger, 1983.

Ramachandaran, R., "Sanctions and Contradictions," *Frontline*. Vol. 17, No. 19, September 16-29, 2000.

Schlesinger, "Fragmentation and Hubris," *The National Interest*. 49, 1997.

Thomas, G. Weiss, "Sanctions as a Foreign Policy Tool," *Journal of Peace Research*. Vol. 36, No. 5, 1999.

STANLEY FOUNDATION REPORTS

Richard, W. Cottam, Khomeini, the Future and the US Options, Policy Paper 38, The Stanley Foundation, Muscatin Iowa, USA, 1987.

Beyond Cold War Thinking: Security Threats and Opportunities, 25th UN of the Next Decade, The Stanley Foundation, 1990.

Change and Stability in the Middle East: How Do We Go There From Here? Vantage Conference, Stanley Foundation, 1991.

Collective Security and the United Nations: An Old Promise in A New Era, 26th UN of the Next Decade Conference, Stanley Foundation, 1991.

The United Nations and The Multilateral Sanctions: New Options for US Policy? 33rd UN of The Next Decade for Peace, US Foreign Policy Conference, Stanley Foundation, 1992.

The UN Role in Intervention: Where Do We Go From Here? 28th UN of The Next Decade Conference, Stanley Foundation, 1993.

Political Symbol or Policy Tool? Making Sanctions Work, 24th United Nations Issue Conference, Stanley Foundation, 1993.

US-UN Relations, Vantage Conference, Stanley Foundation, 1995.

The Future of US Persian Gulf Strategy, 36th Strategy for Peace, US Foreign Policy Conference, Stanley Foundation.

The Persian Gulf: Challenges for A New Administration, 37th Strategy for Peace, US Foreign Policy Conference, Stanley Foundation, 1996.

US Sanctions Policy: Balancing Principles and Interests, 38th Strategy for Peace, US Foreign Policy Conference, Stanley Foundation, 1997.

US-European Policy in the Persian Gulf: Beyond the Friction, The Persian Gulf Project, The Stanley Foundation and the Royal Institute of International Affairs, September 11-12, 1997, Chatham House, London, UK and September 25-27, 1998, Airlie Center, Warrenton, Virginia, USA.

Getting Down to Cases: Enforcing Security Council Resolutions, United Nations of the Next Decade Conference, Stanley Foundation, 1998.

Strategy for Peace, Report of the Fortieth Strategy for Peace, US Foreign Policy Conference, Stanley Foundation, 1999.

Policy Bulletin, Using "Any Means Necessary" for Humanitarian Crisis Response, 36th United Nations of the Next Decade Conference, Stanley Foundation, 2001.

David, H. Saltiel and Jason, S. Purcell, "Using Past Duel Containment: Iran, Iraq and the Future of US Policy in the Gulf," The Atlantic Council of the United States and the Stanley Foundation, Bulletin, Vol. XIII, No. 1, January, 2002.

ANNUAL REPORTS OF THE SECRETARY GENERAL OF THE UN

Javier Perez De Cuellar, "Report of The Secretary General on The Work of The Organization," United Nations, 1990.

Boutros Boutros-Ghali, "An Agenda for Peace," Report of the Secretary General Pursuant to the statement adopted by the

Summit Meeting of the Security Council on January 1992, United Nations, N.Y., 1992.

Boutros Boutros-Ghali, "Building Peace and Development," Annual Report on the Work of the Organization, United Nations, 1994.

Boutros Boutros-Ghali, "Confronting New Challenges," Annual Report on the Work of the Organization, United Nations, 1995.

Boutros Boutros-Ghali, An Agenda for Peace, Second Edition with New Supplement and Related Documents, United Nations, 1995.

Boutros Boutros-Ghali, "The 50th Anniversary," Annual Report on the Work of the Organization, United Nations, 1996.

Kofi, A. Annan, "Renewal Amid Transition," Annual Report on the Work of the Organization, United Nations, 1997.

Kofi, A. Annan, "Partnership With Global Community," Annual Report on the Work of the Organization, United Nations, 1998.

Kofi, A. Annan, "Preventing War and Disaster: A Growing Global Challenge," Annual Report on the Work of the Organization, United Nations, 1999.

Kofi, A. Annan, "Common Destiny, New Resolve," Annual Report on the Work of the Organization, United Nations, 2000.

Kofi, A. Annan, "We The People: The Role of The United Nations in The 21st Century," Annual Report on the Work of the Organization, United Nations, 2000.

Kofi, A. Annan, Annual Report on The Work of the Organization, 2001.

Kofi, A. Annan, "Prevention of Armed Conflict," Annual Report on The Work of The Organization, 2002.

NEWSPAPERS

Hindustan Times (and with its Reference),

Guardian.

New-York Times.

INDEX

H

I

O

P

R